Atonement and Experience

Writings of James Denney

# Atonement and Experience

## Writings of James Denney

Edited and Introduced by

Paul K. Moser and Benjamin Nasmith

PICKWICK *Publications* · Eugene, Oregon

Atonement and Experience
Writings of James Denney

Pickwick Publications
An Imprint of Wipf and Stock Publishers
199 W. 8th Ave., Suite 3
Eugene, OR 97401

www.wipfandstock.com

PAPERBACK ISBN: 978-1-6667-3135-4
HARDCOVER ISBN: 978-1-6667-2376-2
EBOOK ISBN: 978-1-6667-2377-9

*Cataloging-in-Publication data:*

---

Names: Denney, James, 1856–1917 [author]. | Moser, Paul K., 1957–
    [editor] | Nasmith, Benjamin, 1984– [editor]
Title: Atonement and experience: writings of James Denney / edited by
    Paul K. Moser and Benjamin Nasmith.
Description: Eugene, OR : Pickwick Publications, 2022 | Includes
    bibliographical references and index.
Identifiers: ISBN 978-1-6667-3135-4 (paperback) (paperback) | ISBN
    978-1-6667-2376-2 (hardcover) | ISBN 978-1-6667-2377-9 (ebook) Subjects:
    LCSH: Denney, James, 1856–1917. | Theology. | Atonement. |

Jesus Christ — Person and offices. | Revelation — Christianity —
History of doctrines. | Conversion — Religious aspects —
Christianity | Sacrifice | Redemption

Classification: LCC BT453 D46 2022 (print) | LCC BT453 (ebook)

# Contents

## Part 3: Sermons

# Preface

This is a collection of thirteen theological writings of the Scottish theologian and New Testament scholar James Denney (1856–1917). His work had a significant influence on such seminal 20th-century theologians as P.T. Forsyth and H.R. Mackintosh, and it continues to be important for theologians, Biblical scholars, philosophers of religion, and Christian preachers. Forsyth said of Denney: "He has more important things to say than anyone at present writing on theology." Mackintosh said of him: "As theologian and as man, there was no one like him." James Moffatt remarked: "No one can be said even to put you in mind of Denney." A.M. Hunter, Vincent Taylor, and I.H. Marshall also have commented on Denney's important influence.

There is no other collection of Denney's theological essays in print. This collection reduces this deficiency by representing his important work on theology in the Epistle to the Romans and his Pauline Christology. It also includes two of his outstanding sermons that outline his approach to human knowledge of God. The thirteen essays included merit attention in contemporary theology, Biblical studies, and the philosophy of religion. We have contributed a General Introduction that motivates the book and identifies its unifying themes.

P.K.M., Chicago, IL
B.N., Moose Jaw, SK

# Introduction

Paul K. Moser and Benjamin Nasmith

James Denney was born in Paisley, Scotland, and was raised initially as a Reformed Presbyterian and then as a member of the Free Church of Scotland. He was educated at the University of Glasgow (MA, 1879) and the Free Church College, Glasgow (Bachelor of Divinity, 1883). Denney was awarded a Glasgow D.D. in 1895. He was a pastor of a congregation in Scotland from 1886 to 1897, and he then became Professor of Systematic and Practical Theology in the Free Church College, Glasgow. After two years there, he was appointed to the Chair of New Testament Language, Literature, and Theology. In 1915, he became Principal of Free Church College, and he served the College until his death in 1917.[1]

Denney did his main theological work on the topics of divine–human atonement and Christology, with an abiding focus on the role of experience and God's Spirit in atonement and religious belief. The present book represents these areas of attention, in order to capture what motivated Denney in his theology.

## Atonement and Christology

The guiding theme of Denney's theology is a kind of interpersonalism about God in relating to humans. He writes: "The assumption—which is also the experience—of the highest form of religion, as we have it represented in the Christian Scriptures, is the existence of a personal God and of personal relations between that God and man. When these relations are interrupted or

---

1. The most detailed biography of James Denney is Gordon, *James Denney*; see also Taylor, *God Loves Like That!*, chap. 1.

1

deranged by man's action, he finds himself alienated or estranged from God, and the need of reconciliation emerges."[2] The divine atonement for humans, according to Denney, has divine–human reconciliation at its center, and that reconciliation depends on personal interactions between God and humans.

Denney gives top value among religious doctrines to a doctrine of reconciliation: "The doctrine of reconciliation . . . is the most urgent, in a religious sense, of all doctrines; it is the one in which most is revealed of God, and the one of which man has most need to hear. It is, I believe, the doctrine in which the offence of the gospel is concentrated, as well as its divine power to save."[3] He explains what underlies the importance of the doctrine in terms of human sin and guilt and of divine forgiveness of wayward humans.

The role of sin and corresponding felt guilt emerges in human experience, according to Denney: "The sense of being wrong with God, under His displeasure, excluded from His fellowship, afraid to meet Him yet bound to meet Him, is the sense of guilt. Conscience confesses in it its liability to God, a liability which in the very nature of the case it can do nothing to meet, and which therefore is nearly akin to despair."[4] Sin toward God, according to Denney, is thus not just a matter of speculation or imagination. It has, at least in many cases, an experienced reality, and that reality arises in conscience in many cases. A sense of guilt often accompanies that reality, expressing a distressed need to meet a liability. That liability is not restricted to other humans; it involves liability toward God, even if a person is unclear about this. Denney denies that humans can remove this liability on their own. God is needed.

God confronts the human problem of sin and guilt, however much humans deny it, with judgment but not only with judgment. Denney comments on Paul on reconciliation and judgment: "Before he proceeds to explain how reconciliation is achieved by Christ, he exhibits to us the whole world guilty before God (Rom 3:19), subject to His judgment and His wrath, lying under a terrible

2. Denney, *The Christian Doctrine of Reconciliation*, 5.

3. Denney, *Studies in Theology*, 19.

4. Denney, *The Atonement and the Modern Mind*, 84.

responsibility to Him."[5] Such judgment and wrath typically aim at the reconciliation of humans to God and thus are not God's ultimate value. Denney adds: "Alike to Paul and to John, [God's effort through Christ] signified the conviction that the ultimate reality in this world of sinful men was not after all sin, law, judgment, death, or hell, but a goodness in God which bears sin in all the dreadful reality it has for men, and in so doing wins them to trust it, delivers them from sin, reconciles them to itself, and makes them partakers in a divine and eternal life."[6] This goodness of God includes the divine forgiveness of people who sin against God.

Denney identifies a central role for divine forgiveness in reconciliation:

> The heart of the reconciliation lies in the readjustment or restoration of the true personal relation between God and the creature which has lapsed by its own act into alienation from Him; in other words, it consists in the forgiveness of sins. Reconciliation to God comes through God's forgiveness of that by which we have been estranged from Him; and of all experiences in the religion of sinful men, it is the most deeply felt and far reaching. We do not need here to measure what is or is not within its power, but everyone who knows what it is to be forgiven, knows also that forgiveness is the greatest regenerative force in the life of man.[7]

Divine forgiveness of humans ensures that divine judgment is not intended to be God's last word to humans. Instead, a goal of divine–human reconciliation is the final goal for God, even if humans can and sometimes do frustrate it. Divine forgiveness is a central part of this reconciliation, but it seems not to exhaust reconciliation in Paul's perspective.

Denney identifies a crucial role for Jesus in God's dealing with sin and bringing about divine forgiveness aimed at reconciliation. Divine forgiveness of sin, according to Denney, depends on sin being borne. He writes:

5. Denney, *The Christian Doctrine of Reconciliation*, 147.

6. Denney, *The Christian Doctrine of Reconciliation*, 176.

7. Denney, *The Christian Doctrine of Reconciliation*, 6.

> Sin is only forgiven as it is borne. [Christ] bore our sins
> in His own body on the tree: that is the propitiation.
> It is the satisfaction of divine necessities, and it has
> value not only for us, but for God. In that sense, though
> Christ is God's gift to us, the propitiation is objective;
> it is the voice of God, no less than that of the sinner,
> which says, "Thou, O Christ, art all I want; more than
> all in Thee I find." And this is our hope towards God.
> It is not that the love of God has inspired us to repent,
> but that Christ in the love of God has borne our sins.[8]

God does not punish or condemn Jesus, according to Denney, but
God does offer the cross of Jesus as the divine condemnation of sin.
Here he follows a theme from Paul: "By sending his own Son in the
likeness of sinful flesh, and to deal with sin, [God] condemned sin
in the flesh" (Rom 8:3, NRSV, here and in our subsequent Biblical
translations).

Denney connects Jesus's bearing of sin to his perfect obedience:

> It was the condemnation [of sin] in the cross which
> made [Jesus] cry, O my Father, if it be possible, let this
> cup pass from me; it was the anticipation of that expe-
> rience in which, all sinless as He was, the Father would
> put into His hand the cup our sins had mingled. It was
> not possible that this cup should pass. There was no
> other way in which sin could pass from us than by be-
> ing laid on Him; and it was the final proof of His obe-
> dience to the Father, the full measure of His love to us,
> when He said to God, Not my will, but thine, be done:
> and to the disciples, The cup that my Father giveth me
> to drink, shall I not drink it?[9]

The obedient Jesus thus serves as the bearer of human sin for God,
according to Denney. His self-offering to God for this role is accept-
able to God as a result of his perfect obedience as God's beloved
Son.

Denney is cautious about the sense in which Christ's death is
penal. He explains: "That the innocent, moved by love, should suf-

---

8. Denney, *The Christian Doctrine of Reconciliation*, 162.

9. Denney, *Studies in Theology*, 123.

fer with the guilty and for them, is in line with all we know of the moral order under which we live; it is the triumph of goodness in its highest form. But that the innocent should be punished for the guilty is not moral at all."[10] The latter position excludes some familiar views from Denney's perspective on atonement.

Denney elaborates on some noteworthy exclusions from divine atonement:

> It excludes the idea that the Son of God, with whom the Father was well pleased, should be regarded at the same time as the object of the Father's displeasure, the victim of His wrath, on whom the punishment of all the world's sin was inflicted. It excludes all those ideas of equivalence between what Christ suffered and what men as sinners were under an obligation to suffer, which revolt both intelligence and conscience in much of what is called orthodox theology. It excludes all those assimilations of the sufferings of our Lord in the garden and on the cross to the pains of the damned, which cast a hideous shadow on many interpretations of His passion.[11]

So, the crucified Jesus, according to Denney is not "the object of the Father's displeasure, [or] the victim of His wrath." The death of Jesus was not penal in either manner. Denney adds: "While the agony and the passion were not penal in the sense of coming upon Jesus through a bad conscience, or making him the personal object of divine wrath, they were penal in the sense that in that dark hour he had to realise to the full the divine reaction against sin in the race in which he was incorporated, and that without doing so to the utter most he could not have been the Redeemer of that race from sin, or the Reconciler of sinful men to God."[12]

Denney holds that in his cross Jesus identified with sinners in a manner that gave him a realization of God's righteous, holy response to sin. He realized the divine penalty without being "the personal object of divine wrath." Denney adds: "On the cross the

---

10. Denney, *The Christian Doctrine of Reconciliation*, 262.

11. Denney, *The Christian Doctrine of Reconciliation*, 262–63; cf. 272.

12. Denney, *The Christian Doctrine of Reconciliation*, 273.

sinless Son of God, in love to man and in obedience to the Father, entered submissively into that tragic experience in which sinful men realise all that sin means. He tasted death for every man. The last and deepest thing we can say about his relation to our sins is that he died for them, that he bore them in His own body on the tree."[13] If we are going to call this approach "penal," as Denney suggests, we should think of it as indirectly penal.

Denney uses language of "propitiation" for the role of Jesus in divine redemption, but the word "expiation" would be more fitting. He comments: "What is argued for, in connection with the propitiation, especially in Romans 3:25f., is . . . that in Christ as ἱλαστήριον [sacrifice of atonement, NRSV] justice is done not only to the grace of God but to His wrath—to that solemn reaction of God against all ungodliness and unrighteousness of men from which the apostle sets out in the exposition of his gospel (Rom 1:18)."[14] So, Denney has in mind God's vindicating divine righteousness in Christ while responding to human sin without condoning it or leaving it uncovered. God is working in the cross of Jesus on behalf of humans, but God does not need to be persuaded to forgive by Jesus. In addition, no human needs to appease God for divine wrath toward humans. God exercises divine righteousness in Christ as ἱλαστήριον to make a way of redemption for sinners, via a gift of righteous grace.

Denney finds an anchor for divine forgiveness and justification in God's work in the crucified Christ:

> Forgiveness, or justification, in the new era has come to men in Christ, whom God has set forth in his blood as a propitiation; it has come in One who has realised to the uttermost in His own person all that sin meant, One who has drunk the cup our sins had mingled, One who has felt all the waves and billows break over Him in which God's reaction against sin comes home to us sinners. This is of the very essence of the ἱλαστήριον as Paul understands it. It bears witness, of course, to the goodness of God, for it is God who provides it, out of pure love, and it is the way of salvation; but it bears

13. Denney, *The Christian Doctrine of Reconciliation*, 278.

14. Denney, *The Christian Doctrine of Reconciliation*, 157.

witness also to His severity, to His inexorable repul-
sion of evil, to a righteousness on which no shadow of
moral unreality must ever fall.[15]

This comment indicates that God's righteous love underlies the
forgiveness and justification available in Christ. The righteousness
of God calls for the divine atoning action in Christ, for the sake
of justifying the ungodly. This righteousness accompanies divine
love in God's sending Christ to sacrifice himself, on behalf of God,
for humans under the power of sin. God's atonement thus rests on
divine self-sacrifice that manifests perfectly righteous love toward
wayward humans.[16]

Denney opposes any simple forensic or judicial approach to
God's redemptive effort in the cross of Jesus. Instead, he recom-
mends a filial approach based on God's need to maintain divine
righteousness. He remarks:

> Few things have astonished me more than to be
> charged with teaching a "forensic" or "legal" or
> "judicial" doctrine of Atonement, resting, as such
> a doctrine must do, on a "forensic" or "legal" or
> "judicial" conception of man's relation to God . . . .
> There is nothing which I should wish to reprobate
> more whole-heartedly than the conception which is
> expressed by these words. To say that the relations of
> God and man are forensic is to say that they are regu-
> lated by statute—that sin is a breach of statute—that
> the sinner is a criminal—and that God adjudicates on
> him by interpreting the statute in its application to
> his case. . . . If they are to be rational, if they are to be
> moral, if they are to be relations in which an ethical life
> can be lived, and ethical responsibilities realized, they
> must be not only personal, but universal; they must
> be relations that in some sense are determined by law.
> Even to say that they are the relations, not of judge
> and criminal, but of Father and child, does not get us

15. Denney, *The Christian Doctrine of Reconciliation*, 159.

16. For a recent discussion of this theme, see Moser, *Paul's Gospel of Divine Self-Sacrifice*.

past this point. The relations of father and child are undoubtedly more adequate to the truth than those of judge and criminal.[17]

Something must be added to a filial approach to reconciliation in terms of "the relations of father and child." The addition is in God's commitment to divine righteousness in the redemption of humans.

Denney finds the needed addition in the apostle Paul:

> Paul preached the same gospel to the Gentiles as he did to the Jews; he preached in it the same relation of the Atonement and of Christ's death to divine law. But he did not do this by extending to all mankind a Pharisaic, legal, forensic relation to God: he did it by rising above such conceptions, even though as a Pharisee he may have had to start from them, to the conception of a relation of all men to God expressing itself in a moral constitution—or, as he would have said, but in an entirely unforensic sense, in a law— of divine and unchanging validity. The maintenance of this law, or of this moral constitution, in its inviolable integrity was the signature of the forgiveness Paul preached. The Atonement meant to him that forgiveness was mediated through One in whose life and death the most signal homage was paid to this law: the very glory of the Atonement was that it manifested the righteousness of God; it demonstrated God's consistency with His own character, which would have been violated alike by indifference to sinners and by indifference to that universal moral order—that law of God—in which alone eternal life is possible.[18]

Denney's use of (God's) "moral constitution" is more illuminating than his talk of "law." It signifies God's unique moral character of perfect righteousness, and that moral character anchors God's forgiveness and atonement in the cross of Christ. That character is righteous love, and therefore is irreducible to mere love or mere

17. Denney, *The Death of Christ*, 271.

18. Denney, *The Atonement and the Modern Mind*, 75–76.

mercy. The feature of righteousness includes God's intention to make things right in divine–human relations, and that intention goes beyond what is typically meant by "love" or "mercy." A big problem for God and humans, however, is that humans can reject for themselves God's way of making things right. God's Spirit, as Paul claims, can be "grieved" by humans.

## Atonement, Experience, and Spirit

It is one thing for God to establish the actual circumstances for divine–human atonement; it is another thing for humans to appropriate that atonement, to receive it for themselves. If God has established the circumstances in the first-century cross of Christ, we have a historical gap between those circumstances and contemporary inquirers of God. This raises the issue of what bridges the gap. Denney's approach to the human appropriation of divine–human atonement is grounded in morally significant experience, with special acknowledgment of the intervening Spirit of God in current experience. Pneumatology is thus central to his soteriology, and this is a rare virtue for a theology of his time.

Denney comments: "There is certainly no reconciliation but through the historical Christ: there is no other Christ of whom we know anything whatever. But the historical Christ does not belong to the past. The living Spirit of God makes Him present and eternal; and it is not from Palestine, or from the first century of the Christian era, but here and now that His reconciling power is felt."[19] This raises the important issue of how Christ's "reconciling power is felt." We have noted Denney's view that "everyone who knows what it is to be forgiven, knows also that forgiveness is the greatest regenerative force in the life of man." We need to clarify Denney's position, however, on how God or the Spirit of God emerges in human experience for the sake of forgiveness and reconciliation.

Denney draws from Psalm 139 to identify the foundation of human knowledge of God. He explains:

> The being and the personality of God, so far as there
> is any religious interest in them, are not to be proved

---

19. Denney, *The Christian Doctrine of Reconciliation*, 9.

by arguments; they are to be experienced in the kind
of experience here described. The man who can say, O
Lord, Thou hast searched me and known me, does not
need any arguments to prove that God is, and that He
is a person, and that He has an intimate and importunate interest in his life. If that is a real experience, . . .
and if it is not a morbid phenomenon, but one which is
sane and normal, then the *thou* in it is just as real as the
*me*.[20]

Denney adds: "[God] does not put arguments within our reach
which point to theistic conclusions; He gives us the experience
which makes this Psalm [139] intelligible, and forces us also to
cry, 'O Lord, Thou hast searched me and known me.' . . . It is
the overpowering sense that we are known through and through
by another which seals upon our hearts that knowledge of God
on which religion rests."[21] The talk of "forces us to cry" is ar-
guably too strong, but a key role for an experience of divine searching merits attention. Denney attributes the latter experience to the
Spirit of God and to faith in God.

Denney characterizes the Spirit of God in relation to faith in
God:

The Christian God is He who supplies the Spirit (Gal
3:5). To become a Christian is to receive the Spirit (Gal
3:2). To live as a Christian is to walk in or by the Spirit
(Gal 5:16). The Spirit and faith are correlative terms,
and each of them covers, from a different point of view,
all that is meant by Christianity. Regarded from the
side of God and His grace and power in initiating and
maintaining it, Christianity is the Spirit; regarded from
the side of man and his action and responsibility in relation to God, it is faith. The two are coextensive, and
all Christianity is in each. This is vividly expressed in
one of those sentences in which St. Paul concentrates
his whole mind on the greatest things: ἡμεῖς γὰρ πνεύ-
ματι ἐκ πίστεως ἐλπίδα δικαιοσύνης ἀπεκδεχόμεθα [for

---

20. Denney, "Elemental Religion," 3. Also p. 174 below.

21. Denney, "Elemental Religion," 3–4.

> through the Spirit, by faith, we eagerly wait for the
> hope of righteousness.] (Gal 5:5). Here is everything
> that enters into Christianity and determines it to be
> what it is.[22]

Denney adds: "Like the old religion, it has in δικαιοσύνη [righteousness] its hope or goal; but in its attitude to this, nothing is determined by law, in any sense of that word; there are only two powers of which St. Paul is conscious as counting for anything in his soul—the one is divine (the Spirit), the other is human (faith); and though these are distinguishable, they cannot be known apart (cf. 2 Thess 2:13)."[23] We thus may think of faith in God as the fitting human response to God's intervening Spirit, the righteous Spirit of Christ (Rom 8:9–10).

Denney holds that the Holy Spirit emerges in human experience but is not a focus of human faith. He explains:

> In spite of the creeds, there is no such expression in
> the New Testament as believing in the Holy Ghost.
> The Spirit is not an object of faith like Christ or God;
> it is an experience which comes to people through
> faith. Whether we judge from the accounts in the
> Book of Acts or in the Epistles of Paul, it was a vivid
> emotional experience. The figures employed in the
> story of Pentecost—the sound as of a rushing mighty
> wind, tongues like as of fire—are fundamentally true
> and of permanent importance. The Spirit was an
> experience in which believers were the subjects of a
> divine excitement in which their life was raised to a
> new power.[24]

Denney follows Paul in connecting the power of God's Spirit to divine love. He says of Paul:

> All he has to say about the Spirit might be condensed in
> the striking words of Romans 5:5: "The Christian hope
> puts no man to shame, for the love of God is poured

22. Denney, "Holy Spirit," 740.

23. Denney, "Holy Spirit," 740.

24. Denney, *The Christian Doctrine of Reconciliation*, 308.

out in our hearts through the Holy Spirit given to us."
This is what the Holy Spirit does: it fills the Christian
heart with an exultant assurance of the love of God.
The man who has such an assurance—the man whose
heart is full to overflowing with the sense of that love
which God demonstrated to men when He gave His
Son to die for sinners—is full of the Holy Ghost.[25]

The experience of this love, according to Denney, includes an experience of divine forgiveness.

The appropriate human response to God's Spirit is faith in
God. Denney proposes that for a person to have faith in God is:

> to abandon himself to the sin-bearing love which ap-
> peals to Him in Christ, and to do so unreservedly, un-
> conditionally, and forever. This is what the New Tes-
> tament means by faith. It is the only thing which is
> true to the situation in which the sinner finds himself
> when he is confronted with Christ and the work of rec-
> onciliation achieved by Him. To believe in Christ and
> in the sin-bearing love revealed in Him is to do the one
> right thing for which the situation calls. When the sin-
> ner does thus believe he does the one right thing, and
> it puts him right with God; in St. Paul's language he
> is justified by faith. God accepts him as righteous, and
> he is righteous; he has received the reconciliation (Rom
> 5:11), and he is reconciled.[26]

Paul thinks of faith in God as including entrusting oneself to God
(Rom 4:5), and this goes beyond intellectual assent to informa-
tional content. It is, as Denney recognizes, a kind of obedience to
God.

It is noteworthy that Paul regards even Christians as candi-
dates for reconciliation to God. He thus commands the Corinthian
Christians: "Be reconciled to God" (2 Cor 5:20). Perhaps he
thought of such reconciliation and the underlying faith in God
as being a matter of degree after a certain threshold. In any
case, Denney offers an important experience-based approach to

25. Denney, *The Christian Doctrine of Reconciliation*, 309.

26. Denney, *The Christian Doctrine of Reconciliation*, 290.

reconciliation with God, and his approach brings divine–human atonement into the domain of actual human experience and life. Inquirers can find here an opportunity for assessing the veracity of the gospel of atonement on the basis of human experience. Denney's contributions in this regard thus merit careful attention.

## Summary of Chapters

The opening chapters of this book represent Denney's views of Paul's theology in this Epistle to the Romans. In Chapter 1, "The Doctrine of Sin, Part 1," Denney finds Paul's gospel to be centered on divine righteousness, and he considers such righteousness to be responsive to human sin. Law is involved with righteousness and sin, according to Denney, and in a universal manner. He comments: "All men without distinction have such a revelation of God as implies moral obligations toward Him—that is, all are under law. All men, also, have failed to meet these obligations—that is, all are under sin. It is from the last proposition St. Paul starts, and it is in working out its presuppositions that he attains to the universal conception of law" (25). Denney proposes that this universal conception is not merely forensic or judicial, because it involves God's righteous character directly, in a manner that is ethical and interpersonal. God needs to preserve and vindicate this character even when justifying the ungodly, including believers in Jesus. Paul's burden in his Epistle to the Romans is to make sense of this redemptive project.

Chapter 2, "The Doctrine of Sin, Part 2," assesses Paul's understanding of the relation between sin and the Mosaic law in human experience. It identifies Paul's commitment to the universality of sin among humans, without digressing to the historical origin of sin. Sin emerges as stemming from a human moral state that invites divine wrath. Denney finds Paul to acknowledge the following condition in humans: "there is that which reacts instinctively against the law, that which is stimulated by the law into persistent and determined revolt, that which under such stimulus reveals to [us] the exceeding sinfulness of sin" (36). This condition can be recognized through conflicts of conscience, but its resolution calls for something more powerful than conscience: the righteousness of God in Christ crucified and risen.

Chapter 3, "The Gospel a Divine Righteousness," presents Paul's solution to the human predicament of sin and death. The solution comes from God and divine power, not from humans and human power. It comes from God righteousness: that is, "a righteousness which puts the ungodly in the right (Rom 4:5), and constitutes into a people of God those who lay under His judgment (Rom 3:19). A righteousness like this, if such a thing can be, is unmistakably glad tidings for a sinful world; it is a genuine gospel for those who need a gospel" (44). Denney considers the importance for Paul of God's righteousness being appropriated by humans: "this righteousness, which is at least named after God has God as its source, [and] it eventually becomes [ours], and that when this is accomplished [we are] justified—right with God and right in God's judgment" (45). The appropriation is through faith in God, and it rests on a divine gift of grace in Christ crucified, rather than on human earning. Denney thus attends to Romans 3:24–5, to highlight the importance of the death of Christ.

Chapter 4, "Faith and the Righteousness of God," contends that Paul's concern is not with faith in a general sense, but instead with "faith [that] only becomes possible when the object which evokes it is presented to the sinner. There must be an exhibition, through the preaching of the gospel, not merely of Christ, or even of Christ crucified, but of Christ as in his death a propitiation for sin" (54). Faith, in Denney's reading of Paul, is no mere intellectual attitude of assent. He remarks: "when [we] recognise that in Jesus Christ as set forth in his blood the love of God is bearing the sin of the world—when it comes upon [us] that this is the revelation of what God is in relation to sinful [people]; then [we] understand also that there is only one act and attitude by which the sinful [people] can properly respond to God, that, namely, in which [they] give [themselves] up unreservedly to the love demonstrated in Christ" (57). Faith, then, calls for full interpersonal surrender to God and God's will, in Denney's perspective on Paul.

Chapter 5, "The Righteousness of God and the New Life," proposes that "the whole of Christianity is in the faith which abandons itself to the sin-bearing love of God, just as the last truth about God is in the sin-bearing love which offers itself in Christ for the acceptance of faith" (65). It also clarifies Denney's understanding of "propitiation" introduced for his comments on Romans 3: "In the third chapter [Paul] exhibits Christ as a propitiation—God's revelation of a righteousness in which [God's] own character is vindicated, and in which sinners may become right with [God]" (66). Their becoming right with God, according to Denney's reading of Paul, is a matter of faith in God, and that faith is their center for their new life in Christ. Such life, Denney holds, "is not something which has another condition than their faith, it is the assertion of their faith through all things. If we introduce a word from another circle of ideas, and speak of a regenerate life, then we may say that justification regenerates, or that faith regenerates; for the regenerate life of Romans 5:1–11 is nothing but the life of justification and of faith" (66). We might ask how this position relates to Paul's concern for reconciliation with God even among believers (2 Cor 5:20), but we cannot digress.

Chapter 6, "The New Life and the Spirit," gives credit to the Spirit of God for working redemptively in human experience, and this captures Paul's emphasis. Denney comments: "'The love of God,' [Paul] says, 'has been poured out in our hearts through the Holy Spirit given to us.' The experience here ascribed to the Spirit is that assured triumphant consciousness of God's love which enables the Christian to glory in tribulations. It is of God that we have such a conviction about God as this; [God] has wrought it in us by His own divine power; we could never have attained it otherwise" (78). Denney finds a distinctive role for God's Spirit in human conscience. He writes: "Under [the Spirit's] influence conscience becomes not the recorder, nor the avenging angel, nor the worm that never dies, but a kind of genius; the moral world becomes all of a sudden vast, real, enchanting" (80). The moral world also becomes the stage for God's Spirit in bringing life to receptive humans, in a way that the Mosaic law cannot. Denney thus remarks: "for St. Paul there is no such thing as sanctification except through a power which is in every sense of the term supernatural" (86). This power is "supernatural" because it is the power of God's Spirit, the Spirit of Christ.

Chapter 7, "Authority of Christ," takes up the following report of the synoptic Gospels regarding Jesus: "They [the crowds] were astonished at his teaching, for he taught them as one having authority, and not as their scribes" (Matt 7:28–29; cf. Mark 1:22; Luke 4:32). Denney finds that Jesus assumed a kind of practical authority for himself: "he claimed other men, other moral personalities, for himself and his work, and required their unconditional renunciation of all other ties and interests that they might become his disciples. He said, 'Follow me,' and they rose, and left all and followed him (Matt 4:18–22; Matt 9:9)" (90). This authority stems from Jesus's identifying himself with God and God's arriving Kingdom. Even so, people had the option of rejecting Jesus and God's Kingdom, and some took that option. So, the relevant authority is moral rather than coercive toward its goal of lived righteousness in relation to God. Denney regards this authority to emerge in Jesus as judge and revealer for God. It thus bears on human obedience and belief. It also has an indispensable focus, according to Denney: "He did not come to reveal medicine or psychology . . . ; he came to reveal the Father, and his authority has its centre there" (95). Denney spells out this special role for Jesus and his moral authority.

Chapter 8, "Christianity and the Historical Christ," takes up the longstanding issue of how the Christ of history relates to the living Christ of commitment today. Denney notes that "Christ is not for [the Christian] a person who had his being in the past and who exhausted it there; he is a living and present person, with whom he enters into direct and immediate fellowship through the gospel story; it is not a distant past he is dealing with, but a present and eternal life. This, however, is a point of view which mere history cannot attain" (109). Denney thus contends that a Christian "relation to Christ is a relation to a person who is historical, certainly, and who certainly died, but who is certainly not 'as dead as Julius Caesar.' He is far more living than that. In some way or other he belongs as truly to the present as to the past" (114). Denney develops this theme in relation to Jesus as the Son of God, Savior, and Lord. He focuses not on titles but on the factuality of Jesus in these three unique roles on behalf of God.

Chapter 9, "Adam and Christ in St. Paul," examines Paul's understanding of being in Christ as a status for redemption. Denney aims to clarify being in Christ in terms of human experience rather than an abstract status. This matter guides his reflection on union with Christ for redemption. He remarks: "when two persons, two moral natures, are to enter into union with each other, then their union, no matter how intimate and profound it may be, must at the same time be personal and moral" (128). Denney thus asks: "Is not the act in which one person in trust and love 'identifies' himself with another, the most purely 'moral' of all conceivable acts? Is it not the kind of act which, in its motives, its essence, its fruits, most completely manifests the moral nature?" (129). He adds that such language of "identification" is the language of love and moral passion, whatever else it connotes. If we insist on a mystical feature in union with Christ, according to Denney, it is "morality aflame with passion" (130).

Chapter 10, "He that Came by Water and Blood," looks to the Gospel and the First Epistle of John for some concrete tokens of the historical Jesus as the Son of God. According to John's Gospel, Denney finds, "the Son [of God] is the person who has the perpetual fulness of the Spirit and the perpetual power to bestow it, and Jesus is attested by the historical event and experience of his baptism—by his coming by water—to be this person" (134). Similarly, the death of Jesus on the cross should be seen as a demonstration of his being the Son of God. Denney adds: "The water and the blood could not be thought of by John except as implying and declaring the possession and communication of the Spirit by Jesus, and the expiation and conquest of sin" (135). He remarks, furthermore: "There are many who are glad to acknowledge a general debt to the teaching and example of Jesus, but not a special debt to his death; many to whom regeneration, or moral stimulus, is as attractive as expiation is repellent, and who fail to see that in the Christian religion the two cannot be separated" (137). He explains how the writer of John's Gospel and First Epistle of John holds these roles together.

Chapter 11, "Preaching Christ," explores the idea of a unity of substance in the various ways of preaching Christ. Denney's main thesis is: "There is no preaching of Christ, possessed of religious significance, that does not rest on the basis on which the apostolic preaching rested: his exaltation in power, and therefore his perpetual presence. The historical Jesus is indispensable; but if we are to have a Christian religion, the historical must become present and eternal. This it does through the resurrection as apprehended by faith" (146). He adds: "To preach Christ at all we must preach Him as κύριος and μονογενής. The first name secures his unshared place in relation to men, as the latter does in relation to God; and unless he fills such a place, Christianity has no *raison d'être*" (149). He contends that the message Jesus preached cannot justifiably be separated from him as its preacher and representative, indeed as the one in whom it is incarnate. In sum, Denney offers: "To preach Christ means to preach Jesus in the absolute significance for God and man which he had to his own consciousness and to the faith of the first witnesses; and to preach Him as exalted, and as having this absolute significance now and for ever" (150). He documents this conclusion on the basis of apostolic preaching in the New Testament.

Chapter 12, "Elemental Religion," presents what Denney takes to be the best support for God's reality. It arises from Psalm 139: "O Lord, thou hast searched me and known me." Denney remarks: "The being and the personality of God, so far as there is any religious interest in them, are not to be proved by arguments; they are to be experienced in the kind of experience here described. The man who can say, *O Lord, Thou hast searched me and known me*, does not need any arguments to prove that God is, and that He is a person, and that He has an intimate and importunate interest in his life" (174). Denney extends this observation: "Speaking practically—and in religion everything is practical—God alone can overcome atheism, and this is how He overcomes it. He does not put arguments within our reach which point to theistic conclusions; He gives us the experience which makes this Psalm intelligible" (175). Denney elaborates on how God's searching knowledge of us bears on our self-knowledge and on our attitude toward life, including our moral life and hope.

Chapter 13, "Man's Claims in Religion, and God's Response," develops the apostle Paul's thinking on the relation of signs, power, and wisdom to God and divine revelation. Denney's main thesis is: "The power of God to save, the highest and divinest power God can exercise, is the power manifested in His passion and operating through it. The Lord reigns from the tree. This is the paradoxical but ·sufficient answer of God to all who ask signs" (187). Denney turns to some vital questions: "You wish to know the final truth about God? Here it is, eternal love, bearing sin. Can you think of a power so wonderful as that which bears the sin of the whole world? a power so able to regenerate you, and to put the key of life, and of all the mysteries with which it confronts you, into your hand? Can you want anything better to trust, anything worthier to inspire, anything abler to throw upon all the dark places of life the light of hope and joy?" (190). These questions point to the central concern of Denney's theology: the God who loves redemptively in Christ.

# 1

# The Doctrine of Sin, Part 1

The central theological conception of the Epistle to the Romans is that of the righteousness of God. The righteousness of God, however, as the sum and substance of the gospel, is essentially related to sin, and we follow the apostle's order in making sin our first subject of study.

It will not be questioned that the Epistle to the Romans contains a doctrine, or, at least, much of the material for a doctrine, on this subject. The apostle speaks continually in it of "sin" in the singular, and in all sorts of relations. Out of forty-eight cases in which the word ἁμαρτία is used in the Epistle, only three are in the plural; and of these, two (Rom 4:7; 11:27) are quotations from the Old Testament. In the synoptic Gospels, on the other hand, the word is never found in the singular, except in Matthew 12:31, where πᾶσα ἁμαρτία does not form a real exception; it is not sin, but sins, of which Jesus speaks. This of itself is sufficient to show that St. Paul's attitude is that of one who is generalizing on the subject; what Jesus addresses Himself to in the concrete, as it comes before Him in its particular workings, in the lives of individual men, His apostle is trying to grasp in its nature and significance as a whole.

This does not mean that in St. Paul there must necessarily be some loss in truth or reality. A generalization is only unreal to a person who approaches it from the outside; it is not unreal, empty, or unimpressive, to the person who has digested his experience and observation into it. This last is the case in the Epistle. There is no abstract doctrine of sin in it; everything it contains is written out of the apostle's heart; it is profoundly, even passionately, experimental. It is proper to insist on this, because it is sometimes overlooked. The process of generalization is a difficult one, and the forms in which the mind makes its first attempt to express its perception of a universal truth may not be quite adequate to the burden laid on them. One of the most obvious of these forms is personification. Wishing, for instance, to say something which is true not of this or that sin, but of sin in general, the mind projects sin, as it were, to a distance at which it can focus it, and then makes its assertions *as if* sin actually had such an independent existence of its own. It generalizes by the simple process of writing Sin with a capital S, and lending it a quasi-personality. St. Paul himself often does this. He does it, possibly, when he says that Sin entered into the world; he does it certainly when he says that Sin reigned in death, or that there is such a thing as a Law of Sin—a law which Sin enjoins as opposed to the law enjoined by God. But it is a misconception of his mind altogether—a failure to appreciate the psychological conditions under which he worked—when we distinguish on this ground, as many scholars do, an "objective" as opposed to a "subjective" doctrine of sin in certain passages of the Epistle. Perhaps these are words one ought not to use at all; but if they are to be used, we ought to recognise clearly that an "objective" which is not also "subjective" does not belong to science or to experience, but to mythology. Now there is nothing about sin in St. Paul (as I hope will become apparent) which cannot be verified in experience; and the places in which there is even the appearance of an objective conception of Sin, as a power *in rerum natura* but not in this or that human will, are only those in which the apostle, *on the basis of experience*, generalizes by the primitive method of poetic personification. It is needlessly rash to say that in these cases he did not know what he was doing.

Yet everything is not made clear when we say that St. Paul's doctrine of sin was experimental. The question is at once raised, What was the experience in which he gained the insight generalized in this Epistle into a doctrine of sin? Was it his experience as a Pharisee in quest of a righteousness of his own? or his experience as a Christian in possession of the righteousness of God? Or can we perhaps distribute it between the two stages of his life, and maintain that he learned some things about sin by being a sinner, and others only by being saved? The true answer to such questions depends on a perception of what experience is. It is not a *quantum*, but a process, and what it amounted to at any particular moment, supposing it could have been arrested there, changes meaning and value and aspect continually as life moves on. It is not at the instant of doing anything that we know what we have done; it may only be long afterwards, and in the light of very different experiences. This has to be considered especially in such a writing as the Epistle to the Romans. The writer is a Christian apostle. He cannot be anything else; we cannot even imagine him for an instant divesting himself of this character. When he writes of sin, he writes, of course, on the basis of experience; no honest man could do otherwise. But he does not write his autobiography. He does not tell that he stole apples, like Augustine, or that he blasphemed, like Bunyan. He only tells the universal truth about sin, as through experience he has come to know it. But the experience is that of a saved man. At a later point we shall have occasion to consider the teaching of the Epistle about sin and the Christian life, and the attempts to distribute some things the apostle says of sin between the unregenerate and the regenerate man; here it is sufficient to point out that it is the regenerate man who is speaking all the time, and showing us what sin in the light of God universally and essentially is. The doctrine of sin, in other words, is Christian, not pre-Christian or Pharisaic; the whole meaning and issues of sin are not discovered at the feet of Gamaliel, but at the cross of Jesus. Hence St. Paul's writings, intensely personal as they are, do not enable us to reconstruct the Pharisaic consciousness of the man; we know only his Christian consciousness, and how sin and other things were seen and understood there.

St. Paul nowhere gives a formal definition of sin: it was too well known in all its modes to need that. But it is apparent from such passages as Romans 3:20 (διὰ γὰρ νόμου ἐπίγνωσις ἁμαρτίας) and Romans 5:13 (ἁμαρτία δὲ οὐκ ἐλλογεῖται, μὴ ὄντος νόμου) that it has to be defined in the first instance by relation to law. "I had not known sin," he says elsewhere (Rom 7:7), "except διὰ νόμου." No doubt, if we go back to St. Paul's experience as a Pharisee, and the failures of those days (which are surely not excluded by the boasting of Philippians 3:6, "touching the righteousness which is in the law blameless"), the law referred to here is the law of Moses. It was in the form of the law of Moses that law first proved a reality for the apostle. Not, we may suppose, because it was Moses' law; on the contrary, it was the law of God.[1] Formally, Paul made no distinctions in it: he was under obligation to God to keep it all. What we call ritual and what we call moral were alike binding on him. But if we confine ourselves to the Epistle to the Romans, we see that for the conscience of the Christian apostle—for the doctrine of sin, as it is of interest to a Christian man—that which is moral alone comes into view. The ceremonial part of the law has, in point of fact, lapsed: on what principle it is not here needful to enquire. Sin means the violation of the commandments in which the law is unfolded, the neglect or the transgression of its "Thou shalt" or "Thou shalt not." In particular, or so at least it seems on the first retrospect, it means doing what God in His law has forbidden.

To define sin, however, simply as the violation of the law given by Moses would have carried the apostle but a little way in his vocation. He had such a conception both of sin and of righteousness as impelled him to preach the gospel to all men, Gentiles as well as Jews. He brought against all the charge that they were under sin (Rom 3:9). But if sin can only be defined by relation to law, and is, in point of fact, defined for Jews by relation to the Mosaic law, then, in order to put Jews and Gentiles on the same footing as sinners to whom a righteousness of God is essential, Paul must be able in some way to strip law in its Mosaic embodiment of all that is accidental to it; he must be able to generalize the conception of law, and to show that all that is vital in it, everything in virtue of which sin has to be defined in relation to it, has existence among, and validity for, Gentiles as well as Jews. In the Epistle to the Romans this is definitely, though it might seem incidentally, done in various ways.

It is done, for instance, in the passage beginning with Romans 1:19, "That which may be known of God is manifest in them." Here the apostle argues that, in the constitution of nature and in man's

---

1. A curious attempt is sometimes made to represent Paul as disparaging the law, the reason alleged being that he never expressly connects it with God as he does the promises. This is very misleading. It is natural for Paul to speak of the promises *of God* with the emphasis he uses, because it is on the fact that the promises are God's that their inviolability, for which he is arguing, depends. It is natural, too, because as manifestations of His grace the whole explanation of the promises lies in God. But the law has another, though not a less divine, standing. It belongs not to God only, but to the whole constitution of things. It is the law of man and of the world as well as of God.

relation to it, there is such a revelation of God given as puts man under religious and therefore under moral obligations to God, and renders him inexcusable—we may even say, from the theological standpoint of the apostle, was meant to render him inexcusable—if he failed to satisfy these obligations. It is true that the word *law* is not used in this section. But when we are confronted with a revelation of God's eternal power and divinity, binding man to a life of adoring gratitude, and when we see that infidelity to that revelation issues in unutterable moral debasement, how else can we describe the conditions under which men live than by saying that they live under law? True, it is not the Mosaic law. It is not an institution or a code. But it is a divine law, and the Mosaic law can be no more. It connects the life of men as effectively as the Mosaic law with responsibility to God. It produces as surely in the conscience the conviction that they who live in wanton defiance of it are unworthy to live at all (Rom 1:32). Hence the Gentile understands as well as the Jew that the wages of sin is death. This is no survival of primitive mythology, but a spontaneous and universally intelligible expression of the one truth on which all morality rests. The man who is not good—the man whose being does not respond to the revelation of God and fulfil the law involved in that revelation—has no right *to be*. But I repeat, to say this is to say that Law is real for all men.

It is a more explicit generalizing of the idea of law which we find in Romans 2:14ff.: "When Gentiles who have not law (or the law) do by nature the things of the law, these having not the law are a law to themselves," etc. An attempt is made by Feine, in his treatise *Das gesetzesfreie Evangelium des Paulus*, to show that this passage can only refer to Gentile Christians, who are a law to themselves because they have received the Spirit of Christ, in which the law is sublimated and made more potent than the flesh; but both φύσει in verse 14 and κατηγορούντων in verse 15 are inconsistent with such an idea. The Jew rested on his Law, and the point of this passage is that what the law ought to have produced among the Jews and did not was sometimes produced among the Gentiles, where the law of the Jews had never been heard of. The only possible explanation of this is that the law must have some other mode of being besides that with which the Jew was familiar. It must be written elsewhere as well as on the tables of stone or the parchments of the scribes. It must speak from other shrines as well as from the ark or from the cloud on Sinai. It must, in a word, belong to Nature, as well as to history: it must be universal as well as national. This is what Paul is explaining here. There are Gentiles who do "by nature" the things of the (Jewish) law. They have "the work which the law prescribes written on their hearts." They have a conscience which passes judgment on their actions—a conscience which assents to the law of God. Their life is full of moral exercises; their thoughts bring accusations against each other, or make defences. Paul cannot interpret the phenomena of Gentile any more than of Jewish life without subsuming it under the category of Law; but in the very act of doing so, Law loses its limited, Jewish, historical character; it becomes a conception of universal import.

It may also be said that the passage at the end of Romans 2, in which Paul distinguishes the Jew outwardly from the Jew inwardly, rests upon this enlarging and spiritualizing of the conception of Law. The Jew inwardly is in truth a person to whom that which is simply Jewish in the law has no longer importance; it is not its historical but its eternal content, not its national but its divine and human significance, which has justice done to it in his life. The same justice, however, may be done to it in the life of the Gentile: and accordingly, so far from Law being that which separates the Gentile from the Jew, it is, in this its true and abiding meaning, the ground on which Jew and Gentile meet. All men without distinction have such a revelation of God as implies moral obligations toward Him—that is, all are under law. All men, also, have failed to meet these obligations—that is, all are under sin. It is from the last proposition St. Paul starts, and it is in working out its presuppositions that he attains to the universal conception of law.

Nothing is of greater importance for the understanding of the apostle's theology than a correct estimate of this conception. It underlies all his thinking. The moral world would be to him an unintelligible and incoherent place without it; to be more accurate, there could be no moral world without it at all. To banish this generalized conception of law from the relations of God and man is to make religion and morality impossible together. This truth is often overlooked, and the doctrine of the apostle, in consequence,

misrepresented or misread. It is asserted that Paul inherited from
Pharisaism a certain legal conception of the relations of God and
man, a conception essentially false, and that, though he rose above
this conception in his spiritual experience, he was never able di-
alectically to transcend it in his thoughts. In his theologizing, it is
said, he always starts from a forensic and judicial basis. It is this
leaven of Pharisaism which puts out the maturer Christian at every turn. It is this which necessitates the peculiar Pauline theory
of the atonement—a theory which is but an unreal answer to a
question which would never have arisen if Paul had started in his
thinking with a Christian instead of a Pharisaic idea of the relations of man and God.

I venture to say that this whole line of thought is both unjust to
the apostle and untrue in itself. It is unjust to the apostle, for it has
been shown above that the historical Jewish conception of the law
was not that on which his theology was based. That conception, in
the form it had assumed in the Rabbinical schools, might fairly be
said to represent the relations of God and man as "forensic." The
case between them could be stated in terms of statute, and decision
given by reference to the code. But Paul, we have seen, had clearly
transcended this conception even intellectually. He had been able
to generalize the idea of law as something determining the relations of man and God universally, something without which the
moral life of man cannot be construed at all. But in this generalized sense law is not open to be characterized by those invidious
epithets with which we are so familiar. It is not "forensic," it is not
"judicial," it is not even "legal." These question-begging epithets,
as Bentham calls them, are irrelevant to it. It is universal, it is human, it is divine. As the form in which the will of God presents
itself to the consciousness of man, it has an inevitable, searching,
individualizing power of self-application to persons and circumstances to which there is nothing analogous in the "judicial" or
"forensic" sphere. As the moral obligation to which man's consciousness bears witness in the presence of God, it is free from that
element of the arbitrary and conventional which attaches to the
noblest statutes and institutes of man. It is quite unreal to contrast
*legal*, as is habitually done, with *personal*, and to say that the relations of God and man are personal, not legal. It is true they are
not "legal" in the question-begging sense referred to above, but

they are at once personal and determined by law. Apart from their determination by law, which introduces into personal relations a universal element, these relations would be a mere caprice, having no moral meaning or value. It is the determination of the personal by something having universal significance—the combination, in other words, of personality and law—which constitutes the ethical, and it is this on which St. Paul builds. The relations of God and man are ethical—this is his fundamental truth; they are personal relations which live and move and have their being in eternal law; if it were not so, nobody could think of them, and it would not be worth while for anybody to speak of them. But because it is so, law in the universal sense to which Paul has raised it in the interpretation of his gospel is something from which we can never escape. It is the permanent element in all religious dispensations, to which justice must always be done. It is the only principle of moral valuation which the apostle knows. We may exclude from Christianity with the utmost decision all that is legal and Pharisaic, all that is statutory, forensic, judicial, or otherwise opprobrious, but the fact remains that the chief end of Christianity itself is that the righteousness of the law may be fulfilled in us (Rom 8:4). It is not robbing God of His freedom or of His grace, it is not exalting an abstraction of our own minds above the Father of our Lord Jesus Christ, to say that God Himself must in all things do right by this law. He must do right by it even when He works the moral miracle of justifying the ungodly; He must be just Himself in justifying believers in Jesus. And He must do right by it again, and surely will, when He judges men at last according to their works, i.e., according to the manner in which they have in their life responded to and satisfied that law in virtue of which their relation to Him is capable of having moral worth.

# 2

# The Doctrine of Sin, Part 2

Thus far we have been concerned with sin and law as generalized ideas which in their relations to each other fill an essential place in the theology of St. Paul. But we do not really appreciate what he meant by them till we can trace their interaction in his experience, and the moment we attempt to do so the difficulty recurs by which we are so often haunted in the study of the Epistles. St. Paul had his experience of the law under the definite form of the law of Moses; that was for him the most obvious—we are tempted at first to say the only—embodiment of the concept. But the law of Moses cannot be reproduced by us. We cannot put ourselves into the position of a person brought up in a Pharisaic environment, and confronted with the statutes of the Pentateuch and the traditions of the elders; we cannot imagine ourselves called, out of our own resources, and without becoming God's debtors, to achieve by the perfect observance of all these traditions and statutes a righteousness of our own for which we might challenge the approval of God. We cannot imagine this, nor is it needful that we should do so. Life under the law is for us an untried and alien thing, and therefore (so it is argued) the experience of Paul under these conditions, and the theology which he based upon it, can hardly be intelligible and are certainly not authoritative for us.

The answer to this difficulty has already been suggested. That there is an answer is involved in the fact that, peculiar and peculiarly conditioned as the experience of Paul might be, he had been able to eliminate its peculiarities, to universalize it, and on the strength of it to address himself with victorious assurance to the common conscience of mankind. That universal law, which

in a previous paper was shown to determine for him all the relations of God and man, and by doing so to make them relations
of moral import, takes shape variously, according to their circumstances and history, for the imagination and conscience of men. For
Paul the law took shape—it defined itself with divine authority, we
may say—in the law of Moses: for other men it took other, yet analogous, shapes. But all its forms, whatever their adequacy, or inadequacy, owed their authority to representing law in its eternal and
unchanging import. Every law, in other words, appealed to men
because somehow or other the authority of God was felt through
it. It is this which gives sin essentially the same character, no matter what its particular content may be. No things could be more
unlike than the hideous vices of paganism which are pilloried in
the first chapter of Romans, and the pretentious self-righteousness
of the Jews which is exposed in the second; but there is one relation in which they are identical—their relation to the eternal law
of God. Unless Paul had been able to generalize both sin and law
in such a way as to express this, he would have had no universal
gospel to preach, and no theology of it to construct; he would only
have had a curious spiritual autobiography to record. But the mere
fact that he could so generalize proves that his experience under
the Mosaic law is in its very nature akin to something which belongs to human experience in general. Accordingly we do not expect to find what he says unintelligible or unreal; on the contrary
our anticipation, to borrow Bunyan's expression about Luther on
Galatians, is that what he writes will be as though it were written
out of our own hearts.

What, then, does Paul say about the relation and interaction of
sin and law in his own (and therefore in all human) experience?

He has to say much which implies that there is a close connexion between them, much which may seem unflattering to the law,
and he takes care to make plain that for the law in itself he has
nothing but the most religious respect. It is ἅγιος, holy; that is, it
is *God's* law. The commandment in which it is expressed on any
given occasion is holy and just and good. The natural and proper
end of the commandment, that which God has in view in bringing
it into man's consciousness, is life (Rom 7:10). If the law given by
God had only been able to give life, righteousness would no doubt
have been of law, and there would have been no need of the gospel

(Gal 3:21). Nor does Paul say that it is the fault of the law that this result was not attained. On the contrary the law's incapacity is not to be referred to itself, but to the subject with which it has to deal (Rom 8:3). The one thing that has to be borne in mind at every point is that the law of God, defining itself variously to conscience according as the past of men or their surroundings vary, is always conceived as *confronting* those who are to keep it. It is of its nature to be a demand—an absolutely righteous demand, yet in the last resort a demand—not an inspiration.

When a man lives under law in this sense, the first result of it is that he comes to the consciousness of sin. When Paul pronounces the sentence διὰ νόμου ἐπίγνωσις ἁμαρτίας, he pronounces it, no doubt, as a Christian. His Christian intelligence enables him to focus the meaning of his pre-Christian experiences as he might not have been able to do in his pre-Christian days. We cannot deny that there is such a thing as blind, Pharisaic self-righteousness produced under the law; but the law does not produce this, any more than it produces sensuality or other sins. Its true result is an ever deepening consciousness—ἐπίγνωσις is full or adequate knowledge—that the life is not in relation to God what the law demands. It is not right with God; it is wrong with God, and no divine righteousness is realized in it. The Jews had the law of God made real to them, through their Scriptures and their history, with a vividness to which no other nation presents a parallel, and hence it is in Jewish, not in ethnic religious literature, that we find the consciousness of sin most acute. But everywhere the great experiment has the same issue: the law, however our consciousness of it come to us, convicts us of failure. But it reveals its power in another way; as St. Paul puts it, it works wrath (Rom 4:15, ὀργὴν κατεργάζεται). Through it, somehow, the holiness of God, of which it is the expression, reacts against sin; the man who has set himself against the will of God, as it appeals to him through the law, does not discover that the law gives way to him; on the contrary, it abides, and asserts itself against him. The consciousness that God is against us because we have been and are against Him, is the consciousness of His wrath; and there is nothing more real. It is quite true that ὀργὴ) in the New Testament is predominantly an eschatological idea: God's wrath is something that is almost appropriated to the great Day. But eschatological ideas do not arise out of nothing: they are at least the projection in imagination of something which the conscience knows to be real. The manifestation of God's wrath in all its force is by His mercy deferred for a time; but His wrath itself has workings of which the sinner may be painfully conscious long before the last judgment. Even if the sinner is unconscious, the spectator of his life, who is alive to God and to His working in the world, may see the stern and ominous reaction of His violated law—in other words, the wrath which it works—in the debasement and degeneration of the sinner himself. "With the perverse Thou wilt show Thyself forward": this is the truth which receives such appalling illustration in Romans 1:18–32, and which justifies us in regarding the phenomenon there described as a manifestation of the wrath of God. Such wrath is wrought by the law. It is because men are under law and disregard it that it reacts so terribly in their life. The power of God is in it, and it never grows old.

Through the law, then, we get the consciousness of sin; as the rule of the divine reaction against sin, the law works wrath; and the end of the life in which sin and wrath express man's relation to God and God's relation to man cannot be doubted: that life is doomed to death. There is probably no question on which more that is utterly misleading has been written than the question, What did Paul mean by death? Modern minds make distinctions, such as spiritual, temporal, eternal death, and give answers to the question which imply that Paul also had such distinctions present to his mind. There is no indication that he had. Man was man to him, an indivisible whole, and to introduce such distinctions in the interpretation of his writings is only to mislead. It is equally misleading to suggest that the connexion of sin and death for St. Paul rested on a literal interpretation of the opening chapters of Genesis, and that we are only at his point of view when we assume that death was attached to sin in the same way as any penalty is attached by a human legislature to the violation of its laws, and that but for this statutory arrangement man's relation to death might have been quite other than it is. In spite of the references to the third chapter of Genesis in Romans 5:12ff., I venture to maintain that St. Paul never raised the abstract questions here suggested. The story of the Fall and its consequences, including the connexion of death and sin, produces no impression at all until it produces an impression on the conscience, and that impression is one which attests itself. It is not through the study of natural history, but through experience of sin and law and wrath, that we learn the meaning of the words, "The wages of sin is death." The mortality of man is pathetic, but the end of the sinner is tragic. It is not to be assimilated to any natural event; its real nature is only to be discovered in conscience, and to conscience it is never anything but a doom. It has to be interpreted in relation to sin and law, and in this relation it cannot shut out from itself the awful judgment of God. Thoughts and experiences like these, and not reminiscences of the opening pages of the Bible, give authority and poignancy to all St. Paul says of death in connexion with sin. What he says is verified not by appeal to Genesis, but by appeal to the conscience of sinful men.

It is quite unmeaning to say that the theology which rests on the apprehension of truths like these is Paulinism: it is doing even Paul too great an honour to appropriate to him, by such a designation, experiences which every man can verify in his own life. Sin, wrath and death, in their relations to one another and to the holy law of God, are not Pauline, nor Pharisaic, nor Jewish, nor even "legal"; they are human and universal. We know what they mean as well as Paul; and Paul knew that his own experience was not a mystery nor a private property, but something which when uttered would wake echoes in every conscience. He lays great stress on the universality of sin—in other words, on the negative presupposition of the gospel; and in the Epistle to the Romans he has at least four ways of proving it.

(a) First, there is the empirical proof which is worked out in Romans 1 and 2. In Romans 1 Paul adduces evidence of the sinfulness of the Gentiles; in Romans 2 he demonstrates that no appeal to his historical privileges can exempt the Jew from the same condemnation. Strictly speaking, no empirical proof can establish a universal conclusion, but Paul assumes that no serious person will say, Not guilty. He charges all, as he expresses it in Romans 3:9, with being under sin, and he is confident that conscience must give the verdict in his favour.

(b) To this there is added a Scriptural proof in Romans 3:10ff. Formally, this proof is as inadequate as the other. The passages quoted do not refer to all men or to all times, but only to ages in the history of Israel when tyranny or corruption prevailed. But Paul does not think of what they refer to as originally written. It is his own mind he is expressing by them, the mind of a Christian and an apostle about the condition of the human race, and the significant thing is that such a judgment can be expressed in Scripture words. Logically, it may be said, the quotations prove nothing. True; but they are not addressed to the logical faculties, but to the conscience; and the apostle believes that in every man conscience will assent to the impeachment. If everybody who reads the indictment pleads guilty—and that is what he has a right to expect—it does not matter whether there is a logical flaw in it or not.

(c) But Paul has a religious argument for the universality of sin. This is expressed in Romans 3:23f., "All have sinned, and fall short of the glory of God, being justified freely by His grace." There is an inference *backward* from the one mode in which men can be put right with God to the antecedent condition in which they find themselves. If the only mode of justification is the one which Paul had experienced and which he preached—justification for nothing by the grace of God—then plainly there can be no such thing as a justification by works of law; in other words, the true and normal relations of God and man, as the law determines them, have nowhere been satisfied. It may be said that this is reasoning in a circle. "All men have sinned, and therefore justification must be by grace; and again, justification is by grace, and therefore all men must have sinned." But reasoning in a circle is not always wrong. It is not wrong when the circle in which we reason is one which includes within it the whole world of realities with which we are for the time being concerned. Now this is the case here; and when Paul, starting with the primary certainty of his Christian experience, that there is only one way of salvation and that a gracious one, argues to the universality of sin, his circle is quite legitimate. It simply means that the various aspects of reality which make up his spiritual world are consistent with each other, and apart from this it is not easy to see how there could be any assurance of their truth. If there is one gospel to be preached to everybody—and to Paul nothing was more certain—it is an immediate inference that everybody is in the condition which makes that gospel necessary.

(d) But besides his empirical, Scriptural, and religious arguments for the universality of sin, Paul has another, which may perhaps be called a metaphysical argument—the flesh. One is almost afraid to write the word which has been the subject of such rigorous and vigorous treatment, but it cannot be avoided. Whatever else the flesh may be, it is at least something which is common to all men, and which to human experience is universally associated with sin. Whoever says flesh says sin; the flesh is flesh of sin; the works of the flesh are moral horrors, and everybody in some shape or degree knows what they are. The flesh, it is not too much to say, represents for Paul the virulence and constitutional character as well as the omnipresence of sin; it carries in it always the emphasis of despair. It must be admitted that this is curiously unlike the way in which the flesh is spoken of in the Old Testament. There it is a graphic expression for the natural weakness of man; it does not aggravate the sinfulness of sin, but is rather put under the head of extenuating circumstances. "He, being full of compassion, forgave their iniquity, and destroyed them not; yea, many a time turned He His anger away, and did not stir up all His wrath. And He remembered that they were but flesh, a wind that passeth away, and cometh not again." How could any one deal rigorously with such creatures? This is the tone, too, in which Jesus speaks, extenuating the fault of the disciples, who slept through His agony in the garden: "The spirit indeed is willing, but the flesh is weak." But if Paul's conception of the flesh cannot be explained from the Old Testament, or from the words of Jesus, just as little can it be traced to a dualistic psychology of Hellenic origin. What we find in such dualistic psychologies is the antithesis of the material and the intellectual; it may be felt as a burden, or a limitation, or in some other way a restraint on man's becoming what he would become; but nothing is more remote from such philosophical dualism, even in the finest moral natures, than the passion of abhorrence, condemnation, and despair with which Paul speaks of the flesh. The truth is that when he speaks of the flesh, it is not an antithesis that he is dealing with, but an antagonism; the flesh belongs not to his psychology—he has no such thing—but to his moral and religious experience; it is that in him which does not subject itself to the law of God, and cannot, but lives in the perpetual revolt of sin. That there is that in him which can be so characterized is as sure to him as that he is a human being, and it is as sure for others as for himself. Just because a man is what he is he finds himself in standing antagonism with the law of God. That is what Paul means by being in the flesh; and it is a conclusive demonstration of the universality of sin. For a man to say he knew no sin would be as much as to say that he had no part in the nature common to man.

It may be objected here that this, as an argument for the universality of sin, begs the question. So it does, if a man has no conscience. But if a man recognises in himself what Paul is talking about when he talks of the flesh—and it is assumed by the apostle, and surely with reason, that men *will* recognise it, not indeed as psychological theory, but as moral fact—then it does not beg the question. It wakes up in the conscience, the only place in which it can be felt, a sense of the dreadful, inevitable, pervasive, constitutional antipathy of man to the law of God; it gives him a new revelation of the depth and intensity of sin; the *misera necessitas peccandi*,[1] as Augustine called it, closes in on him and all his kind. It is in expounding the law and the flesh in their interaction that Paul says the most daring and paradoxical things about sin. The law, he indirectly suggests in Romans 8:3, might have done something great for man, but it was weak through the flesh; the flesh disabled it. Instead of subduing the flesh, the law irritated it. It acted, in point of fact, in a way that seemed to defeat its own end. All that its "Thou shalt not" produced from the flesh was "I will." The forbidden fruit is the very fruit we want to eat. Paul does not hesitate to say—what must have seemed impious to a Jew, and is startling even for him—that this was God's intention in the reign of law. He meant it, by evoking the instinctive antipathy of the flesh, to multiply transgressions, and so to bring man to despair. No doubt it is the Mosaic law of which Paul says this, both in Romans 5 and Galatians 3; but that does not make it meaningless for us. The instinctive revolt against the law which imposes its restraint on our nature is not a Jewish but a human experience; and whatever the law be which brings this characteristic of our nature into consciousness, it does for us what the Mosaic law did for Paul, and we understand his experience through our own. For us, as for him, such an experience is God's way of shutting us up to another mode of attaining righteousness than that of works of law. Such a

1. [Wretched necessity of sinning.]

nature stands in no proportion to our calling; it leaves us face to
face with an impossible problem, sold under sin.

It is common to ask at this point how Paul conceived man's
nature to have become what it is, or whether he conceived it to
have been what it is from the beginning. These are questions to
which no answer is supplied; they are questions, indeed, which it
would have been as impossible for Paul to answer as it is for us.
We never knew ourselves to be anything else than what we are,
and we cannot go out of our nature as it is to scrutinize it in assumed antecedent conditions. In man as he is—and that is man
in the only sense in which we know anything about him—there is
that which reacts instinctively against the law, that which is stimulated by the law into persistent and determined revolt, that which
under such stimulus reveals to man the exceeding sinfulness of
sin. This is what Paul means by the flesh, and it has simply to be
taken as it stands. Its origin is not explained by such propositions
as Romans 5:12, "Through one man sin entered into the world"; or
Romans 7:9, "I was alive apart from law once, but when the commandment came sin sprang to life, and I died." These propositions
have precisely the same value: the first applies to humanity, indi-
vidualized in its natural head, the same mode of conception which
the second applies to the life of the writer himself. But in both cases
it is a mode of conception which may be said to belong to ideal biography. We cannot go back in our life to a happy time when we
had no conscience of sin, and no idea of what the flesh means; we
know what the flesh means as soon as we have a conscience at all,
and memory reaches no further, if indeed it reaches as far. Similarly we cannot go back in the history of man to a paradisaical
condition in which sin had not entered and in which there was no
trace of antagonism to law, no disproportion between man's nature and his vocation; as far as history is concerned, it has nothing
to say of any such state. Alike in the individual and in the race
the moral state has simply to be accepted: questions of origins are
hopelessly beyond our reach.

But by St. Paul it is accepted, and this is the point to be emphasized, *as a moral state*. Its moral character is of the very essence
of it. It never occurs to the apostle that because man is what he is,
and because his nature, so far as it is known in experience, betrays
uniformly this antipathy to the law, therefore man is discharged

of all moral responsibility. The facts for him have their whole being and meaning in the moral sphere; to say "the flesh" is not to pronounce man's acquittal, it is to exhibit the profound and hopeless character of his sin. To know what the flesh means does not prompt self-exculpation: it wrings from the sinful soul the cry, "O wretched man that I am! who shall deliver me out of the body of this death?"

One can imagine beforehand a way in which deliverance might come. If the law lost its external provocative character—if it ceased to be, as something which merely confronted man with its demands, and became instead a νόμος δυνάμενος ζωοποιῆσαι, an inspiring force; or if man's nature was changed—if the flesh ceased to be, and instead of ruling man and making the law ineffective was itself reduced to impotence, then the deliverance might come. In the Christian experience of possessing the Spirit both these results are combined. The Spirit is, in a word, a νόμος δυνάμενος ζωοποιῆσαι, or what is the same thing, a δύναμις through which the law passes into act; it is the union of law and impulse, in which the strife of sin is finally overcome. But this is anticipating. In the end the law as an external thing does pass, and its place is taken, and the ends it vainly sought to secure are secured, by the Spirit. But it does not pass unhonoured. Even in its external and imperfect forms, of which the Mosaic law is the highest example, it represented the will of God; and it is the will of God to which (in reacting against the law) human nature has shown itself opposed. It is impossible for any one who sees this to believe that God can ignore it. It is impossible for him to believe that God asks men to forget it without more ado, and to dismiss from their life, not understood and not used, the painful experiences of sin, law, wrath, the flesh, death. The law as an outward thing passes, but between its passing and the coming of the Spirit stands the whole body of Christian facts centring in the death and resurrection of Jesus. These facts are the condition of the Spirit's coming; its coming is not direct, but mediated through them. The power to live a holy life is not poured into a sinful nature claiming immediate fellowship with a holy God; it is bestowed on such a nature, according to Paul, only through Jesus Christ and Him crucified. The righteousness of God, which is the answer to the whole necessities of the sinful world, is not revealed *in vacuo*. It is not transmitted into human nature by the vibrations of some sort of spiritual ether, as one might infer from the comparisons which are sometimes used to illustrate it; it is demonstrated in Jesus Christ set forth as a propitiation, through faith, in His blood. It is this which we have next to study in all the relations suggested by what we have seen of sin, the flesh, and the law.

# 3

# The Gospel a Divine Righteousness

The study of St. Paul's doctrine of sin, with its correlated ideas of law, wrath, the flesh and death, enables us to understand the situation which the gospel has to meet. It is not man without qualification to whom it is addressed, but sinful men, and men whose sin has the constitutional, desperate and fatal character which we have seen. It is such men who are confronted with the problem: How shall we be righteous with God? They can find no answer for it. The answer, when it is found, is *a revelation* (Rom 1:17); it comes from heaven, and bears the name not of men but of God. "I am not ashamed of the gospel . . . a righteousness of God is revealed in it" (Rom 1:16–17).

Whatever the righteousness of God may be in itself, it is surely clear that it is something of which we must eventually be the subjects. In whatever sense it is God's, there must be some sense in which it also becomes ours. It is we sinners who have to be justified by it, and if it were not available for our justification there would be no gospel in it for us. The apostle expresses this in various ways. The connexion of Romans 3:22 and Romans 3:24 implies that it is in virtue of this δικαιοσύνη θεοῦ revealed in the gospel that we are justified. In 2 Corinthians 5:17 he speaks of "the abundance of the gift of righteousness." In 2 Corinthians 5:21 he argues that the end of all God's reconciling work—the very meaning of the death of His Son—is that we should become the righteousness of God in Him. It is a fixed point therefore to begin with, that whatever δικαιοσύνη θεοῦ may be, abstractly considered, the δικαιοσύνη θεοῦ which is the content of the gospel revelation is something which is destined to become man's. But what does this phrase mean, into which Paul condensed the whole of Christianity?

One set of attempts to explain it proceeds, it may be said, philologically. It assumes that δικαιοσύνη θεοῦ must mean what it bears on its face: the righteousness which belongs to God, which is His essential attribute, an integral element in His nature or His character. In this sense, however, a revelation of the righteousness of God would only mean a revelation that God was righteous; and it may well be doubted whether such a revelation would constitute a gospel for men in the condition described by Paul. Hence it is usually assumed that the revelation of God's righteousness in the gospel includes in particular a revelation of the fact that this righteousness is not self-contained, so to speak, but self-communicating; it is God's, but it issues forth from God and imparts itself to men. Sometimes, as for instance in Sanday and Headlam's Commentary,[1] this is connected with passages in Isaiah which speak of God's righteousness as "going forth"; or, to use the language of these scholars, "as projected from the divine essence and realizing itself among men." Without raising the question whether the Old Testament writer meant anything of this kind when he spoke of God's righteousness as "going forth," the religious truth of the conception which is thus associated with St. Paul's phrase need not be disputed. It conveys the same lesson as our Lord's word to the young ruler: "There is none good but one, that is, God." All goodness comes from Him; in men it is a stream fed from that central fountain. St. Paul would have been the last man in the world to deny this, but it may fairly be questioned whether the conception stands in a sufficiently close relation to the necessities of sinful men to constitute a gospel; and so far as the writer is aware, no one has even attempted to connect it in any specific way with St. Paul's conception of the cross. It is by no means equal to the requirements of the case to say with Sanday and Headlam that to St. Paul "it seems a necessity that the righteousness of God should be not only inherent but energizing, that it should impress and diffuse itself as an active force in the world"; and then to add to this, as by way of supplement, that

1. Sanday and Headlam, *A Critical and Exegetical Commentary on the Epistle to the Romans*, 35.

there is "one signal manifestation" of it, "the nature of which it is difficult for us wholly to grasp, in the death of Christ." This is not merely "one signal manifestation" of it; on the contrary, so far as the righteousness of God in St. Paul constitutes his gospel, it has no meaning whatever but that which it has as manifested at the cross. We may be getting to know God, perhaps, but we are certainly not getting to understand the apostle, when we provide an indefinite background like this for the glad tidings of "Jesus Christ and Him crucified." St. Paul's gospel—for δικαιοσύνη θεοῦ is his gospel in brief—is something far more specific than the idea that God's righteousness overflows upon man, or that God makes us partakers in His own character, and does so the more eagerly and urgently because otherwise we have no character at all. The ultimate objection to such an interpretation of the righteousness of God is that it does not appreciate the ethical character of the situation. To St. Paul, the problem presented to God by the sin of the world is a moral problem of tremendous difficulty, and it is hardly too much to say that this is an attempt to solve it by ignoring the moral difficulties altogether. The righteousness of God is here conceived as acting after the analogy of a physical force. It "goes out," "energizes," "diffuses itself," as the light and heat of the sun, irrespective of moral conditions. It is its nature to do so and it can never do anything else. But in spite of the Biblical comparison of God to the sun, moral problems can never be solved by the categories of physics, and the gospel of St. Paul grapples far more closely with the moral necessities of the case. His δικαιοσύνη θεοῦ as concentrated in Christ crucified has essential relations to sin and law and death which are here left out of sight. Another attempt or series of attempts to get at the meaning of the expression may be distinguished from the last as historical. It aims at establishing a connexion in import as well as in form between St. Paul's language and that of the Old Testament. Its most distinguished representative was Ritschl, and it has been elaborately set out again by the lexicographer Cremer in his *Paulinische Rechtfertigungslehre*. Not that Cremer is entirely at one with Ritschl: indeed he pursues him all along with a sort of protesting criticism, the relevance or justice of which it is often not easy to discern. But they agree in trying to attach Paul's sense as well as his words to the Old Testament in something like the following fashion. They point out that God's righteousness is manifested when He acts as judge, and that when He does so it is always to see right done, to vindicate those who are in the right, to establish righteousness in the earth. Ritschl illustrates this conception principally from the Psalms: a notable instance is Psalm 35:23–28: "Judge me, O Lord my God, according to thy righteousness: and let them not rejoice over me. . . . Let them shout for joy, and be glad, that favour my righteous cause" (literally, my righteousness). And my tongue shall talk of thy righteousness and of thy praise all the day long." Here the righteousness of God is that principle in the divine nature in virtue of which God cannot suffer wrong to triumph over right; when His people are wronged, it is in virtue of His righteousness that He vindicates or, as it may be expressed, justifies them. He pleads their cause and puts them in the right before all. Hence the appeals which we have in the Old Testament to the righteousness of God, not as something to be dreaded by His people, but as their one sure hope. "In thee, O Lord, do I put my trust . . . deliver me in thy righteousness" (Ps 31:1). "Quicken me, O Lord, for thy name's sake: in thy righteousness bring my soul out of trouble" (Ps 143:11). Hence also the use of the word "righteousnesses" to describe the great acts in which God interposed in His people's cause and maintained their right in the world: "There shall they rehearse the righteousnesses of the Lord"—the various manifestations of His righteousness—"the righteousnesses of his rule in Israel" (Judg 5:11; cf. 1 Sam 12:7). And hence also the combination, so frequent in the latter half of the Book of Isaiah, of righteousness and salvation. "My salvation is near to come, and my righteousness to be revealed" (Isa 56:1). "My salvation shall be for ever, and my righteousness shall not be abolished" (Isa 51:6).

In the line of passages like these it is argued, especially by Ritschl, that God's righteousness is no abstract, and especially no legal retributive justice, but essentially gracious. It is not something to which justice must be done in order that grace may be free to act; it is itself grace in action for the vindication or justification of the people of God. It is in this sense that δικαιοσύνη θεοῦ is to be interpreted in St. Paul.

Here again, as in the former instance, we may admit the religious truth of the representation. Granted that it is God's people with whom we have to deal, and especially God's people wronged by the world, we can understand that God's righteousness is that to which they would appeal for salvation. Like Christ, reviled and insulted, they would commit themselves to Him who judges righteously (1 Pet 2:23) and trust in Him to plead their cause. Paul perhaps has this connexion of ideas in mind when he refers to the persecutions and afflictions endured by the Thessalonians as "a manifest token of the righteous judgment of God" (2 Thess 1:5): they speak plainly of the way in which the Righteous Judge must interpose to do the injured believers justice and to punish their foes. Even when there is no conception of a hostile world against which the cause of God's people has to be made good, we find the righteousness of God spoken of in a way to which Ritschl can appeal in support of his interpretation. "Wherever there is a people of God at all, there is a relation between them and God which involves obligations on both. sides, and God's fidelity to these obligations is called His righteousness. It may have its most signal manifestation when His people have been false to the obligations on their side, and in this case it is closely related to the forgiveness of sins. God does not renounce His people when they err or sin in human frailty and then come to Him in penitence; He fulfils the covenant obligations as far as they are binding on Him, and He shows His righteousness in doing so. This is the explanation of those combinations which at first surprise a modern reader: "Deliver me from bloodguiltiness, O God, thou God of my salvation; and my tongue shall sing aloud of thy righteousness," i.e., of Thy fidelity to all that is involved in the promise to be the God of Israel (Ps 51:14); or the precisely similar passage in the New Testament: "If we confess our sins, he is faithful and righteous to forgive us our sins"; i.e. true to the obligations involved in His relation to us as Christians (1 John 1:9). In passages like these a righteousness of God is undoubtedly spoken of which is a gracious thing and which is exhibited in the forgiveness of sins: the only question to be answered is whether it can be identified off-hand with that δικαιοσύνη θεοῦ which is Paul's gospel to a world lost in sin.

To the present writer it does not seem doubtful that the answer must be in the negative. In every case to which this line of interpretation can appeal, the righteousness of God is manifested in relation to a people of God. God does right by them, it may be in achieving their deliverance from oppressors—this is "salvation" in the sense of the Old Testament; it may be in forgiving the sins of which they repent, and which are not in themselves a renunciation of their covenant with Him. No doubt the righteousness of God in this sense is sometimes spoken of as manifested to the world. "The Lord hath made known his salvation: his righteousness hath he openly shewed in the sight of the nations" (Ps 98:2). But this does not mean what Paul means when he speaks of the gospel of a divine righteousness being made known to all nations for the obedience of faith; it means that God has delivered His people from their enemies, and given an unmistakable demonstration on the stage of universal history of His fidelity to His covenant. "All the ends of the earth have seen the salvation of our God" (Ps 98:3) means "have seen the salvation he has wrought *for us*"; "the mercy and the faithfulness" which He has "remembered toward the house of Israel." There is nothing here of the nature of gospel to those who are not the people of God. In spite of parallelism of language, there is not in such passages any real correspondence of thought with St. Paul. He does not preach his gospel to people who can make appeal to God to do right by them: he preaches to those who are hopelessly in the wrong before God. He does not preach to those who can think of themselves as somehow God's people, and who can count on God's fidelity to all that this means; he preaches to those who are not God's people, who can count on nothing, and to whom his gospel is the one unqualified miracle of the world. And the righteousness of God which he preaches is neither the vindication of the good when they are wronged, nor the faithfulness of God to His people even when they have failed in their duty to Him. It is something far more wonderful and profound. It is a righteousness infinitely more gracious and more compelling than either—a righteousness *which puts the ungodly in the right* (Rom 4:5), and constitutes into a people of God those who lay under His judgment (Rom 3:19). A righteousness like this, if such a thing can be, is unmistakably glad tidings for a sinful world; it is a genuine gospel for those who need a gospel; and this, one may venture to say, is not yielded by either of the other interpretations. This too, it is not too much to add, is decisive: the evangelist is in the last resort the judge of evangelical theology. If it does not serve his purpose it is not true.

To grasp the apostle's meaning, it is necessary to follow the exposition which he himself gives of it in Romans 3:21ff. and to remember at the same time that when Old Testament words are used in the New Testament they cease *ipso facto* to be Old Testament words and carry in them a New Testament meaning. We take for granted only what has already been made clear: that this righteousness, which is at least named after God has God, as its source, that it eventually becomes man's, and that when this is accomplished man is justified—right with God and right in God's judgment; and with these assumptions we proceed to an examination of the classical passage (Rom 3:21–26).

We notice first that the divine righteousness of the gospel is manifested χωρὶς νόμου, apart from law. This does not mean that it has no relation to the universal moral elements in the relations of God and man; on the contrary, it is part of the apostle's object to prove that in the way in which this righteousness comes justice is done to all these elements, so that God in revealing it not only "justifies" the believer in Jesus but is Himself "just." The new religion may be χωρὶς νόμου, but it does not annul law; it sets law on its feet (Rom 3:31). It is χωρὶς νόμου in the sense in which a Jew laid stress on his fulfilment of the law, or a Gentile on his life according to the law of nature, as constituting a claim upon God, in response to which He must acknowledge them to be in the right or righteous before Him: for the divine righteousness which the gospel proclaims all men have to become God's debtors: it is a divine gift, not a human achievement. It is χωρὶς νόμου only in the sense that to its presence in the world man's fulfilment of law contributes nothing. Although it is χωρὶς νόμου it is "witnessed to by the law and the prophets," that is, by the Old Testament. Although the gospel is a new revelation belonging to the present age (νυνὶ δὲ Rom 3:21, τῷ νῦν καιρῷ Rom 3:26), Paul is aware that revelation from first to last is a unity, and therefore consistent with itself. It is one God who is revealing Himself in it all along. In an age when criticism is illustrating the differences of a formal kind which exist in the record of revelation, this is a truth to be emphasized. The Old Testament and the New Testament are at bottom one, and will stand or fall together. It is their oneness which is the ultimate proof of their divinity. The unity of Scripture and its inspiration are correlative terms, and its unity consists in this, that it all attests the gospel. It is a complete mistake to try to solve difficulties about inspiration by striking out here and there what is not inspired, or by distinguishing a human element from the divine (as if there were anything in Scripture which was not thoroughly human even while divine), or by attempting to grade the various Scriptures according to the degree of inspiration they exhibit: we believe Scripture to be inspired because when we approach it with the one question on the answer to which the possibility of religion depends—How shall a sinful man be just with God?—from first to last it has one and the same answer. And because Scripture is the only authority in the world which has a consistent and convincing answer to give, we believe that inspiration belongs to it alone. We ought to notice in passing that the particular Scriptures to which Paul refers in support of this assertion are not those of which such copious use has been made by writers like Ritschl, Häring, Cremer, Sanday and Headlam, and others, to explain the antecedents and associations of his phrase δικαιοσύνη θεοῦ. He does not quote any of the numerous passages from the Psalms or II. Isaiah in which God's righteousness is spoken of as "going forth," and has been represented as "energizing," or "enclosing and gathering into itself human wills." Probably he did not read the Psalms and Isaiah in this sense; at all events it is by appeal to passages of quite a different kind that he demonstrates the consistency of the Christian gospel with the ancient revelation of God.

The divine righteousness of the gospel thus asserted becomes available for men—becomes men's in short, so that they stand right with God in virtue of it—through faith. It is a righteousness of God through faith in Jesus Christ coming to or extending over all who have faith. What faith means as the appropriation of the divine righteousness will be considered in next paper; here it is only referred to for the light it casts on the nature of that righteousness itself. It emphasizes the fact that it is a gift, something which men may receive but which they cannot produce. If "the gift of righteousness" is the true way to describe it (Rom 5:17), then the only way to have it as our own must be to "take" it. It cannot be ours if we leave it, and we are not able to earn it. This is what is implied in the emphasis here laid on faith.

At verse 24, as is well known, there is a certain irregularity in the apostle's grammar, but the connexion of his ideas is not obscured. The sentence beginning δικαιούμενοι δωρεὰν τῇ αὐτοῦ χάριτι is virtually an exegesis of the 22nd verse. When sinful men believe in Jesus Christ, and the divine righteousness manifested in Him becomes theirs, this is what happens: they are justified freely by God's grace. They become right with Him, righteous in His sight, and they owe it to His pure unearned goodness. He has brought into being and put within the sinner's reach the very thing the sinner needs, and which, though he cannot produce, he can still appropriate—a "righteousness," namely, which because it is of God is properly described by His name, δικαιοσύνη θεοῦ, and not by the name of those for whom it is destined.

Paul cannot speak of the grace which underlies the gift of righteousness without going on to magnify it. That is what he does when he says that we are justified freely by His grace "through the redemption that is in Christ Jesus." It is possible to argue that what ἀπολύτρωσις (redemption) suggests is not the cost of liberation or emancipation, but the fact. Certainly the fact suggested by the word is not to be overlooked; to overlook it is to miss the meaning of justification. To be justified freely by God's grace is to be emancipated from a former state and its liabilities; it is to have our relation to God and our standing with Him changed, no longer determined by such powers and expressed in such words as Sin, Condemnation, Curse, Law, Death, but determined by Christ alone. But whenever we say "by Christ alone,"—whenever we think of the ἀπολύτρωσις as being ἐν Χριστῷ Ἰησοῦ—the cost of it comes into view. Paul preached no vague and unembodied redemption to sinful men; the divine righteousness which he offered, and which meant this great emancipation from law, sin and death, he could only offer in Christ, and, as the next words show, in Christ crucified. There are modern theologians who hold that the Son has no place in the gospel, which is simply the revelation of the Father; but their gospel is certainly not that of the greatest of apostles. He did not preach his "divine righteousness," referring casually, as he might think it necessary or becoming, to Christ's authority; he preached a redemption *in Christ Jesus*, he preached Christ as Himself made righteousness to us.

Nor is he content with a merely impressionist view of Christ, as it has been called; he thinks out the problems involved in the sin-

ner's emancipation and justification in Him; he unfolds that interpretation of Christ which explains His power and sovereignty in
his own heart and gives him His gospel of justification to preach;
Christ Jesus he says, *whom God set forth as a propitiation through faith*
*in His blood.* Alike by those who accept and by those who reject it
this is felt to be the heart of St. Paul's theology and of his gospel.
Happily for him the two things did not fall apart. The profound-
est truth he knew was the most joyful message he could proclaim.
Happily too he did not feel it necessary to apologize for the love
of God; it did not seem incredible to him that that love should do
things for men, in Christ, that fill the soul with fear and wonder.
"By terrible things in righteousness wilt thou answer us, O God of
our salvation." We can admit that when St. Paul wrote, "Christ Jesus, whom God set forth as a propitiation in his blood," he touched
on one of the ultimate truths which, as Dr. Hort says, become apparent not by the light we can shed on them, but by the light which
they shed upon everything else; but even so he does not leave us
unable to grasp his meaning. No doubt it has points of attachment
in the Old Testament. Stress need not be laid on the fact that the
LXX uses ἱλαστήριον, the "mercy seat" of our English version; if
St. Paul had meant this he must have indicated it more definitely.
But when he combined the two expressions ἱλαστήριον and ἐν τῷ
αὐτοῦ αἵματι he certainly conceived of Christ's death as sacrificial;
none but sacrificial blood had propitiatory power. The question
remains however: Does it carry us any way into his mind to say
so? Do we know what he meant or felt when he assimilated the
death of Christ to a sacrifice? Does he read the meaning out of the
sacrificial system into the death of Christ, or, having discovered
the profound import of Christ's death, does he suddenly become
aware that here is the one sacrifice by which propitiation is made
for ever, and adopt the language of the ancient ritual to find access
for his thought to his hearers' minds?

In so far as these questions invite us to follow the psychological
genesis of Paul's thoughts we probably do not require to answer
them. One point is clear: he saw himself, and taught his contemporaries to see, an essential correspondence between the death of
Jesus and the propitiatory sacrifices of the Old Testament. But in
what did that correspondence consist? It consisted in this, that in
both cases a connexion was assumed between the sacrificial death

and sin. The victim's death was in the last resort due to sin: to put it in the simplest possible form, it was a death for sin. It is not unusual to hear this peremptorily denied, and the legitimacy of putting Christ's death in any relation to the ancient sacrificial system summarily ruled out of court. Wellhausen's *obiter dictum* that the cultus is the pagan element in the religion of Israel has met with a wonderfully wide and uncritical acceptance even among evangelical theologians. But it has the falsehood of all epigrams written on its face. The cultus in the religion of Israel is like the cultus in any other; it is pagan or something else than pagan, just as the religion does not or does possess the power to interpret, to spiritualize, to transfigure it. "Purge me with hyssop, and I shall be clean: wash me, and I shall be whiter than snow" (Ps 51:7). That is the language inspired by the cultus, and interpreting it; is there anything pagan in that? No doubt an institution like sacrifice would mean many different things in the course of its long history. It would mean one thing in the primitive ages explored by Robertson Smith, another in those to which the later strata of the Pentateuch belonged; one thing to the man who killed his victim with his knife, but how much more to the man who, to use the words of a great preacher, killed it with his soul! It is not necessary to go into these distinctions, nor when we consider the extent to which the ritual and sacrificial elements in the Old Testament have served to mould alike the religious thinking and the adoring worship of the New—recall only the Epistle to the Hebrews and the Book of Revelation—can we take seriously the proposal to set them aside as pagan and irrelevant to Christianity. The simple truth is that here, at the very heart of his gospel, in interpreting the one truth on which the hope of sinful men depends, Paul finds no language to express himself in but language prompted by the sacrificial system. And when the other New Testament writers come to the same place they do the same thing. In John, it is "Behold the Lamb of God which taketh away the sin of the world." In Peter, "He bore our sins in his own body to the tree"— "a lamb without blemish and without spot." In Hebrews, "He put away sin by the sacrifice of himself." And the Apocalypse is full of "a lamb as it had been slain." The idea in all this is not ambiguous: it is that the death of Christ is essentially related to sin—has to be defined by relation to it, as the death of the propitiatory sacrifice had to be.

When Paul says here that "God set forth Christ a propitiation in His blood," he only allows for a moment what for his readers at least is the illuminating idea of atoning sacrifice to fall upon the death of Christ. But what he means is precisely what he means when he says in other places, without the sacrificial figure, "Christ died for our sins; God made him to be sin for us; he became a curse for us; he was delivered up for our offences." All that sin meant for us—all that in sin and through it had become ours—God made His, and He made His own, in death. He *died* for us. This death, *defined as it must be by relation to our sins,* is that in virtue of which Jesus Christ is a propitiation for sin. Without it and without this interpretation of it St. Paul would have no gospel to preach. The word has been abused, and false inferences have been drawn from it, but is there a word in the world which covers the essential truth of this gospel better than the word *substitution*? αὐτὸς ἡμῶς τὰς ἁμαρτίας ἀνήνεγκεν, *He* bore *our* sins.

Further light is thrown on the idea of propitiation when we notice the double purpose it secures. It is its aim and its result that God should be at once just and the justifier of him who believes in Jesus. This second result is the one which we should regard as being immediately in view—the securing of a divine righteousness for the sinful. But it is the peculiarity of a propitiation that it does this in a way which at the same time secures the righteousness of God Himself. What does this mean? What is the righteousness of God Himself which has to be secured in this connexion? Is it His righteousness regarded as a self-imparting quality to which justice is not done as long as there is sin in the world which it has not overcome? We have already seen the limits of this conception, and there is no way of deducing from it the specific propitiation which Paul preaches, or indeed any propitiation whatever. A divine righteousness is the gift which God offers to man in Christ for his salvation, but salvation—and especially the salvation of the New Testament—is never traced to the righteousness of God as its source. Is then the righteousness of God Himself, as one of the ends to be secured by the propitiation, that fidelity of God to His covenant obligations, which we have seen is sometimes the meaning of the word? The answer must again be in the negative: if this were the case, the distinction between δίχαιον and δικαιοῦντα would disappear; for according to this view it is precisely in justifying that God shows Himself faithful, in vindicating the right of His people that He is exhibited as a righteous God. Setting aside then both of these interpretations, nothing remains but to look to the context. There we see that the righteousness of God Himself is conceived as something affected by "the passing over of the sins done aforetime in the forbearance of God." There has been in the moral administration of the world a temporary suspension of God's ultimate judgment on sin, and so far His righteousness has been obscured and may be called in question. It is not apparent, men may say, that God does judge sin with an uncompromising judgment. But according to the argument of St. Paul in this passage, a propitiation not only enables God to put the gift of a divine righteousness within the sinner's reach, but at the same time to silence this doubt; even in justifying the guilty God's uncompromising judgment upon sin is set in the clearest light. Now what is the immediate inference from this when we consider that God has set forth Christ as a propitiation in His blood? It is that the death of Christ must be defined in relation to sin, and to God's ultimate judgment on sin, in such a way that no one looking at it and knowing what it means can say any longer God is not righteous; He is more or less indifferent to evil. It would not be a propitiation to St. Paul—it would lack one of the essential constituents of propitiatory virtue—if it did not embody unequivocally God's condemnation of sin. Hence such a condemnation is part of the essential significance of the cross.

The apostle does not expand his thoughts here, but the connexion of ideas cannot be mistaken. All that sin means for man—all the doom that it involves—is summed up in death, the awful experience in which God's condemnation of sin becomes finally real to conscience; and *He died* for us. He made our doom His own. He took our condemnation upon Himself. He did it in obedience to the will of the Father, and in doing so. He acknowledged the justice of the divine order which binds together death and sin. No one who knows what He did can think again that God is indifferent to this order. On the contrary, its inviolableness is maintained even in bringing sinful men salvation. There is no such idea in Christianity as that of God condoning sin. God condones nothing: His mercy itself is of an absolute integrity. He is a righteous God, even in justifying the ungodly; and the propitiation which He sets forth in Christ Jesus, dying in His sinlessness the death of the sinful, is the key to the mystery.

Once more, is not the word which spontaneously rises to our lips to express this the word substitution? The aversion to it which prevails so widely has many causes. Partly it is due to its abuse, and if the abuse can be guarded against should not weigh in our minds. Partly it is one form of the aversion to the very idea of mediation in religion. Substitution is mediation in the most acute and defiant form and provokes the most vehement opposition from those who reject mediation *ab initio* and prefer religion without the sense of personal debt to Christ. Partly again it rests on what are regarded as distinctively moral grounds. Substitution is quite frankly pronounced immoral. It is not possible, without anticipating what has to be said in a later discussion of faith, to give the whole answer to the moral protest, but it is not too much to deprecate the summary and angry rejection of an idea which has played the part which substitution has in evangelical preaching, and which has, to say the least, such specious points of attachment in apostolic doctrine. What we usually mean by the sphere of morality is the sphere of mutual obligation; you are morally bound to do something for me and I for you, and we have a moral right to require the fulfilment of these bonds. Manifestly in the sphere of such relations there is no room for such an action as the death of Christ if it means what Paul takes it to mean. But even human life gives scope for acts in which the limits of such moral obligation are transcended—acts which are not moral, but far higher than moral; acts immediately inspired of God, the understanding of which is to morality as the discovery of a fourth dimension would be to geometry. It is only in this sense that the substitution of Christ is not moral. It transcends the moral world because it has to recreate it. Substitution, in short, is mediation raised to its highest power, exalted and glorified by love to its most compelling intensity. No one who accepts the idea of mediation in religion at all is in the right to reject it *a priori* here. To do so is to declare that he can measure the love of God beforehand and tell all that it can or will do. But it is not beforehand that we know anything about redemption. *"Hereby perceive we love."* Who could have told beforehand that a divine righteousness would come to sinful men in Christ Jesus set forth by God as a propitiation in His blood?

# 4

# Faith and the Righteousness of God

The righteousness of God, which for St. Paul is equivalent to the gospel, is hardly presented to us, in the Epistle to the Romans, as a thing in itself. No doubt there is a sense in which it is independent of the relation of any man to it; it is *there*, there in Jesus Christ set forth by God as a propitiation in His blood, whether men look that way or refuse to look. It is as real as the presence of the Son of God in the world, as real as His death upon the cross, whether men comprehend it and appropriate it or not. But although the δικαιοσύνη θεοῦ must have this outwardness and independence, since otherwise the evangelist would have nothing to preach, St. Paul habitually thinks and speaks of it in relation to that human act or experience in which it becomes man's. That act is faith. Apart from faith, the revelation of God's righteousness is nothing to us; through faith, all that it is and means becomes ours. Hence it is a divine power to save in the case of every one who has faith (Rom 1:16); it is revealed "from faith to faith"; that is, according to the most probable interpretation, faith is from first to last the condition on which we appreciate the revelation, and make its blessings our own (Rom 1:17); the end of an apostolic ministry is to produce among men that submission to God's way of salvation which can be described as the obedience of faith (Rom 1:5): even the propitiation which Christ is in His blood is expressly characterized as a propitiation "through faith" (Rom 3:25), as though the apostle would warn us against ascribing any magical virtue to the propitiatory death where faith in it was wanting. The subject of this paper is faith in relation to the righteousness of God, as St. Paul exhibits it in the Epistle to the Romans.

St. Paul himself nowhere gives a definition of faith, the reason being presumably, as Pfleiderer suggests, that he does not employ the word in any other than the current sense, or at least is not conscious of doing so. Where the gospel is spoken of as a message which the apostle delivers, to believe naturally means to accept his testimony, to receive his message as true; where it is identified with a person, with God as its source, or with Christ as its mediator, then the acceptance of the message is elevated into some kind of trust reposed in God or in Christ. In a sense religious faith always has God as its object, and means reliance upon Him in the character in which He has revealed Himself. It may be reliance on a word which God has spoken, holding fast to such a word as the one thing which cannot be shaken in a world of unrealities: such was the faith of Abraham, who lived as if the only reality in the universe were this, that his seed should inherit Canaan, and that through him all the families of the earth should be blessed. It may be reliance on a deed which God has done, a deed in which His character is so exhibited as to evoke the confidence of men. If we regard the presence of the Son of God in the world, including His death and resurrection, as one such great revealing act of God, we can understand how Peter speaks of Christians as those who "believe in God through Christ" (1 Pet 1:21). Such faith might be indefinitely rich in content, as rich as the life of Jesus recorded in the Gospels and as the innumerable impulses to trust which spring out of it. If, again, the act of God is that central and decisive one—the setting forth of Christ as a propitiation in His blood—in which He deals with the sin of the world for man's salvation, then the corresponding faith is that sinner's faith on which Paul concentrates attention as the condition of being right with God. It is really this last which we have to consider. The generic use of the terms "faith" or "believing" by the apostle may be disregarded; the point of interest is his specifically Christian use of them—that is, his use of them in relation to the revelation of the δικαιοσύνη θεοῦ in the propitiation of Christ.

The first point to notice is that such faith only becomes possible when the object which evokes it is presented to the sinner. There must be an exhibition, through the preaching of the gospel, not merely of Christ, or even of Christ crucified, but of Christ as in His death a propitiation for sin. Without this, there is not, for the apostle, any possibility whatsoever of faith, or salvation, or even of what some people would call Christianity. This is the one and indispensable foundation for everything Christian. It is sometimes asserted that there are really two ways of putting the gospel in Paul: first, a forensic or judicial way; and second, an ethical or mystical way. To the forensic gospel, Christ is in some sense man's substitute, and faith means the acceptance of what He has done for us; to the mystical or ethical, He is in some sense man's representative, and faith means identification with Him in His death and life. Often, it is added, the "forensic" is the inferior type of gospel, a type in which the form, borrowed from Pharisaism, does great injustice to the Christian contents; it is the ethico-mystical gospel which really answers to the experience of Christian men. The conception of faith, too, which answers to the forensic gospel, and to the substitutionary Christ of the propitiation, is indefinably empty and unreal—it is a mere abstraction; the faith, on the other hand, which corresponds to the gospel of ethical identification with Christ, is the rich and powerful moral force in which the Christian actually lives and moves and has his being. The same criticism, too, is passed on the issues of faith in the respective cases. The righteousness of God in the "forensic" gospel is only, it is said, an imputed righteousness; some sort of unreality clings to it; to build our life on it is to build on a false bottom, and in point of fact it has constantly led to moral disasters; whereas the divine righteousness of the ethico-mystical gospel is as real as the union with Christ, and if at any given moment defective enough, it has yet the promise and potency of perfection in it.

This whole line of argument seems to me not only mistaken in itself, but conspicuously and even wantonly unjust to St. Paul. That the apostle in the Epistle to the Romans says all that has been said above about union with Christ through faith is not to be questioned; but (1) he does not say it as a substitute for what he has said before about faith in Christ set forth by God as a propitiation in His blood; nor (2) does he say it in blank forgetfulness of this, or in no relation whatever to it. It is assumed in all such criticism of the apostle that in Christ on His cross, *independent of His propitiatory character*, there is that which will draw sinful souls into mystical union with Him. This, it is very safe to say, the apostle would at once have denied. And he would have been in the right in denying it. There must be something in the death of Jesus on the cross, more than in other deaths, which draws men into union with Him; what is it? In what does the attractive, subduing, constraining power of that death lie? Those who set the ethico-mystical theory of faith and salvation against what they call the forensic, or who make the two independent of each other, have no answer: the power of the death of Jesus to draw men into mystical union with Him is merely impressionist; the rationale of it is to seek. But Paul *has* an answer. The death of Christ has power to draw sinners into union with Him because it is in point of fact—such is the marvellous love embodied in it—*their* death which He dies. The seat of the attraction in Christ, in virtue of which sinners are drawn into ethico-mystical union with Him, the point of contact which sinners have in the Sinless One, is nothing else than this, that He has come into our place, that on the cross He is taking our responsibilities, bearing our sins, dying our death. Here is the love of Christ which takes hold of men, and draws them into the ethico-mystical union. But put this aside, and there is no force to produce this union, in the case of Christ, any more than in the case of other sufferers for righteousness' sake, whose story impresses our hearts. The union with Christ in His death, therefore, which is represented as an alternative to Christ's propitiation for our sins and the acceptance of it by faith, is in reality no such thing; neither is it a thing independent of the propitiatory death; it is its effect, or rather its fruit. It is Christ our Substitute, Christ who bore our burden, Christ who made our sins His own when He died our death upon the tree, it is that Christ and no other in whom the power dwells, and by whom it is exercised, to draw sinners to Himself and make them one with Him in death and life. The sixth, seventh, and eighth chapters of Romans are not a new gospel for those who do not care for the third, fourth and fifth; they are not an accidental, or a much needed, supplement to those chapters, having yet no organic connexion with them; they are vitally involved in them, *and in nothing else*. Apart from the significance of Christ's death, as exhibited in Romans 3—5, the power of it as exhibited in Romans 6—8 is baseless, inexplicable, incredible. All Christianity, including the mystical union with Christ, has the atonement and faith at the foundation of it, and it can have no other foundation. To St. Paul there is only one gospel, and his construction of it is one: it is no thing of shreds and patches, but a seamless garment. The true connexion of his ideas is perfectly put in the glorious lines of that great mystic, St. Bernard—

> *Propter mortem quam tulisti*
> *Quando pro me defecisti;*
> *Cordis mei cor dilectum,*
> *In te meum fer affectum!* [1]

As a comment on the connexion between Romans 3, 4, 5 and Romans 6, 7, 8—on the relation of the substitution of Christ to ethical identification with Him—of Christ for us to Christ in us or we in Him—this for truth and power will never be surpassed. But blot out the first two lines and the inspiration of the third and fourth is gone. Precisely so, I venture to say, blot out the "forensic" representation of St. Paul's gospel, and the "ethico-mystical" one has the breath of its life withdrawn. There is no regeneration if you give the go by to the atonement; it is the atonement received by faith—that is, it is justification—which regenerates.

But to return. If faith is only possible when the object which evokes it is presented to the sinner, it is no less true that the object presented to the sinner in the gospel is fitted to evoke faith. There is nothing arbitrary in making faith the condition of salvation. When a sinner knows what Christ on the cross means—when he accepts the apostolic testimony that this is not merely a murder or a martyrdom, but a propitiation—when he recognises that in Jesus Christ as set forth in His blood the love of God is bearing the sin of the world—when it comes upon him that this is the revelation of what God is in relation to sinful men; then he understands also that there is only one act and attitude by which the sinful man can properly respond to God, that, namely, in which he gives himself up unreservedly to the love demonstrated in Christ. If he had another hope, he cannot keep it; he lets everything go, that he may unconditionally surrender to this. If he had no other hope, then this is his refuge from despair; a love to which sin is as tragically real as it is to him, and which makes his sin its own. Can a man with a bad conscience buy that? Can he earn it? Can he pay for it? Can he do anything but commit himself unconditionally to it,

---

1. [Through death, how you support me, When you withdraw on behalf of me, Beloved heart of my heart. Carry my affection in you.]

knowing that only so can he be right with God? Can he think that
there is anything else in the world on which a sinner may hope
to build up a good life than this assured love of God bearing the
world's sin? The questions answer themselves. To St. Paul faith, in
the specifically Christian sense, is the act, or if we prefer it the state,
of the soul in which the appropriate response is being made to the
revelation of God's righteousness in the propitiation of Christ. For
such a soul, that propitiation, or the revelation of God which is
made in it, is the universe; nothing else counts. The soul is given
up to it; it is absorbed, overcome, determined through and through
by it; its past does not count; its future is divinely assured; in the
great renunciation and abandonment of faith it is at last right with
God; it counts on Him, and He undertakes for it. This is the experience which St. Paul has in mind when he speaks of justification
by faith. The justified man is one whose relation to God is determined not by sin, or by the law, but by Christ who died for sin,
and by faith in Him and His atoning death. The criticisms of the
Pauline gospel of justification by faith, ancient and modern, are
innumerable, but in the main they are of two kinds. First, it is asserted that the whole conception of propitiation (to which faith is
here made relative) implies a "legal" and therefore a false conception of God's relations to man. This has been already considered in
the papers on sin and law. Secondly, it is asserted that the "legal"
justification of man, secured through the substitution of Christ, is
without moral contents, and contains no moral guarantees for the
sinner's future life. This is in effect answered in the representation given above of what justifying faith truly is, and it will be
more fully dealt with below when we consider what St. Paul himself says about faith establishing the law. To get a more adequate
idea of the faith through which man becomes right with God it
is only necessary to study the passage in Romans 3:27ff. in which
the apostle, at the close of his demonstration of the significance of
Christ's death, points out the characteristics of the Christian religion as based upon faith in it.

"Where," he asks, "is boasting, the boasting with which Pharisaism is so familiar? It is at once shut out. How is the religion—
the divine institute—to be characterized, which so summarily excludes it? Is it to be characterized by works? No. It is to be characterized by faith. For our conclusion is that a man is justified by

faith apart from works of law." It is implied in this, of course, that faith is not a work of law. There is nothing meritorious in it, nothing on the ground of which the believing sinner may claim acceptance with God as his due. It implies a relation to God into which such ideas cannot possibly intrude. But although boasting (καύχη-σις) in this sense is excluded, it is introduced in another, and introduced through faith. The believing man, justified by his faith, makes his boast in the Lord (Rom 5:1–3). Καυχᾶσθαι is a favourite Pauline word; and exultation, triumphant assurance, glorying in God, are the characteristics of the apostle's faith. He knew perhaps better than any one who has ever lived what that word means: The joy of the Lord is your strength.

There has been much theological discussion as to the relation of assurance to faith, and the motives of the usually meticulous treatment of the problem (the desire not to wound tender, timid consciences, not to encourage presumption, not to blunt the zeal for sanctification) are honourable enough; but it is certain that out of regard for them the apostolic mood has often been completely lost. When a man has his eye fixed on Christ, set forth by God as a propitiation in His blood, is it a sin for him to be *sure* of God's love to the sinful? Can he be *too* sure of it? Is it presumptuous of him to be *perfectly* sure? Is not the presumption rather in doubting it? All great evangelists have felt that without an *initial assurance* of God's love, an assurance which is not so much an added perfection of faith as the very soul of faith, the sinner never does justice to God, never is truly made right with Him, never gives the gospel a chance, or gets for himself the inspiration the gospel can give. What Paul means when he cuts faith off completely from works is to emphasize its sole sufficiency for the religious life, a sufficiency of course conditioned by its object, but once its object is apprehended, unconditional. As long as the sinner holds on, though it were but with his finger-tips, to something in which the initiative and the credit are his own, he does not abandon himself unreservedly to the mercy of God in Christ; and until he does this he can never know what incomparable impulses of strength and gladness dwell in the atonement. Yet it is in these alone that his hope of a future life of virtue lies. This is the answer to all the timid qualifications of the doctrine of justification by faith alone. Reduced to their simplest terms, and exhibited in their true meaning, they are neither more nor less than attempts to take moral guarantees from the sinner *before* he is allowed the benefit of the gospel. But the very meaning of the gospel—and here we see with what propriety justification by faith is treated as identical with the gospel—is that the sinner is not in a position to give any such guarantees. Allow him unconditional access to Christ the propitiation, allow him an initial unconditioned assurance of the sin-bearing love of God, and all moral guarantees will be found in that. The gospel does not demand such guarantees, because it is its business to provide them.

This truth, which is often missed by moralizing critics of St. Paul, has been grasped in some fashion by every branch of the Christian Church. The moralist is apt to be a legalist without knowing it, and he is slow to understand that morality may be transcended without being endangered; or rather that, in the case of men who have a bad conscience through sin, morality *must* somehow be transcended by an unconditional grace, if such men are ever to have the chance of being moral again. But this unconditional grace—this grace which is here, antecedent to any moral guarantee the sinner can offer, requiring of him nothing but that he abandon himself to it, and giving him the assurance that if he do so all will be well—this unconditional grace is what is represented alike in the Lutheran doctrine of justification by faith alone, in the Calvinistic doctrine of sovereign electing grace, and in the Romish doctrine of the grace contained in the Sacraments. All these doctrines mean, at bottom, the same thing. They mean that in the work of man's salvation an unconditioned initiative belongs to God, and that all that is required of man is the unreserved abandonment of himself to what God has done. That is faith in the sense of St. Paul, and it contains everything because it contains God the Saviour in the revelation of His grace. Faith is the abandonment of the soul to that revelation in the assurance of its utter truth. It is not an antecedent condition, a work of law which a man must make good out of his own resources before he can receive the gospel; it is nothing else than the acceptance of the gospel. That is why it puts a man right with God, and has all joy, and all moral possibilities, in it.

Next to the all-sufficiency of faith—for this is what is really meant by the exclusion of "works" from the initiation of the Christian life—St. Paul insists on the universality of it as a religious principle. The inseparable association of "faith" and "all" is very striking in the Epistle. The obedience of faith is to be won among all the nations (Rom 1:5); the gospel is the power of God to every one who has faith (Rom 1:16), to Jew first and also to Greek; the righteousness of God is through faith in Christ Jesus, upon all that believe, without distinction (Rom 3:22); any Christian is adequately described as one who has faith in Jesus (Rom 3:26). It is in this line that St. Paul asks, when he has finished his exposition of propitiation and faith in their relations to each other, Is God—that is, the God who has set forth Jesus as a propitiation in His blood—a God of Jews only? Does that great demonstration of love appeal to something national, so that only those born in a certain line, and trained in a certain tradition, can respond to it? Far from it. That to which the great propitiation appeals is neither Jewish nor Greek, neither ancient nor modern, neither oriental nor occidental; it is simply human. God in His propitiation undertakes for sin, and appeals to the sinner for unreserved trust: that is the whole matter. As a religious principle the faith which is the response of the sinful soul to the atonement abolishes all national distinctions; the only realities in its world are the Redeemer God, and the soul in which His love evokes the response of faith. Paul was conscious of this inference from the very hour of his conversion: it pleased God, he says, to reveal His Son in me, *that I might preach Him among the nations* (Gal 1:16). It was not a Jew who was saved on the way to Damascus, but a sinner; and the same appeal, made to the same necessity, and evoking the same response, was independent of all national limitations. The cross, as St. Paul interprets it, speaks a language to which conscience gives every man the key; if we make it out at all, we see this, and know that there is but one way in which circumcision and uncircumcision alike, or ancient and modern alike, or cultured and uncultured alike, can become right with God, and face life with assurance and joy.

It might seem an immediate inference from this that all that was Jewish passed out of religion, or, to use words that were natural then, though in some respects too big for this meaning, that faith abolished the law (Rom 3:31). No doubt the inference is in some sense, or even in various senses, just. As it has been put above, the revelation of God made in Christ the propitiation is the whole world to the sinful soul, and the response of faith which it evokes is the whole of religion. As far as the law means anything that is national, historical, statutory, it is made void by faith: Christ is the end of it to every one who believes (Rom 10:4); the Jewish religion is superseded. We are not under law any longer; it is not a system of precepts and of prohibitions by which our life is ruled; we are under grace; the life we live is that which grace calls into being through faith; not restraint but inspiration is the Christian's watchword, not Sinai but Calvary is his holy mount. But where Paul discusses the connexion of faith and propitiation, what he is concerned to maintain is that faith does *not* annul the law, but rather sets it on its feet. What is the conception of law implied here?

It may be plausibly argued: if we look to the sequence of Romans 3 and 4, that what Paul wishes to prove is that the way of being right with God which we discover in the Old Testament, which in a large sense may be called Law, is not subverted but confirmed under the Christian dispensation. In other words, he wishes to prove that in all ages men have been justified in the same way— that Abraham, for instance, the father of the Jews, is the spiritual ancestor of all believers, the type of that attitude to God which has its final and perfect exemplification in Christian faith, because that faith is a response to the final and perfect revelation of God. There is a great truth in this. God has one people through all the ages, and at bottom their attitude to Him is one. That is why we can understand the Old Testament and use it as a religious book. In this sense, an argument that faith does not annul but confirm the law would be an argument in support of our Lord's words, I came not to destroy, but to fulfil. But if we consider both what precedes (Rom 3:21–26), and what comes after (e.g., in Rom 8:4), we shall probably be inclined to the conclusion that what St. Paul means in Romans 3:31 is something quite different. Law to a Jew, and for that matter to most men, is a symbol of the distinction between right and wrong, a guarantee of righteousness; and what he asserts is that faith is so far from annulling that distinction (as some of his adversaries asserted then and have asserted ever since), that it actually establishes it. There is nothing, the apostle maintains, to which the distinction of right and wrong is so inviolable as faith; there is nothing which does such signal justice to that distinction;

there is nothing which is so productive of genuine righteousness; nay, there is nothing else which can produce righteousness at all.

One could conceive the apostle challenging his opponents to look at an empirical proof of this. The only good man, he might say, is in point of fact the pardoned man, the man whose heart has been made tender, and his conscience sensitive, by submitting to have his sins forgiven for Christ's sake. To humble oneself to receive the reconciliation which comes at the cost of the atonement is to pass through the only experience in which one becomes a new creature; and short of becoming a new creature, no man ever does justice to the demand of the law. You may think you are fulfilling the law while the hardness of your heart leaves you insensible to what it is; it is only when the great appeal of Christ's propitiation melts your heart and casts it into a new mould that you begin to see what goodness is, and to be a good man. Faith in the atonement is not hostile to righteousness; it is the fountain of all righteousness worthy of the name. Religion, it might be otherwise put, though it transcends morality, does not extinguish it; on the contrary, the only genuine morality is born of it.

Again, we might conceive the apostle, when accused of annulling the law by faith, pointing to Christ Himself, and to His undisputed character. Sainte Beuve quotes some one who says that the last enemy to be overcome by the believer is the great God Pan. He means that sense of the unity of all things in which the sense of their differences is lost. Nature and spirit, necessity and freedom, the personal and the impersonal, even good and evil, are fluctuating and evanescent distinctions; they shade off into each other by imperceptible degrees, and even the critical line which marks off good and evil wavers and vanishes as we try to fix it. This is the mood which really annuls "law," and makes righteousness not a reality or a hope, but an illusion and a despair. And in the very world in which this mood overcomes men, and they say it is all one, we come suddenly upon Christ crucified, dying to establish the difference which their minds are weariedly giving up. Whoever else may ignore the claim of righteousness, the just demand of law, the believer in Jesus dare not: for Jesus resisted unto blood, striving against sin, and showed us in doing so that righteousness is as real as His passion, and the demand of the law more sacred than life itself. How can faith in Him make Law void?

But the conclusive argument of the apostle would certainly be an appeal to his doctrine of propitiation. The faith which is charged with subverting the law of God is a faith which has Christ set forth in His blood as its object and inspiration. Now what is the meaning of that object? According to the apostle, it is Christ bearing sin, Christ accepting and making His own in all their tragic reality the responsibilities in which sin had involved us. How, then, can the faith which such a Christ evokes but have the moral characteristics of that propitiation in its very substance? How can it do anything else than treat as absolutely real that righteousness of God to which the propitiation which is its abiding source is the most signal homage? Faith begotten by Christ, set forth as a propitiation in His blood, is faith to which sin is all that sin is to God, holiness all that holiness is to God, law all that law is to God; it is so far from subverting morality that in a world of sinful men it is the one guarantee that can be given for a genuinely good life. It is with such an impression of it on his heart that St. Paul writes: I am not ashamed of the gospel, for it is a divine power to save in the case of every one who has faith; for in it a divine righteousness is revealed of which faith is the very element.

# 5

# The Righteousness of God and the New Life

Through faith in Christ, set forth by God as a propitiation in His blood, man is justified. His relation to God is determined not by sin, or by any of the powers or ideas which in St. Paul's mind form part of the same whole as sin, such as the law, the curse, or death; it is determined completely and exclusively by Christ. The sinner who is ignorant of Christ, or who refuses the obedience of faith, is in the wrong with God; the sinner from whom Christ the propitiation has won the great surrender is in the right with God. He is in that attitude to God which alone answers to the truth of what God is, as God has revealed that truth in giving His Son a propitiation for the sins of the world.

Now to be right with God in this sense is not a part of religion, it is the whole of it. The righteousness of God which Paul preached was not an element in his gospel; his gospel was exhausted in it. The justification of the sinner was not a preliminary to something higher, it was not a condition without which real salvation could not be attained; it was itself salvation. In the very nature of the case it could not be supplemented, and it did not need to be; it has in it the promise and the potency of all that can ever be called Christian. The man who has once apprehended, in Christ or His cross, the true dimensions of the love of God, and in whose heart that unconditioned love, bearing his sins, has called forth the response of unconditional faith, has in principle nothing more to learn about God, and nothing more to receive from Him. His faith in God's love, the faith by which he is made right with God, is his life. The whole of Christianity is in the faith which abandons itself to the sin-bearing love of God, just as the last truth about God is in the sin-bearing love which offers itself in Christ for the acceptance of faith.

This is the point of view from which St. Paul, in the Epistle to the Romans, first enlarges on the life of the justified. In the third chapter he exhibits Christ as a propitiation—God's revelation of a righteousness in which His own character is vindicated, and in which sinners may become right with Him. In the fourth chapter he shows that the way of being right with God which he preaches—the way not of meritorious works which claim as of right God's approbation, but of unconditional reliance upon God in Christ—is no new thing, subversive of all the true religion that has ever been known in the world, but one in principle with the piety of the Old Testament. He points especially to the identity of Abrahamic and of Christian faith in this, that both are trust in a living God who can quicken the dead (Rom 4:17). This is the Scriptural way of saying that both are faith in omnipotence. But in the case of Christian faith, the omnipotence has been demonstrated in a way which gives it a peculiar character. It has been shown in raising from the dead One "who was delivered for our offences and raised for our justification." In other words, it has been shown in the service of the love of God, dealing with the sin of the world for man's redemption. It is not omnipotence *simpliciter* in which the Christian trusts, it is omnipotent *grace*. And when we say this, we see again how trust in such grace is not a part of the Christian life, but the whole of it. Hence we cannot be surprised when St. Paul at this point actually brings the whole Christian life into view as the life of the justified, a life which has its inspiration and all its characteristic qualities and virtues simply in this, that it is the life of men who through faith in the omnipotent grace revealed in Christ are completely and once for all right with God. It is not something added to their justification, it is something involved in it. It is not something which has another condition than their faith, it is the assertion of their faith through all things. If we introduce a word from another circle of ideas, and speak of a regenerate life, then we may say that justification regenerates, or that faith regenerates; for the regenerate life of Romans 5:1–11 is nothing but the life of justification and of faith. It does not matter for our present purpose whether we read ἔχωμεν or ἔχομεν in Romans 5:1, or take καυχώμεθα in Romans 5:2–3 as indicative or subjunctive, though the indicative in all three seems to me the more probable; peace with God, access to God, a secure standing in grace, power to glory even in tribulations and to make them subservient to spiritual good, and a hope of glory which does not make ashamed because it rests on the assurance of God's love, a love poured out in our hearts through His Spirit—all this is included in the life of the justified. It does not occur to the apostle to ask, What is the connexion between justification and the new life? How is the new life mediated to the man who through faith in Christ set forth as a propitiation has become right with God? These are not real questions for him. The new life, as Romans 5:1–11 exhibits it, is not communicated or evoked in any special way at all. It is the spontaneous manifestation of what justification is and means. It is justification asserting itself as a reality in all the relations, and under all the changing and trying conditions, of our being. "We have received the reconciliation" (Rom 5:11): everything is in that.

It is worth while to notice that this point of view underlies all that Paul has yet to say, and emerges through what might seem at the first glance inconsistent with it. To believe in a love of God which is deeper than sin, and makes propitiation for it, is everything; whoever has this faith has justification and the life of the justified in one. Hence the love of God appears both at the beginning and at the end of all that St. Paul has to say about the new life (Rom 5:5ff.; Rom 8:32ff.), and in both places it appears in that immensity which belongs to it as a love which has made propitiation for sin. The *whole* of the Christian life is *one* indivisible response to *this* love. It is a love with every promise in it, and in both the passages referred to it is made the basis of all Christian inferences. When we are sure of this love, the love which enables the ungodly to become right with God, much more, argues the apostle in Romans 5, may we be sure that all our other necessities will be looked to by God. The same argument is repeated in Romans 8. "He that spared not His own Son, but delivered Him up for us all, how shall He not also with Him freely give us all things?" But to argue in this way from the love which makes atonement to all other demonstrations of God's love which may be necessary for the sinner—in other words, to argue that the whole love of God is given in the love which justifies the ungodly—is precisely the same as to argue that the justification in which this atoning love is received, and in which the sinner becomes right with God, includes in itself the whole of salvation, and that the justified man has only to assert and manifest himself as what he is, in order to be equal to all the demands of life. The new life is in no sense added to justification; justification itself, in St. Paul's words, is *justification of life* (Rom 5:18). It is a mistake to draw distinctions which the apostle does not draw, and to say that life here means eternal life in the transcendent, not the ethical, sense: its may fairly be questioned whether St. Paul could have made out what this means. Life may be rich, but it is simple and indivisible; and when justification is qualified by life we must take it in its wealth of meaning certainly, but in its simplicity as well. A self-contained justification, an impotent negative justification, without fruit or outlook, is not the apostle's idea. To him justification is related to life and to be characterized by it. We may say, if we please, that it has immortality in view, but we must say also that it regenerates. Everything in Christianity is vitally in it, vitally connected with it and dependent on it, its vital manifestation. It follows, of course, that independent of it there is nothing of vital Christianity at all.

This interpretation of St. Paul's teaching on justification may seem to some to leave no room for anything in the Epistle to the Romans after Romans 5:1–11. When the apostle has reached this point, it may be argued, he has said all he has to say; he has made his gospel known to his readers in all its breadth and length and depth and height. And there is no doubt that the connexion between the part of the Epistle with which we have been engaged, and the part which follows, is difficult to grasp. By some it is simply denied. Ritschl, for instance, argues that Paul keeps the two points of view which they represent—that of justification by faith, and that of the bestowment of the Holy Spirit on believers—quite apart. He traces their course, so to speak, side by side, and makes the attainment of salvation at last equally dependent on the one and on the other, but he never combines them. Holtzmann agrees with Ritschl in this, but makes a certain allowance for the lines of thought crossing each other; and though he holds that Paul never clearly defined their relations, he thinks there are certain ideas common to both (such as faith, the Spirit, and redemption) which assist us in bringing them into connexion. Weiss makes a connexion by the simple process of addition. First, we are justified by faith—not indeed in the sense of justification explained above, but in some more negative and impotent sense; then we receive the Spirit, as the power of the new life, in baptism; and it is the sum of these which is the Christian salvation. None of these views can be willingly accepted by one who reads the first part of the Epistle as it has been read in these papers, and who has on general grounds a prejudice in favour of St. Paul's coherency. We might rather be disposed to argue that in Romans 3:9—5:11 he is propounding his gospel in its purely religious significance— remembering, of course, that in a religion which puts a man right with God everything is included; that in Romans 5:12-21 he digresses to bring out its significance in the spiritual history of humanity, and particularly to show that the great figures in that history are Adam and Christ, and its great ideas Sin and Grace, Death and Life, as compared with which Moses and his Law have only a subordinate and transient importance; while in Romans 6—8 the ethical significance of the gospel is asserted against plausible objections which would find in it an excuse for sin. But this is to give an exaggerated importance to Romans 5:12-21, which in spite of the enormous place it has filled in the history of dogma is hardly more than an *obiter dictum* in the Epistle to the Romans. What is really before the apostle's mind from Romans 5:11 onwards is the ethical vindication of his gospel. That gospel was attacked on the ground of reverence for the law, and the main purpose served in his argument by this much disputed passage is to put the law in its place. The law is not what the Jews who slandered him (Rom 3:8) supposed. It is a vanishing quantity between Sin and Grace, as Moses is a vanishing personality between Adam and Christ. But after his preliminary discounting of its importance (in which the law can only be taken in the historical sense) he comes to face the real objection which was in the minds of his opponents. The law they were concerned about was not to be disparaged as the law of Moses: to them it was the law of God. It represented the interest both of God and man in righteousness, and their assertion was that Paul's gospel of a justification for the ungodly was inconsistent with its claims. It set righteousness at nought. It not only tempted men to say, Let us do evil that good may come, let us continue in sin that grace may abound; it justified them in so saying, and would end in their so doing. This is the situation to which Paul addresses himself in Romans 6:1ff.

Let it be observed that what is assailed is St. Paul's doctrine of justification. Now that which is assailed is that which has to be defended. Nothing will serve the apostle's purpose except a demonstration that justification as he understands it is vitally related to the holy will of God, as it is expressed in the law, and to the doing of that will in life. To show that there is *more* in Christianity than the δικαιοσύνη θεοῦ which he has consistently identified with his gospel, and to argue that morality is guaranteed in another way of which he has as yet said nothing, but which this objection reminds him to set forth, is both irrelevant and absurd. It is as if he tacitly pleaded guilty to the charge made against his gospel, and then by an afterthought got past it; as if he said, Yes, my gospel of a divine righteousness would be open to these charges if it stood alone; but it does not stand alone. It is supplemented by a reception of the Holy Spirit in which a divine life is communicated to us and maintained in us; and as we walk after the Spirit the righteousness of the law is fulfilled. Such a connexion, or rather such a want of connexion, such an incoherence, in the apostle's thoughts is incredible. A gospel of justification, which has no relation to morality, and of new spiritual life which has no vital connexion with justification, is a gospel like Mephibosheth, lame on both its feet. It needs a great deal of courage to ascribe it to a mind like St. Paul's, even in the company of such distinguished scholars as those referred to above.

But indeed it is not necessary to do so. The apostle states the objection of his opponents, apparently in their own words, Shall we continue in sin that grace may abound? Then he repels it with moral indignation: μὴ γένοιτο. The very idea is shocking. Then— and this is the essential point—he demonstrates its inconsistency with his gospel. This is the purport of Romans 6:2: men who like us died to sin, how shall we continue to live in it? It seems to be taken for granted, by many if not by most interpreters, that the idea of dying to sin is a perfectly new one, having no relation to anything which precedes and intelligible only in the light of what follows. I venture to dissent altogether from this view. Dying to sin is not a new nor an incomprehensible idea to any one who has understood Romans 3:25f., and who knows what that faith is in which the sinful man abandons himself to the mercy of God in Christ crucified. It is our death which Christ dies as He bears our sins on the cross, and when we commit ourselves in faith to the mercy of God which is revealed there, to that mercy and to no other, we make that death our own. Sin becomes to us in the very act of believing all that it is to Christ; we are dead to it as He is dead; it is a thing foreign to the world into which our faith introduces us, as it was foreign to Him who died for it. St. Paul does not here supplement his gospel of justification; he only brings out its contents on the basis of experience, and shows how adequate they are to answer the objections made to it in the name of morality. Every man, he argues, who knows what it is to be justified by believing in Christ who died for sins knows *ipso facto*, in his own soul, what it is to die to sin. It is Christ *dying* for sin who evokes faith, and the faith which He evokes answers to what He is and to what He does; it is a faith which has a *death* to sin in it. But this is the same faith which justifies, and St. Paul's argument rests entirely on the fact that it is the same. Unless the faith through which the sinner becomes right with God involves in it this death to sin, and what is not a separate thing, but only the other side of the same, a being alive to God, he has no reply to his opponents at all. It is out of his faith that this argument is constructed. The very same experience in which he becomes right with God through Christ—that is, the experience of faith—is an experience in which he becomes a dead man, so far as sin is concerned, a living man, so far as God is concerned. Not that this is the ground on which he finds acceptance with God, or in view of which God justifies him; nothing could be so direct a contradiction of Pauline theology as the idea that God justifies us because the germ of sanctification or of new life is present in the soul and can be counted on to develop. It is the one unconditional mercy of God in Christ crucified which evokes the one response of faith—a faith in which, as one indivisible experience, the believing sinner becomes right with God and dead to sin. And it is the abiding assurance of this justifying mercy, a mercy in the acceptance of which sin dies, or the believer dies to sin (for the two are one), on which the new life depends. The joy of justification is not the initial impulse by which the boat is pushed from the shore; if St. Paul can be trusted, it is the very element on which it floats; it is the inspiration of the new life from beginning to end, and that life itself can be exhaustively described as the life of justification.

The whole answer of St. Paul to the charge that his gospel led to immorality is contained in that exclamation—*men like us who died to sin!* As has been remarked already, it is no answer, unless the dying to sin is necessarily involved in that very act of believing in which a man is made right with God. Paul knows from experience that it is so involved, but he can imagine his assertion being doubted; and if it is doubted, where is the proof? In the nature of the case there can be no conclusive proof but the experimental one—the actual holiness of the justified, the fulfilment of the law by sinners who have received the reconciliation freely, and with no moral guarantees either asked or offered by way of preliminary. But in the nature of the case also such an experimental proof can hardly be given, and all St. Paul can do to satisfy those who are sceptical about the death to sin involved in faith is to point to the rite in which faith is declared, and to show that it also has the death in question written on its face. The rite is that of baptism. It is plain from the apostle's language that all Christians were baptized, and it ought not to be necessary to say that in the New Testament baptism and faith are correlative ideas; the meaning of baptism is the meaning of faith, and that is why Paul can appeal to it here as a way of bringing out what is involved in faith. What, then, is the light which baptism—which is only an illustration of faith, a picture in which the contents of faith are presented to the eye—throws upon the subject in hand? In what way does it support the assertion that faith involves a death to sin, and is therefore inconsistent with a continued life in it?

Baptism supports this assertion inasmuch as, in the form in which it was familiar to the Church, it is a picture of death, burial, and resurrection. These things are in baptism as in a picture, but they are in faith in their reality. What is in the picture for the eye to see is in faith as the experience of the soul. We were baptized into Christ's death, means that when we were baptized our faith was evoked by and concentrated on that death; in its atoning power, a power which belongs to it because it is really our death borne by Him, it takes hold of us and conforms us to itself; we make it our own in the very act of believing, and in Christ through faith we die to sin. This is the faith which baptism presents to the senses; if it is not this, what, St. Paul asks, is it? What other interpretation can you put on the sacrament than that it enshrines and exhibits this spiritual experience? Paul does not refer to baptism because there is something in it which is not to be found in faith, but for precisely the opposite reason. He refers to it because it brings out the fact that in faith—the faith which justifies—the only faith he knew or could think of, the faith which is identical with the Christian religion and which is confessed in baptism—there is involved (at least in idea) a death to sin which is the only absolute guarantee for a life fulfilling the law.

The ideal or theoretical vindication of St. Paul's gospel is therefore quite complete. He knew in his experience that justifying faith meant death to sin, and the symbolism of the sacrament exhibited this meaning to all. But the ideal is one thing; the reality, even where it has touched the ideal at the central and vital point, is another. The new life is indeed, we may say, guaranteed by the death to sin involved in faith and represented in baptism; it is guaranteed by it, yet it lies beyond it, and as the end contemplated in it, it has an independence of its own. "We were buried with Him by our baptism into death, that like as Christ was raised from the dead by the glory of the Father, even so we also should walk in newness of life." Religion is not a substitute for morality, it has it in view; and though it is a guarantee for it, morality must be freely and morally produced. Hence the exhortations to right conduct with which the remainder of Romans 6 is filled. It is as if the apostle said to his readers, "It is of no use to argue the case; all that can be done is by well doing to put to silence the ignorance of foolish men. Baptism *is* a picture of death and resurrection, and in faith there *is* a corresponding reality; there is a death to sin, and a being alive to God. This it is impossible for us to doubt, but there can be no theoretical demonstration of it; let us demonstrate it, therefore, in act. *Reckon* yourselves to be dead to sin, and alive to God in Jesus Christ. Remember what you *are*; be yourselves, and every mouth which reproaches the gospel will be stopped."

It is a highly remarkable fact that all through this chapter, in which the apostle is dealing with the morality of the new life, there is no mention of the Holy Spirit. Christianity is explained in its entirety out of Christ and faith. It consists, first and last, of experiences generated in the believer by the cross. The fundamental one

is death to sin; in the assurance that he has shared with Christ at
this point, the apostle is confident that he will share with Him all
through. "If we died with Christ, we believe that we shall also live
with Him." It is probably a mistake to speak in this connexion of
a mystical union with Christ as a transcendent reality on which all
such experiences are dependent. It is the experiences alone with
which the apostle is dealing, and it does not make them in any degree more intelligible to provide them with an unrealizable background. To believe in Christ who died for our sins, and who died
our death in doing so, is to die ourselves to sin; it is to receive
"justification of life"; it is to have the love of God shed abroad in
our hearts; it is to know that we are under grace, and that neither sin nor death can have dominion over us any more; it is to
have as the ever present, all determining power in our moral life
the sense that for these unspeakable blessings we are debtors to
Christ who died. We owe them absolutely, and without any qualification, to Him, and our new life is inspired and sustained by the
sense of this obligation. As the apostle puts it in another epistle, it
is a life not to ourselves, but to Him who for our sakes died and
rose again, and to the God whose love He revealed in doing so.
This is the connexion in which the one reference to the Holy Spirit
stands which we have yet found in St. Paul's treatment of justification. "The love of God is shed abroad in our hearts through the
Holy Spirit given unto us" (Rom 5:5). It is this love of God to us,
which, through the response of love evoked by it in our hearts, is
the guarantee for a good life. Love begets love—to be more specific, grace begets gratitude; and gratitude is the inspiration of all
Christian goodness. This, much more than anything suggested by
the idea of a mystical union with Christ, or an indwelling of the
Spirit, seems to me the point of view from which the apostle contemplates the problem raised in Romans 6. We cannot continue in
sin, his argument runs; to do so would be inconsistent with our
whole relation to Christ. It would be inconsistent with the death
to sin which is involved in faith, and represented, as in a picture,
in baptism; it would be inconsistent with our sense of debt to Him
who died for our sins that we might be in bondage to them no
more; it would be inconsistent with our hope of the glory of God.
All this, I repeat, is intelligible, and it is on the level at which the
apostle writes throughout this section. Whatever it may be proper

to say of the Holy Spirit, or of union to Christ, or incorporation in Him, must be said on the basis of such experiences and within their limits.

# 6

# The New Life and the Spirit

The conception of the Spirit is by far the most difficult thing to master in the theology of St. Paul. Partly this may be due to the fact that the word is sometimes used in a more popular, at others in a more specific, not to say technical sense; partly to its meaning being determined, here by Old Testament associations, there by the ecstatic accompaniments of primitive Christianity, and yet elsewhere by some Hellenic or semiphilosophic influence; partly to the Spirit's having in one place a physical or hyperphysical mode of manifestation, and in another being purely ethical. But all these difficulties and many others are covered if we say that in St. Paul Spirit is in the last resort coextensive with Christianity. It is one of the ways in which anything and everything Christian can be described—all such things are experiences of a man who is in the Spirit, or who is led by the Spirit, or who walks after the Spirit. To describe them in this way is to describe them by reference to God, or to the divine power which is their source. Of course God in this case is not conceived abstractly or *in vacuo*; the God whose Spirit is the explanation of all things Christian is the God who has been manifested for our salvation in Christ, and the Spirit to which all that is Christian is due is not an undefined divine power, it is definitely Christ's Spirit. St. Paul identifies the two, when he says to the Corinthians, The Lord is the Spirit; just as our Lord Himself identifies them, when with reference to the mission of the Comforter, He says, I will not leave you bereaved: I come to you. The difficulty of dealing with St. Paul's mind on this subject is that spirit is not the only term he uses with this universal scope. Just as everything Christian can be defined in terms of

Spirit, when we refer it to God as its source, so everything Christian can be defined in terms of Faith, when it is referred to man's response to God as its condition. It is natural, when we think (as we habitually do) of man's responsibility to God in connexion with the gospel, to put faith in the forefront, and to make the reception of the Spirit depend upon faith, and often St. Paul himself does so. But, on the other hand, it is through the Spirit that the love of God which in Christ crucified makes its appeal to man is shed abroad in our hearts, and to that love faith is only the response. Hence it is hardly real to argue about the relations of faith and the Spirit. They are alternative ways of describing all Christian experiences, according as we regard them as explicable through man's abandonment of himself to God, or through God's gracious and powerful operation on and in man. The only difference, so far as the Epistle to the Romans is concerned, is that Paul gives the primacy to faith in speaking of justification, probably because at the initial stage of Christianity the emphasis has to be laid on the sinner's assuming or refusing to assume, by a free act of his own, the proper relation to God; while a similar primacy is given, when the subsequent life is dealt with, to the Spirit, probably because the dominant consciousness of the believer is that all his experiences now originate in a power which he can only call divine.

To say that faith and the Spirit are co-extensive terms, each covering the whole area of Christian experience, though looking at it in different relations, is as much as to say that no one could write fully of either without bringing under review all that St. Paul would have acknowledged as Christian. It is not the purpose of this paper to do anything so far reaching, but to examine the subject of the Spirit so far as it is presented in the first eight chapters of Romans. The one point of supreme importance is, that to St. Paul, as to all early Christians, the Spirit was not a subject of doctrine, but of experience. A doctrine of the Spirit is an anachronism in the New Testament, in a sense in which the doctrine of atonement is not. The apostolic question is not, Do you believe in the Holy Ghost? but, Did you receive the Holy Ghost? To appreciate the experience which the apostle designates on every occasion on which he uses the word, or indicates that the thought is in his mind, may be difficult, but it is only in so far as we do so that we do anything at all. Of all trivialities which vex the mind of man, few are more distressing than those which are sometimes made to pass muster as a doctrine of the Spirit.

St. Paul first uses the word—in the part of the Epistle which deals with the life of the justified—in Romans 5:5. "The love of God," he says, "has been poured out in our hearts through the Holy Spirit given to us." The experience here ascribed to the Spirit is that assured triumphant consciousness of God's love which enables the Christian to glory in tribulations. It is of God that we have such a conviction about God as this; He has wrought it in us by His own divine power; we could never have attained it otherwise. The love of God referred to, as the apostle immediately goes on to explain, is the love manifested in Christ's death for sinners; it is in making this live, and in enabling us to realize that it is ours—actually bestowed by the Father on us—that the divine power of God reveals its presence in our hearts. The connexion of ideas here is precisely that which we find in our Lord's own teaching in John 14—16. There is no ministry of the Spirit outside of Christ. The Spirit does not speak of Himself. His work is witness bearing, and it is in giving the soul the sense of what Christ's death means for sinners—in other words, by making the atonement live as the Alpha and Omega of all we mean when we say God—it is by this, and not by any mystical, blankly or vaguely super natural process, that He gives us a divine assurance of God's love.

It is the experimental character of all St. Paul has to say about the Spirit which in all probability explains its absence in Romans 5:12–21. In the famous parallel between Adam and Christ we have a theological interpretation of history on the grandest scale; but though there are points of attachment to experience in it—as in the words "all have sinned" in Romans 5:12; or, "they that receive the abundance of the grace" in Romans 5:17—it is on the whole speculative rather than experimental. The apostle's intellect is stirred by the vast conceptions of the unity of the race in sin and in redemption, in Adam and in Christ, and it is his own experience, and still more his own hope, as a Christian man, which turns the parallel into a contrast, and annuls the reign of sin in the surpassing glory of the reign of grace; but in spite of this experimental prompting, and this Spirit-born assurance, there is something in this passage which is at least as much philosophical as it is divine, and the want of any reference to the Spirit is not surprising.

It is in proportion the more surprising when we find the Spirit absent throughout Romans 6. It may, indeed, be questioned whether it is absent. Does not the use made of baptism, it may be asked, in the beginning of that chapter, necessarily involve the introduction of the Spirit? Is not the connexion between baptism and the Spirit normal throughout the New Testament, so that whenever the first is mentioned we are not only entitled but obliged to assume the second? Without questioning this in the least, it must be pointed out that it is not on any such relation between baptism and the Spirit that the apostle's argument proceeds. As has been explained in a previous paper, he refers to baptism, not because it enables him to bring in the Spirit, but because it enables him to bring out what is involved in faith. The idea underlying all he says is not that baptism brings the gift of the Spirit and so of a divine life which must expel sin, but that baptism exhibits to the very senses the truth that the faith which is, declared in it involves a death to sin, with which continued life in sin is irreconcilable. Paul refrains from speaking of the Spirit in this connexion because in the first instance he is not going to speak of the death to sin from the point of view of Christian privilege, but from that of Christian responsibility. This death to sin is involved in faith, the great free act of surrender, on the part of man, to the sin-bearing love of God in Christ crucified; to take this act seriously, to live by faith, faith in the Son of God who loved us and gave Himself for us—the whole security of Christian morality lies for St. Paul in that. No doubt he could have put this in another light, and explained the Christian's freedom from sin by reference to the divine Spirit dwelling in him. But that does not prove that we have a right to introduce the Spirit here, where St. Paul does not. It only proves that he has various ways, which have an independence of their own, of interpreting or rendering the same experience. He can be theological, or religious, in a strict sense, and then he speaks of the Spirit; he can be psychological, or ethical, and then he speaks of faith, or love, or even of gratitude. That in which all his thoughts, and all his modes of expression unite, is Christ. Faith and Spirit alike are words which have no meaning but in relation to Him, and He gives what is to all intents and purposes the same meaning to both. The faith which abandons itself to Christ is at the same time a receiving of the

Spirit of Christ, or of what to experience is the same thing, Christ in the Spirit; there are not two things here but one, though it can be represented in the two relations which the words faith and Spirit suggest. Where human responsibility is to be emphasized, it is naturally faith which is put to the front; where the gracious help of God is the main point, prominence is given to the Spirit. But whether we say faith or Spirit, we say something which derives its whole meaning from Christ. It is He who evokes faith, and who in evoking faith becomes a divine spiritual presence in man.

It is the essential relation of the Spirit to God which probably explains the fact that in almost every passage in which it occurs, in the seventh and eighth chapters of Romans, there is a contrast expressed or implied to some condition or experience which is merely human. It has always to be defined by contrast. It is power as opposed to weakness, freedom as opposed to bondage, adoption as opposed to servitude, holiness as opposed to the flesh of sin, life as opposed to death. The very fact that the Spirit is co-extensive with Christian experience makes vain any attempt to be systematic in the treatment of it within narrow limits; but a survey of the relevant passages in Romans 7 and 8 will serve to bring out those characteristics of Christian experience in which the apostle was most vividly conscious of the presence and power of God.

The first is Romans 7:6: we serve in newness of the Spirit, not in oldness of the letter. The καινότης, newness or freshness, is that which belongs to or is characteristic of the Spirit, and in the experience of the Christian it is due to the Spirit. It is because he possesses the Spirit that the Christian does not find the service of God stale. In his pre-Christian days it was otherwise. When God was represented for him by "the letter," there was no freshness in His service; it sank into the heavy routine of custom, or into a punctilious and scrupulous conformity to law, in which spontaneity, and with it life, was lost. But the Spirit is characterized above everything by moral originality and freshness. Under its influence conscience becomes not the recorder, nor the avenging angel, nor the worm that never dies, but a kind of *genius*; the moral world becomes all of a sudden vast, real, enchanting. In a higher sense than that of the Psalmist the word comes true, "Thou sendest forth Thy Spirit, they are created, and Thou renewest the face of the ground."

When we consider the contrast in this passage between spirit and letter, it is a little surprising to find St. Paul say in Romans 7:14: We know that *the law is spiritual*. Law and Spirit, we are apt to think, are mutually exclusive terms. The Christian lives in the Spirit, and therefore he is *not* under the law. But with all his disparagement of the law in certain relations or for certain purposes St. Paul never forgets that the law is of God. That is what he means here by calling it πνευματικός. It is spiritual in its essence, though not in its form, and hence there can be none but a spiritual fulfilment of it. A creature like man, who is σάρκινος—a creature of flesh sold under sin—can make nothing of it. If his vocation is expressed in the law, then his nature stands in no proper proportion to his vocation; the position is one in which he is doomed to endless defeat. The law which is "spiritual" in essence has its spiritual virtue neutralized by the form in which it addresses itself to man. It may be in itself spiritual, but it does not come to him with the power which properly belongs to spirit. Spirit, according to Paul, is essentially life-giving ζωοποιοῦν: but, as he says elsewhere, no such thing has been given as a law able to give life (νόμος δυνά-μενος ζωοποιῆσαι, Gal 3:21). Had there been such a thing, had there been a law which brought along with it the power to fulfil its own requirements—in other words, had there been a law which was "spiritual" in the full sense of the term—righteousness would no doubt have come by it; man would not have been left to fulfil his vocation alone; as it rose before his mind the power of God would have risen simultaneously in his heart to realize it. But with all his recognition of the fact that the law came from God and enshrined His will, St. Paul had no experience of this kind to connect with it; life under the law, spiritual as he acknowledged the law to be, and delighting in it as he did "after the inner man," had been for him a life of uninterrupted frustration, ending in despair; all his experience of Spirit as the divine power through which the law is accomplished dates from his acquaintance with Christ.

This is the point to which we are brought at the beginning of Romans 8. The Spirit is here described in Romans 8:2 as "the Spirit of life,' or perhaps as "the Spirit of the life in Christ Jesus." This latter way of connecting the words, though it is supported only by a minority of scholars (including Pfleiderer and Lipsius), seems to me, grammatically speaking, far more Pauline than the other;

but in respect of meaning there is no appreciable difference. When Paul says "the Spirit of life," he has in a manner said everything he has to say on the subject. That the life in question is one with Christ's life is involved in all that has already been said about the relations of Christ and the Spirit. "Spirit," standing by itself, is a blank unintelligible form; whatever meaning and content it has in the New Testament must be derived from Christ. If it is to be characterized as "the Spirit of life," because through it life has come to us in divine power (as it had to St. Paul), then whether the very words of the passage connect that life with Christ or not we can only hold that it is the same life in which the Son of God triumphed over sin and death. And the gift of the Spirit means our participation in His triumph. "The law of the Spirit of the life in Christ Jesus set me free from the law of sin and death."

We have seen already that the Spirit is essentially opposed to anything legal; no contrast in St. Paul's mind is sharper than that of πνεῦμα and γράμμα, spirit and letter. Yet the Spirit is not antinomian. There is a *law* of the Spirit. It does indeed transcend everything statutory. To its inexhaustible originality in discovering the will of God all legal enactments are inadequate. But it legislates, nevertheless. It lays down at every moment and at every step the proper course of conduct for man to follow. It can do this because of its relation to Christ. It is His Spirit, and the law of His life is inherent in it. Hence there is nothing mystical in the Spirit any more than there is in the Gospels, nothing in it which opens the door to antinomianism or to moral anarchism any more than there is in the history of Jesus. It is so far from the possibility of any such perversion that justice is done to the law by those and by those only who walk after the Spirit. It is in them that the righteous demand of the law is fulfilled. The law, which is spiritual, never gets justice done to it till man becomes the possessor of the Spirit, and then it gets justice done to it, not by any legal exertions of man, not by "works of law" which he achieves, but by the divine impulse of the Spirit which brings his natural impotence to an end, and carries out the mind of Christ in his life. The just demand of the law, as St. Paul finally puts it, is fulfilled *in* those who walk after the Spirit, *in* them, not *by* them. The sense of debt to God, the consciousness that it is to the life and power He has given that this change is due, is conveyed not only by the reference to the Spirit, but by this self-denying choice of the preposition.

It is not necessary to enter here into an examination of the difficult and complicated sentence in Romans 8:3. Thus much is certain, apart from details: it is the Spirit which does for man what the law could not do, and the Spirit can only be given through the life and through the atoning death of Jesus. In that life and death the dreadful problem of man's sin was effectually dealt with, and it is on the basis of this effectual dealing, or, to use the old expression, it is on the ground of Christ's finished work that the divine power is given which brings life and righteousness to men. It brings life and righteousness to men just because the virtue of that finished work is in it; separate "spirit " from this, and it is an empty word; you may say what you please of it, for you are dealing with an unknown quantity in an empty space. All the legitimate meaning of spirit lies in Christ and His atonement, and in the experiences begotten through them in believing souls.

The Spirit, throughout the eighth chapter, is contrasted sharply with the flesh. It is as though the two could not be defined at all except by antagonism to each other. Those who are after the flesh mind the things of the flesh; those who are after the Spirit, the things of the Spirit. The mind of the flesh means death, the mind of the Spirit life and peace. The mind of the flesh means enmity against God; the mind of the Spirit means God's own mind in man. I have explained in a former paper the sense in which "flesh" is to be understood in such passages as these. On the one hand it includes a reference to man's nature, in which there is no special moral emphasis; man as σὰρξ is σάρκινος, a creature of flesh, a weak and ineffective creature, who has a task before him too great for his powers. On the other hand, it includes a reference to man's nature in which *is* a special moral emphasis; man as σὰρξ is not only σάρκινος, a creature of flesh, but σαρκικός, a creature abandoned to the flesh and enslaved by it. "Flesh" not only suggests the inadequacy of his nature to his calling, but at the same time the depravation of his nature through the engrossment and absorption of it all in its lower elements, a depravation by which sin has become virulent and so to speak constitutional in him, so that the disproportion between what he is and what God meant him to be grows continually greater and more desperate. At one point or another, flesh may be used in one or other of these references mainly, or its meaning may be coloured by the consciousness of both; but over the whole area in which it can be spoken of it is confronted, defeated, and annulled by Spirit. When God comes to us through the Spirit, all that we were without God comes to an end; all that we were striving in vain to become for God is assured of consummation. As against the sinfulness of the flesh, the Spirit is a divine power which ensures righteousness; as against the death which is all that sinful flesh has to look forward to, the Spirit is the divine power which brings the earnest of immortality.

To enter into the details by which St. Paul illustrates his faith and experience in this connexion would carry us too far. But it is well worth while to notice the verses (Rom 8:9–11) in which his whole mind upon the subject is condensed. *"You,"* he says to believers, "are not in the flesh, but in the Spirit, if, as I assume, the Spirit of God dwells in you." "The Spirit of God" is the simplest description which can be given of the Spirit; it is indeed so simple as to be almost tautological, for the Spirit in experience is nothing but God powerfully and effectively working upon man. But for those who have received the gospel, God is not undefined; He has been revealed in His Son, and "the Spirit of God," as the apostle proceeds, becomes almost without his noticing it "the Spirit of Christ." "If any man has not the Spirit of Christ, he is not His." Nothing could show more clearly than this how the Godhead of Christ, as the Lord and giver of the Spirit—that is, of divine life and power—was assumed by the apostle. But at the next turn of the sentence, the Spirit disappears, and we come upon "Christ in you," which is evidently to be taken as precisely the same thing. Of course Christ *can* only be in us through the Spirit, but it is equally important to remember that that which is in us through the Spirit—the Spirit of *God*—can be nothing but Christ. This divine Presence and Power in the soul makes all that is Christ's ours. It does not, indeed, save the body from dying: the doom of sin is not retracted within this area, though it is ultimately reversed. But it is stronger than all the weakness, and than all the badness of human nature. It puts to death the doings of the body. The malignant powers of Sin and Death, which had so long imposed their will on wretched men, are deprived of their sovereignty. The law of God, which is holy and just and good, instead of encountering in human nature nothing but the malignant flesh, which it provoked to greater malignity, or the approving but impotent reason, is borne to its fulfilment on the flood of a new life quickened in the believer by the power of God. If the grave is not shut, it is opened. "If the Spirit of Him who raised Jesus from the dead dwells in you, He who raised from the dead Christ Jesus shall make also your mortal bodies live through His Spirit dwelling in you."

The Spirit is connected with immortality, in the Epistle to the Romans, in yet another way. Not only as a spirit of life, or as the Spirit of Him who raised Christ from the dead and gave Him glory, but as the Spirit of sonship, it has this forward look. Sonship, or adoption, of course includes far more than this. It is defined at first by contrast with δουλεία and φόβος, servitude and fear. It is the Spirit which breaks out in the loud and joyful cry, unheard from human lips, in the glorious confidence and liberty of the New Testament, till the Spirit of Christ taught it, Abba, Father. But in the filial relation there is an infinite hope, and St. Paul rarely dwells on the one without glancing at the other. "The Spirit itself bears witness with our spirit that we are the children of God; and if children, then heirs." In this sense the Spirit itself is the firstfruits, or the earnest of the inheritance to be revealed. It is not in spite of having it, but because of having it, that Christians sigh in themselves, waiting for the adoption—that is, for the fulfilment of all it means—even the redemption of the body. The Spirit, in spite of all that is said about its immanence and its essentially ethical character, always represents in St. Paul what we mean by the supernatural. It represents not only what God is as a presence in man, but what God is as a power transcending all that man's experience has yet disclosed. The Spirit is as completely supernatural as the Lord of Glory from whom it comes, and the issue of its indwelling is not only victory over sin, but conformity to the image of the Son. The Spirit is life, and all that is called death is swallowed up in its victory. St. Paul did not and could not make our distinctions between ethical and physical, or ethical and transcendent, or ethical and supernatural, or however otherwise we may phrase them. He did not distribute the working of the Spirit along these as along different lines. For him "spiritual" was a word which had only one synonym—"divine"; and in the divine will and power, as revealed in the life, death, and resurrection of Jesus, all such distinctions were transcended. No one can apply them to the manifestation of Christ as that stood present to the mind and faith of St. Paul, and therefore it is equally impossible to use them to any real purpose when we are trying to grasp his conception of the Spirit. Some Christians seem to have the idea that if you ignore heaven you can lay greater stress on holiness; the New Testament does not favour the idea. To St. Paul, at all events, holiness and heaven, the ethical and the transcendent, are one in Christ and in His Spirit; and to an adequate sense of what Christ and His Spirit are—in other words, to an adequate apprehension of the divine—the mode of being in which Christ now lives and reigns is as real as sanctification; indeed, for St. Paul there is no such thing as sanctification except through a power which is in every sense of the term supernatural. The light of heaven, using the term heaven as a little child uses it, lies on every particle of genuine Christian morality. And it does so because all such morality is produced by the Spirit of Him who raised up Christ from the dead, and who is making us heirs together with Him.

The last reference to the Spirit in this part of the Epistle is that which connects it with prayer. The new Christian life is a mystery even to him who lives it. There are depths in it which he cannot fathom; he cannot tell whence it comes and whither it goes; sure as he is that it is of God, it brings a vocation and a responsibility with it which exceed his grasp; even when he would commend himself to God for help and guidance he does not know how to begin; his mind will not concentrate itself on anything, and words desert him. This incapacity, which comes with the gift of the Spirit, the Spirit itself relieves. "In like manner the Spirit also helpeth our infirmity; for we know not how to pray as we ought; but the Spirit itself maketh intercession for us with groanings which cannot be uttered." Perhaps there may be a reference in these words to the speaking with tongues, when men prayed in the Spirit while the understanding was unfruitful; but I can hardly think so. Such speaking with tongues seems to have been usually of an ecstatic or rapturous character, a thanksgiving to which others might say Amen, or a declaration of the mighty works of God; here, on the contrary, we seem, to be in a region where there is not indeed less intensity but surely less liberty in utterance. The only passage in Scripture which occurs to me as a parallel to this is the one in the 53rd chapter of Isaiah: "He shall see of the travail of his soul and shall be satisfied." The prophecy had its supreme fulfilment in Christ, and it is by reference to Christ that we must interpret all that is said of the Spirit. Through the Spirit, as it is spoken of here, we can see something of what Christ's soul travail means. St. Paul knew himself what it was to enter with measureless passionate sympathy into the difficulties of the new life in inexperienced souls, who were finding the new life itself the most baffling, unmanageable thing in the world. "My little children, of whom I am again in travail until Christ be formed in you." It is this same passionate sympathy with the same baffled inexperience, lost in the very wonder and mystery of that divine life into which it is being initiated, that Paul here, out of his own experience, ascribes to the Holy Spirit of God. Is not such sympathy "the love of the Spirit" (Rom 15:30), by which most surely "the love of God is shed abroad in our hearts" (Rom 5:5), so that, as the apostle goes on immediately to say, "We know that all things work together for good to them that love Him"? It is through an experience of God's presence and power like this—so intimate, so condescending, so sympathetic, yearning so to take care of us when we cannot take care of ourselves, to inspire us when we cannot think, to intercede for us when we cannot pray, to undertake for us when consciousness and will fail—that we catch something of the breadth and length, and depth and height, and of the love which passes knowledge.

# 7

# Authority of Christ

The first recorded comment on the teaching of Jesus is that of Matthew 7:28f. (Mark 1:22; Luke 4:32): "They were astonished at his teaching, for he taught them as one having authority, and not as their scribes." The scribes said nothing of themselves: they appealed in every utterance to tradition (παράδοσις); the message they delivered was not self-authenticating; it had not the moral weight of the speaker's personality behind it; it was a deduction or application of some legal maxim connected with a respectable name. They claimed authority, of course, but men had no immediate and irresistible consciousness that the claim was just. With Jesus it was the opposite. He appealed to no tradition, sheltered Himself behind no venerable name, claimed no official status; but those who heard Him could not escape the consciousness that His word was with authority (Luke 4:32). He spoke a final truth, laid down an ultimate law.

In one respect, He continued, in so doing, the work and power of the prophets. There was a succession of prophets in Israel, but not a prophetic tradition. It was a mark of degeneration and of insincerity when self-styled prophets repeated each other, stealing God's words every one from his neighbour (Jer 23:30). The true prophet may have his mind nourished on earlier inspired utterances, but his own message must spring from an immediate prompting of God. It is only when his message is of this kind that his word is with power. No mind was ever more full than the mind of Jesus of all that God had spoken in the past, but no one was ever so spontaneous as He, so free from mere reminiscence, so completely determined in His utterance by the conditions to which it was addressed. It is necessary to keep both things in view in considering His authority as a teacher. Abstract formulae about the seat of authority in religion are not of much service in this connexion. It is, of course, always true to say that truth and the mind are made for each other, and that the mind recognizes the authority of truth because in truth it meets its counterpart, that which enables it to realize its proper being. It is always correct, also, to apply this in the region of morals and religion, and to say that the words of Jesus and the prophets are authoritative because our moral personality instinctively responds to them. We have no choice, as beings made for morality and religion, to do anything but bow before them. The difficulty is that the "mind," or "conscience," or "moral personality," on which our recognition of the truth and authority of Jesus' teaching is here made dependent, is not a fixed quantity, and still less a ready-made faculty; it is rather a possibility or potentiality in our nature, which needs to be evoked into actual existence; and among the powers which are to evoke it and make it actual and valuable, by far the most important is that teaching of Jesus which it is in some sense allowed to judge. We may say in Coleridge's phrase that we believe the teaching of Jesus, or acknowledge its (or His) authority, because it "finds" us more deeply than anything else; but any Christian will admit that "find" is an inadequate expression. The teaching of Jesus does not simply find, it evokes or creates the personality by which it is acknowledged. We are born again by the words of eternal life which come from His lips, and it is the new man so born to whom His word is known in all its power. There is a real analogy between this truth and the familiar phenomenon that a new poet or artist has to create the taste which is necessary for the appreciation of his work. Dismissing, therefore, the abstract and general consideration of the idea of authority in religion, our course must be (1) to examine the actual exercise of authority by Jesus in the Gospels, referring especially to occasions on which His authority was challenged, or on which He gave hints as to the conditions on which alone it could be recognized; (2) by way of supplement we can consider the authority of the exalted Christ as it is asserted in the Epistles and exercised in the Church through the New Testament as a whole.

1. *The exercise of authority by Jesus on earth.*—(a) The simplest but most far-reaching form in which Jesus exercised authority was the

*practical* one. He claimed other men, other moral personalities, for Himself and His work, and required their unconditional renunciation of all other ties and interests that they might become His disciples. He said, "Follow me," and they rose, and left all and followed Him (Matt 4:18–22; 9:9). He made this kind of claim because He identified Himself with the gospel (Mark 8:35; 10:29) or with the cause of God and His Kingdom in the world, and for this cause no sacrifice could be too great, no devotion too profound. "He that loveth father or mother more than me is not worthy of me. He that loveth son or daughter more than me is not worthy of me. Whosoever he be of you that renounceth not all that he hath, he cannot be my disciple" (Matt 10:37; Luke 14:33). Nothing is less like Jesus than to do violence to anyone's liberty, or to invade the sacredness of conscience and of personal responsibility; but the broad fact is unquestionable, that without coercing others Jesus dominated them, without breaking their wills He imposed His own will upon them, and became for them a supreme moral authority to which they submitted absolutely, and by which they were inspired. His authority was unconditionally acknowledged because men in His presence were conscious of His moral ascendency, of His own devotion to and identification with what they could not but feel to be the supreme good. We cannot explain this kind of moral or practical authority further than by saying that it is one with the authority which the right and the good exercise over all moral beings.

Not that Jesus was able in every case to carry His own will through in the wills of other men. Moral ascendency has to be exercised under moral conditions, and it is always possible, even for one who acknowledges its right, to fail to give it practical recognition by obedience. When Jesus said to the rich ruler, "Sell all that thou hast, and give to the poor, and thou shalt have treasure in heaven: and come, follow me" (Mark 10:21), He failed to win the will of one who nevertheless was conscious that in refusing obedience he chose the worse part. "He went away sorrowful"—his sorrow implying that it was within the right on the part of Jesus to put him to this tremendous test. He acknowledges by his sorrow that he would have been a better man—in the sense of the gospel a perfect man—if he had allowed the authority of Jesus to have its perfect work in him. These are the facts of the case, and they are ignored by those who argue that it is no man's business to part with all he has for the sake of the poor; that property is a trust which we have to administer, not to renounce; that the commandment to sell all cannot be generalized, and is therefore not moral; and that it is, in short, an instance of fanaticism in Jesus, due to His belief in the nearness of the Kingdom, and the literal worthlessness of everything in comparison with entering into it at His side. There is nothing here to generalize about. There is a single case of conscience which Jesus diagnoses, and for which He prescribes heroic treatment; but it is not in the patient to rise to such treatment. The high calling of God in Christ Jesus is too high for him; he counts himself unworthy of the eternal life (Act 13:46). The authority of Jesus is in a sense acknowledged in this man; it is felt and owned though it is declined. Where the authority lay is clear enough. It lay in the Good Master Himself, in His own identification with the good cause, in His own renunciation of all things for the Kingdom of God's sake; it lay in His power to reveal to this man the weak spot in his moral constitution, and in the inward witness of the man's conscience (attested by his sorrow as he turned away) that the voice of Jesus was the voice of God, and that through obedience to it he would have entered into life. It lay in the whole relation of these two concrete personalities to each other, and it cannot be reduced to an abstract formula.

This holds true whenever we think of the moral or practical authority of Jesus. It is never legal: that is, we can never take the letter in which it is expressed and regard it as a Statute, incapable of interpretation or modification, and binding in its literal meaning for all persons, all times, all social conditions. This is plain in regard to such a command of Jesus as the one given to the rich ruler: no one will say that this is to be obeyed to the letter by all who would enter into the Kingdom of God. But it is equally true of precepts which are addressed to a far wider circle, and which are sometimes supposed (like this one) to rest in a peculiar sense on the authority of Jesus. Take, e.g., the case of the Sermon on the Mount in Matthew 5:21–48. From beginning to end this may be read as an assertion of the moral authority of Jesus, an authority which is conscious of transcending the highest yet known in Israel. "It was said to them of old time . . . but I say unto you." On what do the words of Jesus throughout this passage depend

for their actual weight with men? They depend on the consciousness of men that through these words the principle of morality,
for which our nature has an abiding affinity, is finding expression.
But just because we are conscious of this principle and of the affinity of our nature for it, we are free with regard to any particular expression of it; the particular words in which it is embodied
even by Jesus do not possess the authority of a statute to which
we can only conform, but about which we must not think. When
Jesus says, "Whoso shall smite thee on the right cheek, turn to him
also the other; to him that would go to law with thee and take
thy coat, leave also thy cloak": it is not to keep us from thinking
about moral problems by giving us a rule to be blindly obeyed, it is
rather to stimulate thought and deliver us from rules. His precepts
are legal in form, but He came to abolish legalism, and therefore
they were never meant to be literally read. When they are literally
read, conscience simply refuses to take them in. They are casuistic
in form, but anti-casuistic in intention, and their authority lies in
the intention, not in the form. What the precepts of non-resistance
and non-retaliation mean is that under no circumstances, under
no provocation, must the disciple of Jesus allow his conduct to
be determined by any other motive than that of love. He must be
prepared to go all lengths with love, and no matter how love is
tried, he must never renounce it for an inferior principle, still less
for an instinctive natural passion, such as the desire for revenge.
Put thus, the moral authority of Jesus is unquestionable, and it asserts itself over us the more, the more we feel that He embodied
in His own life and conduct the principle which He proclaims. But
there is nothing in this which binds us to take in the letter what
Jesus says about oaths, or non-resistance, or revenge; and still less
is there anything to support the idea that His words on these subjects are part of a fanatical renunciation of the world in the region
of honour as well as of property,—a literal surrender, in view of the
imminence of the Kingdom, of all that makes life on earth worth
having. It is not uncommon now for those who regard the Kingdom of God as purely transcendent and eschatological to match
this paradoxical doctrine with an ethical system equally paradoxical, a system made up purely of renunciation and negation, and
to fasten it also upon Jesus; but it is hardly necessary to refute either the one paradox or the other. What commands conscience in

the most startling words of Jesus is the truth and love which dictate them, but to recognize the truth and love is to recognize that no form of words is binding of itself. It is the supreme task of the moral being to discover what in his own situation truth and love require; and there is no short cut to the discovery of this, even in the Sermon on the Mount. Jesus is our authority, but His words are not our statutes: we are not under law, even the law of His words, but under grace—that is, under the inspiration of His personality; and though His words are one of the ways in which His moral ascendency is established over us, they are only one. There is an authority in Him to which no words, not even His own, can ever be equal.

The final form which this practical or moral authority of Jesus assumes in the New Testament is the recognition of Him as Judge of all. Probably in the generation before that in which He lived the Jews had come to regard the Messiah as God's vicegerent in the great judgment which ushered in the world to come; but what we find in the New Testament in this connexion is not the formal transference of a piece of Messianic dogmatic to Jesus; it is the moral recognition of the moral supremacy of Jesus, and of His right to pronounce finally on the moral worth of men and things. Experiences like that which inspired Luke 5:8 ( "Depart from me, for I am a sinful man, O Lord"), John 4:29 ( "Come see a man which told me all things that ever I did"), John 21:17 ("Thou knowest all things, thou knowest that I love thee"), are the basis on which the soul recognizes Christ as Judge. The claim to be Judge appears also in His own teaching (Matt 7:22ff.; 25:31ff.; Luke 13:25ff.); and if the form of the words in the first of these passages has been modified in tradition in order to bring out their bearing for those for whom the evangelist wrote, no one doubts that their substance goes back to Jesus. It is He who contemplates the vain pleas which men will address to Him "in that day"—men who with religious profession and service to the Church have nevertheless been morally unsound. The standard of judgment is variously represented: it is "the will of my Father which is in heaven" (Matt 7:21) or "these sayings of mine" (Matt 7:24) or it is what we might call in a word "humanity" (Matt 25:35; 25:42): and in its way each of these is a synonym for the moral authority of Jesus. As far as we are sensitive to their demands we are sensitive to His moral claim. Into the representations of Jesus as Judge outside of the Gospels it is not necessary to enter.

(*b*) The authority of Jesus comes before us in another aspect when we think of Him not as commanding but as *teaching*, not as Legislator or Judge, but as *Revealer*. In the first case, authority means His title to obedience; in this case, it may be said to mean His title to belief.

Perhaps of all theological questions the nature and limits of this last authority are those which have excited the keenest discussion in recent times. On the one hand, there are those who, fixing their minds on the Divinity of Jesus, regard it as essentially un-Christian to question His utterances at any point. Whatever Jesus believed, or seemed to believe, on any subject is by that very fact raised above question. The mind has simply to receive it on His authority. Thus when He refers to Jonah (Matt 12:38ff.; Luke 11:29ff.), the literal historicity of the Book of Jonah is guaranteed; when He ascribes the 110th Psalm to David (Matt 22:41ff. and parallels), critical discussion of the authorship is foreclosed; when He recognizes possession by unclean spirits (Mark 1:23ff. and often), possession is no longer a theory to explain certain facts, and therefore open to revision; it is itself a fact: it gives us a glimpse into the constitution of the spiritual universe which we are not at liberty to question. On the other hand, there are those who, while they declare their faith in the Incarnation, argue that it belongs to the very truth of the Incarnation that Jesus should not merely be man, but man of a particular time and environment; not man in the abstract, but man defined (and therefore in some sense limited) by the conditions which constitute reality. He had not simply intelligence, but intelligence which had been moulded by a certain education, and could only reveal itself through a certain language; and both of these are conditions which (while essential to historical reality) nevertheless involve limitation. Hence with regard to the class of subjects just referred to, those who are here in question feel quite at liberty to form their own opinions on relevant grounds. They do not, as they think, set aside the authority of Jesus in doing so: their idea rather is that in these regions Jesus never claimed to have or to exercise any authority. Thus in the first two instances adduced above, He simply takes the Old Testament as it stands, and He appeals to it to confirm a spiritual truth which He is teaching on its own merits. In Matthew 12:38ff. He is reproaching an impenitent people, and He refers to the Book of Jonah for a great example of repentance, and that on the part of a heathen race; the men of Nineveh who repented will condemn His unrepentant contemporaries in the day of judgment. In Matthew 22:41ff. He is teaching that the essential thing in Messiahship is not a relation to David, but a relation to God; and He refers to the 110th Psalm, and to David as its author, as unintelligible except on this hypothesis. In both cases (it is argued) the truths which rest on the authority of Jesus are independent of the Old Testament appeal which is associated with them. That repentance is an essential condition of entering into the Kingdom of God, and that there is no responsibility so heavy as that of those who will not repent even when Jesus calls, are truths which are not affected though the Book of Jonah is read as an allegory or a poem; that the fundamental thing in the person of Jesus is not His relation to David (which He shared with others) but His relation to God (which belonged to Him alone), is a truth which is not affected though the 110th Psalm is ascribed to the Maccabaean period. In other words, the authority of Jesus as a revealer of God and of the laws of His Kingdom is not touched, though we suppose Him to share on such matters as are here in question the views which were current among His contemporaries. It is not denying His Divinity to say this; it is rather denying His humanity if we say the opposite. Parallel considerations apply to the belief in possession which Jesus undoubtedly shared with His fellow-countrymen, and in fact with His contemporaries generally. Possession was the current theory of certain morbid conditions of human nature, physical, mental, and probably in some cases also moral; but the one thing of consequence in the Gospel is not that Jesus held this or any other theory about these morbid conditions, but that in Him the power of God was present to heal them. Our theory of them may be different, but that only means that we belong to a different age; it does not touch the truth that from these terrible and mysterious woes Jesus was mighty to save. It does not matter that His notions of medicine and psychology were different from ours; He did not come to reveal medicine or psychology—to "reveal" such things is a contradiction in terms; He came to reveal the Father, and His authority has its centre there.

There is, no doubt, great, possibility of error in arguing from such abstract ideas as "Divinity" and "humanity," especially when they are in some way opposed to one another in our minds: however we may define them, we must remember that they were in no sense opposed or inconsistent in Christ. He was at once and consistently all that we mean by divine and all that we mean by human, but we cannot learn what that was by looking up "divine" and "human" in the dictionary, or in a book of dogmatic theology. We must look at Jesus Himself as He is presented to us in the Gospels. And further, we must consider that there is a vast region of things in which there neither is nor can be any such thing as authority—the region, namely, which is covered by science. Now questions of the kind to which reference has just been made all belong to the domain of science. The nature of the Book of Jonah, the date and authorship of the 110th Psalm, the explanation of the morbid phenomena which the ancients ascribed to evil spirits inhabiting the bodies of men: these are questions for literary, for historical, for medical science. It is a misleading way of speaking about them, and needlessly hurts some Christian feelings, to say that the authority of Jesus was limited, and did not extend to such matters. The truth rather is that such matters belong to a region where there is no such thing as authority, or where the only authority is that of facts, which those in quest of knowledge must apprehend and interpret for themselves. It is a negation of the very idea of science to suppose that any constituent of it could be revealed, or could rest upon authority, even the authority of Jesus. Hence in regard to all such subjects the question of Jesus' authority ought never to be raised: it is not only misleading, but unreal. On the other hand, when we come to the authority which Jesus actually claims as a revealer of God, and of the things of His Kingdom, we find that it is not only real but absolute—an authority to which the soul renders unreserved acknowledgment.

This is brought out most clearly in Matthew 11:27. Here Jesus speaks in explicit terms of His function as Revealer, and we see at once the absoluteness of His authority, and its sphere. "All things have been delivered unto me by my Father, and no one knoweth the Son save the Father, neither doth any know the Father save the Son, and he to whomsoever the Son willeth to reveal him." Whatever else these words express, they express Jesus' sense of absolute competence in His vocation: He had everything given to Him which belonged to the work He had to do, and He was conscious of being equal to His task. If we try to interpret "all things" by reference to the context, then whether we look before or after we must say that the "all things" in view are those involved in the revelation of God: in the work of revelation, and especially in the revelation of Himself as Father, God has no organ but Christ, and in Christ He has an adequate organ. The passage anticipates John 14:6, "I am the way, the truth, and the life: no man cometh unto the Father but by me." It is in a word like this—*I am the truth*—that we find the key to the problems which have been raised about the authority of Jesus as a Teacher or Revealer. The truth which we accept on His authority is the truth which we recognize in Him. It is not announced by Him from a world into which we cannot enter: it is present here, in Him, in the world in which we live. It is not declared on authority to which we blindly surrender; it is exhibited in a Person and a Life which pass before us and win our hearts. To put it otherwise, the truth which we owe to Jesus, and for which He is our authority, is not information; it is not a contribution to science, physical or historical—for this we are cast by God on our own resources; it is the truth which is identical with His own being and life in the world, which is embodied or incarnate in Him. It is the truth which is involved in His own relation to God and man, and in His perfect consciousness of that relation: it is the truth of His own personality, not any casual scientific fact. He does not claim to know everything, and it would be difficult to reconcile such a claim with true manhood; but He does claim full knowledge of the Father, and not His words only, but His whole being and life are the justification of His claim.[1]

---

1. Loisy (*L'Évangile et L'Église*, 45f., *Autour d'un petit Livre*, 130f.) has attacked Matthew 11:27 on the ground that the unique divine Sonship which it ascribes to Jesus is of a sort which it was not historically possible for Him to conceive or assert. Jesus, he holds, could only have used "Son of God" in the Messianic official sense of Psalm 2:7; here, therefore, where the meaning is clearly more than official, it cannot be the voice of a Jewish Messiah which is heard, but the voice of the Christian consciousness in a Gentile environment: the larger Church has universalized the Jewish conception, elevated the official Son—the Messianic King—into a Son by nature, and put its own faith and its own experience of Jesus into Jesus' own lips. Perhaps it is enough to say in refutation of this, that the words here in question, as found both in Matthew and Luke, in all probability

The authority of Christ as a Teacher and Revealer has been called in question mainly in connexion with His words about the future. There is no doubt that these present great difficulty to those who believe in Him. They seem to say quite unmistakably that certain things will happen, and happen within a comparatively short time, which (if we are to read literally) have not happened yet. "Ye shall not have gone through the cities of Israel till the Son of Man be come" (Matt 10:23); "Verily I say unto you, there be some of them that stand here which shall in no wise taste of death till they see the Son of Man coming in his Kingdom" (Matt 16:28; cf. Matt 24:29-35; Mark 13:30 f.; Luke 21:27f.). The coming of the Son of Man in His Kingdom was conceived quite definitely by the apostolic Church as a supernatural visible coming on the clouds of heaven, and it is a strong measure to assume that in cherishing this hope, by which the New Testament is inspired from beginning to end, the early Church was completely misapprehending the Master. He must have said something—when we consider the intensity of the apostolic hope, surely we may say He must have said much—to create and sustain an expectation so keen. But there are considerations we must keep in mind if we would do justice to all the facts. (1) The final triumph of His cause, which was the cause of God and His Kingdom, was not for Jesus an item in a list of dogmas, but a living personal faith and hope; in this sense it has the authority of His personality behind it. It was as sure to Him as His own being that the cause for which He stood in the world would triumph; and it is as sure for everyone who believes in Him. (2) He Himself, with all this assurance of faith, explicitly declares His ignorance of the day and hour at which the final triumph comes. He longed for it intensely; He felt that it was urgent that it should come; and urgency, when expressed in terms of time, means imminence; but the disclaimer of knowledge remains. The one thing certain is that He spoke of the time as uncer-

belong to Weiss's "apostolic source," the oldest record of words of Jesus; and that the same unique relation of "the Father" and "the Son" is implied in Mark 13:32, the genuineness of which no one doubts. Schmiedel (*Encyc. Bibl.* ii. 2527), without disputing the words in Matthew 11:27, tries by recurring to the Western text to reduce them to the "official" Messianic meaning which Loisy could recognize as possibly historical. Harnack, on the other hand, treats them as authentic, and indeed as the most important and characteristic words of Jesus on record for determining His thought regarding Himself (*Das Wesen des Christentums*, 81).

tain, as sometimes sooner than men would expect, and sometimes later: the moral attitude required being always that of watching.[2]

(3) When Jesus bodied forth this hope of the future triumph of His cause, and of His own glorious coming, He did it in language borrowed mainly from the Old Testament apocalypse, the Book of Daniel. It would be hard to say that the apostles completely misunderstood Him when He did so, but it is hard for anyone in using such language to say what is literal in it and what has to be spiritualized. No one in reading Daniel 7 takes the four great beasts, and the sea out of which they rise, literally; why, then, must we be compelled to take the human form and the clouds of heaven, literally? The Book of Acts (Act 2:16–21) sees in the experience of the Church at Pentecost the fulfilment of a prophecy in Joel (2:30) which speaks of "blood and fire and vapour of smoke, of the sun turning into darkness and the moon into blood," though no such phenomena actually accompanied the gift of the Spirit. May not modern Christians, and even the early believers, have taken poetic expressions of the living hope of Jesus more prosaically than He meant them? (4) We must allow for the possibility that in the reports of Jesus' words which we possess, the reporters may sometimes have allowed the hopes kindled in their own hearts by Jesus to give a turn or a colour, quite involuntarily, to what they tell us. They might not be able to distinguish precisely between the hopes they owed to Him and the very words in which He had declared His own assurance of victory. And finally (5), we must remember that in a spiritual sense the prophecies of Jesus have been fulfilled. He came again in power. He came in the resurrection, and He came at Pentecost. He filled Jerusalem with His presence in the early days of the Church as He had never done while He lived on earth; from the very hour when they condemned Him (Matt 26:64) it was possible for His judges to be conscious of His exaltation and of His coming in power. It may be that in all prophecy, even in the prophecy of Jesus, there is the element which we can call illusive, without having to call it delusive. To be intelligible, it must speak the language of the age, but it is going to be fulfilled in another age, the realities and experiences of which transcend the conceptions and the speech of the present. Even if this be so, it does not

2. Bruce, *The Kingdom of God*, 278; Wendt, *The Teaching of Jesus*, 1:127.

shake our faith in Jesus and His authority. The truth which is in-carnate in His person is the truth of the final—and who will not sometimes say the speedy?—triumph of His cause. We may mis-conceive the mode of it, even when we try to guide ourselves by His words; but the important thing is not the mode but the fact, and of that we are as sure as we are sure of Him.

(c) Besides the authority which He exercised in establishing His ascendency over men, and that which we recognize in Him as the Truth, we may distinguish (though it is but part of His revelation of the Father) the gracious authority exercised by Christ in *forgiv-ing sins*. That He did forgive sins is not to be doubted. The nar-rative in Mark 2:1–12 makes this clear. Jesus no more *declared* that the paralytic's sins were forgiven than He declared that he was not lame: the meaning of the whole incident is that His word *conferred* with equal power the gift of pardon and the gift of bodily strength. The one miracle of redemption—"who forgiveth all thine iniqui-ties, who healeth all thy diseases"—reaches through the whole of human nature, and Jesus has authority to perform it all. It is in this sense that we must interpret passages like Luke 7:47 ff; Luke 23:43 as well as Mark 2:17, Luke 15, and ultimately Matthew 18:18 and John 20:23. There is not anything to be said of this authority but that it must vindicate itself. No one can believe that Jesus has au-thority to forgive sins except the man who through Jesus has had the experience of forgiveness. The divine love that dwelt in Jesus, that received sinners and ate with them, that spent itself to seek and save the lost, that saw what was of God in men and touched it: that divine love made forgiveness not only credible to sinners, but real. It entered into their hearts with God's own authority, and in penitent faith and love the burden passed from their consciences and they were born again. When He was challenged by the scribes, Jesus appealed to the physical miracle, which was indisputable, in support of the spiritual one, which lay beyond the reach of sense; but it was only the scribes, not the forgiven man, who needed this seal of His authority to pardon. Those whom He forgave had the witness in themselves, and ultimately there can be no other. The authority which Jesus exercised in this gracious sense He extended to His disciples alike during their brief mission while He was on earth (Mark 3:15; 6:7–13), and in view of their wider calling when He was exalted (Matt 18:18; John 20:23).

Some light is thrown upon the authority of Jesus if we consider the occasions on which it was challenged, and the way in which Jesus met them.

(α) It was tacitly challenged wherever men were "offended" in Him. To be offended (σκανδαλίζεσθαι) is to stumble at His claims, to find something in Him which one cannot get over and which is incompatible with absolute surrender to Him; it is to deny His right to impose upon men the consequences (persecution, poverty, even death) which may be involved in accepting His authority (see Matt 11:6; 13:21; 13:28ff.; 15:12; 24:10; 26:31; the other Gospels here add nothing to Matthew). Sometimes Jesus met this tacit challenge by pointing to the general character of His work as vindicating His claims. This is what He does in the case of John the Baptist (Matt 11:2–6). Whether we read this passage—"the blind receive their sight, the lame walk," etc.—in the physical or the spiritual sense, the works in question are the signs that God's Anointed has come, and it can only mean loss and ruin to men if they fail to see and to acknowledge Him as what He is. Sometimes, again, Jesus encountered those who were "offended" in Him with a severity amounting to scorn. When the Pharisees "stumbled" because His word about things that do and do not defile cut straight across their traditional prejudices, He did nothing to conciliate them. "Every plant that my heavenly Father hath not planted shall be rooted up. Let them alone. They are blind guides of blind men. And if the blind man leads the blind, both shall fall into the ditch" (Matt 15:13f.). In reality the "offence" in this case meant that sham holiness would not acknowledge true; and in this situation it can only be war *à l'outrance*. As a rule, however, Jesus only speaks of men being offended, or offended in Him, by way of warning; and He assumes that to the solemn tones of His warning conscience will respond. His authority is inherent in Himself and His actions, and cannot with a good conscience be repudiated by any one who sees what He is. This is the tone of Matthew 13:21; 24:10; 26:31.

(β) It is a more explicit challenge of His authority when Jesus is asked to show a sign, or a sign from heaven (Matt 12:38f.; 16:1f.; Luke 23:8; John 6:30). This was the recurrence of the temptation of the pinnacle, and Jesus consistently rejected it. He never consented (not even in the case of the paralytic of Mark 2:1–9, see above) to present the physical as evidence for the spiritual. The proof of the authority with which He spoke did not lie outside of His word, in something which could be attached to it, but in the word itself; if it was not self-attesting, nothing else could attest it. This is put with peculiar force in the Fourth Gospel. It is true that an evidential value is recognized in the miracles, but it is only by an afterthought, or as a second best: "though ye believe not me, believe the works" (John 10:38); "believe that I am in the Father and the Father in me; or else, believe for the very works' sake" (John 14:11). The main line of thought is that which deprecates faith based on signs and wonders (John 4:48). When the multitudes ask, "What sign doest thou then? our fathers did eat the manna in the wilderness," the answer of Jesus virtually is, "I am the bread of life. . . . He that eateth *me* shall live by me . . . the words that I speak unto you are spirit and are life" (John 6:30ff.). In other words, the authority of Jesus does not depend upon any external credentials; it is involved in what He is, and must be immediately apprehended and responded to by the soul. What enables men to recognize Jesus as what He is, and so to acknowledge His authority, is, according to the representation of John 6—10, a need in their nature or state which He can supply. If we wish to be sure that He is the Christ, the King in the Kingdom of God, the way to certainty is not to prove that He was born at Bethlehem of the seed of David (John 7:42), nor that He came into the world mysteriously (John 7:27), nor that He has done many miracles (John 7:31): it is to see in Him the living bread (chap. 6), the living water (chap. 4 and John 7:37), the light of the world (chaps. 8 and 9), the Good Shepherd (chap. 10), the Giver of Life (chaps. 5 and 11). These are ideas or experiences which are relative to universal human needs, and therefore they are universally intelligible; every one who knows what it is to be hungry, thirsty, forlorn, in the dark, dead, knows how to appreciate Jesus; and apart from these experiences no cleverness in applying prophetic or other theological signs to Him is of any value. All this is strictly relevant, for it is through experiences in which we become debtors to Jesus for meat and drink, for light and life, that we become conscious of what His authority means.

(γ) Once, at least, the authority of Jesus was challenged in a quasi-legal fashion. When He drove the traders from the Temple, the chief priests and the elders of the people came to Him, saying, "By what authority doest thou these things, and who gave thee this authority?" (Matt 21:23ff.; Mark 11:27ff.; Luke 20:1ff.). Formally, by His counter question about the Baptist, Jesus only silences His adversaries; but more than this is meant. If, He suggests, they had been true to the earlier messenger of God, they would have had no difficulty about His claims. If they had repented at John's summons, and been right with God, then to their simple and humble hearts Jesus' action would have vindicated itself; as it is, to their insincere souls He has no advance to make. The ambassador of an earthly king has credentials external to his person and his message, but not the ambassador in whom God Himself visits His people. His actions like His words speak for themselves. Throughout the Fourth Gospel it is an affinity of spirit with Jesus on which the recognition of His authority depends. It is those who are of God (John 8:47), of the truth (John 18:37), those who are His sheep (John 10:4f.; 10:26), who hear His voice: those who are not of God, especially the insincere, who seek honour from one another (John 5:44), are inevitably offended in Him.

2. Thus far we have considered the authority of Christ as it was exercised, acknowledged, or declined during His life on earth. But the New Testament exhibits much more than this. It is not merely as historical, but as *exalted*, that Christ exercises authority—in the Church. In all its aspects the authority which we have studied in the Gospels reappears in the Epistles. It is perpetuated in the Christian society in an effective, if somewhat undefinable way.

What strikes one first in the New Testament literature, apart from the Gospels, is the almost complete absence of *literal* appeal to Jesus. The apostles, whatever be the explanation, do not, except on rare occasions, *quote* the Lord. It is true that when they do so, His word is regarded as decisive in a sense in which even the word of an apostle is not (cf. 1 Cor 7:10 with 7:12; 7:25; 7:40). It is true also that passages like Romans 12, 13, and much in the Epistle of James, could only have been written (in all probability) by men who not only had the Spirit of Christ, but whose minds were full of echoes of His words. Nevertheless the fact remains that Jesus is hardly appealed to formally as an authority in the New Testament writings. There could be no more striking proof of the fact that Christianity was apprehended from the first as a free and spiritual religion to which everything statutory was alien. Not even the word of Jesus had legal character for it. What Jesus sought and found in

His disciples was a spiritual remembrance of Himself. His words were preserved not in a phonograph, or in a stenographic report, but in the impression they made, in the insight they gave, in the thoughts and experiences they produced in the lives of living men. They were perpetuated not merely by being put on record, but still more by being preached. Now to preach is not only to report, but to apply; and the application of the word of Christ to new circumstances inevitably and unconsciously brings with it a certain or rather an uncertain amount of interpretation, of bringing out the point, of emphasis on this or that which at the moment demands it. What we wish to know is whether the men whose ministry perpetuated the word of Christ, and perpetuated it in this free and spiritual fashion, had the qualifications demanded by their task. Could Christ so fit them for their ministry that they should be under no legal constraint, and yet should never be unfaithful to His meaning, or misrepresent Him or His work? In other words, could He in any sense transmit His authority to His witnesses, so that it should be felt in them as in Him?

The answer of the New Testament is in the affirmative, and it is not too much to say that the New Testament as a whole is the proof that this answer is right. "We have the mind of Christ," says St. Paul (1 Cor 2:16), and again (in 2 Cor 13:3), "Ye seek a proof of Christ speaking in me"—a proof which he is quite ready to give. He was conscious that in the discharge of his apostolic ministry he was not alone: Christ was in him pleading His own cause. Of course the authority of Christ in this case cannot be other than we have already seen it to be in the earthly life of Christ. Its range is the same, and its recognition is conditioned in the same way. The apostle is no more bound literally to reproduce Jesus than Jesus is bound literally to reproduce Himself. He is no more bound than Jesus is to prove the truth of his message by credentials external to it. He no more hesitates than Jesus does to trace the rejection of his message, the refusal to call Jesus Lord, to a want of moral affinity with Jesus which is the final definition of sin. "If our gospel is veiled, it is veiled in them that are perishing, in whom the god of this world hath blinded the minds of the unbelieving" (2 Cor 4:3f.). It is not possible to say beforehand, on the basis of any doctrine of inspiration, whether there are elements in the apostolic writings, and if so what, which have no authority for us. Nothing in them has legal or statutory authority, and spiritual authority must be trusted to win for itself the recognition which is its due. There is something to be said for the distinction that while the testimony of the apostles to Jesus—a testimony resting on their experience of what He was and of what He had done for them—is perennially authoritative, the theology of the apostles—a theology conditioned by the intellectual environment in which they lived and to which they had to vindicate their message—has only a transient importance. The difficulty is just to draw the distinction between testimony and theology; as a matter of fact, the two things interpenetrate in the New Testament, and there is a point at which the distinction disappears. To insist upon it as if it were absolute is really to introduce again into Christianity (under the form of the apostolic testimony) that legal or statutory or dogmatic element from which Jesus set all religion free. It is better to read the apostles as men through whose minds Christ pleads His own cause in the Spirit. The minds may be more or less adequate instruments for His service; they may be more adequate in some relations, and less so in others; but they are indivisible, and it is not helpful in the long run to introduce into them the schism of testimony and theology. We must let them tell upon us in their integrity, and acknowledge their authority whenever it proves irresistible. (More detailed consideration of this point will be found in the article on "Preaching Christ").[3]

The part of the New Testament which raises in the acutest form the question of the authority of Christ—or perhaps we should say here of His apostle—is the Fourth Gospel. It is practically agreed among scholars that the style of the discourses in that Gospel is due to the author, not to the speakers. Every one speaks in the same style—John the Baptist, Jesus, the evangelist himself. The words of an actor in the history (Jesus, for example, in the first part of chap. 3, and the Baptist in the latter part) pass over insensibly into words of the historian. The first person plural is used by Jesus (e.g., John 3:11; 9:4) where it is tempting to say that it is the Christian consciousness which is expressed, the common mind of the Church which owes its being to Him. Further, Jesus says things about Himself in the Fourth Gospel to which there is no

3. [Chapter 11 of this volume.]

parallel in the other three. He speaks plainly of His pre-existence, of the glory which He had with the Father before the world was, of an eternal being which was His before Abraham was born; He makes Himself the content and the subject of His teaching— "I am the bread of life, the light of the world, the resurrection and the life"; He identifies Himself in a mysterious way with the redeeming purpose and power of God—"I and the Father are one," "He that hath seen me hath seen the Father." It may be difficult for the historian, on purely historical grounds, to prove that Jesus uttered all the words thus ascribed to Him, and if the difficulty presses, the authority of the words may seem to disappear. But is this really so? May not the Fourth Gospel itself be the fulfilment of one of the words in question—"I have many things to say unto you, but ye cannot bear them now. But when he is come, the Spirit of truth, he shall guide you into all the truth: for he shall not speak from himself, but whatsoever things he shall hear, these shall he speak . . . He shall take of mine, and shall announce it to you" (John 16:12f.). These words would not be satisfied by a merely literal reproduction of what Jesus had uttered: they imply that with the gift of the Spirit will come a profounder insight into all that He had meant, and ability to render a more adequate testimony to the truth embodied in Him. Twice in the Gospel (John 2:22; 12:16) the writer tells us expressly that after Jesus was glorified the disciples remembered incidents in His career and saw a meaning in them unnoticed at the time; and this principle may well reach further. When Jesus fed the multitudes, He did not, so far as the Synoptics record, say anything to explain His act; all they were conscious of was that He had compassion on their hunger. But the Spirit-taught apostle, long afterwards, saw what He meant, and felt that if they had only had ears to hear as the bread passed from hand to hand, they would have caught the voice of Jesus— "I am the bread of life." So when He opened the eyes of the blind, what He meant was, "I am the light of the world"; and when He raised the dead, "I am the resurrection and the life." If John did not hear Him say so at the moment, he heard Him afterwards, and the authority of the words need not be less though we have to think of them as spoken, not by the historical Christ in Galilee or Judaea, but by the exalted Christ through His Spirit in the soul of the beloved disciple. They would be in this case a sublime illustration of what

St. Paul calls "Christ speaking in me." The peculiarity that they are put into the lips of Jesus Himself, in connexion with definite scenes and incidents in His earthly life, was possibly quite intelligible to those who first read the Gospel; they knew that it was a spiritual Gospel, and that it was never intended to be taken as a literal record of Jesus' discourses, but as an inspired interpretation of all that He was and did. Read in this light, it has its authority in itself, as the other New Testament books have, and as Jesus Himself had when He spoke with men face to face; and it is an authority, as experience proves, not less potent than that which is claimed and wielded by Christ in any other of His witnesses. If we compare it with the other Gospels, which have in a higher degree the character of literal transcripts of word and deed, we may even say that it is a fulfilment of the words found in the lips of Jesus in John 14:12, "He that believeth on me, the works that I do shall he also do: and greater works than these shall he do; because I go to the Father." Faith in Jesus has never achieved anything surpassing the witness—the true witness—of this Gospel to the Son of God. The final and supremely authoritative testimony to Jesus is no doubt that which is given in His being and in His work in the world; but so dull of eye and slow of heart were the disciples, that had He put all the import of this into words they could not have taken it in. What He could not say on earth, however, He was able to say by His Spirit from heaven; and when that one of the disciples who was able to hear puts what he has heard into the Master's lips, he is only giving Him His own. The authority of the word of Jesus here, as everywhere in the New Testament, lies in itself, and in the fact which it interprets. It is an authority which has never failed to win recognition, and it may be said of it with emphasis, "Every one that is of the truth heareth this voice."

# 8

# Christianity and the Historical Christ

Not long ago the favourite cry in advanced theological circles was Back to Christ. Christ, it was taken for granted, was the only authority and the only guarantee for Christianity. The religion which traced its origin to Him had become entangled, in the course of its history, with much which was indifferent or alien to the mind of the Master; and the one conclusive way of getting rid of all this was to return to the Master Himself. When it began to be realised that much of the theological lumber, as it was called, which some people wished to get rid of, had unquestionable roots in the New Testament, there were timid minds which began to have misgivings; but the bolder spirits in the new movement rather enjoyed the audacity of disparaging the apostles in the name of the Lord. What they wanted was to get behind them all, behind Peter and Paul and John, to the very man of Nazareth; the historical Jesus was their watchword; everything in the Christian religion was to be legitimated by appeal to Him alone.

Well, times change. There is no doubt something comforting in this idea of basing religion on the historical Saviour. History, we say to ourselves, is the region of fact, as opposed to speculation— of reality as opposed to fancy. When we are dealing with history we know where we are; we come in contact with things which make their own appeal, and evoke an appropriate but free and rational response. But when the mind devotes itself to history, in the sense of that which simply happened in the past, it has disconcerting experiences. Such experiences, which greatly disturb the assurance with which it embarked on the return to Christ, can be put in three ways.

(1) The sense of distance, which grows upon the mind as it thinks of things or persons simply as historical, weakens the impression they make on us, and therefore their value for religious purposes. As a historical person Jesus lived far away and long ago. Even if the gospel story of His life is literally true, how distant He is. He lived in the ancient world—further back than our national life or our language reaches, behind modern science and civilisation, behind the barbarian invasions and the fall of the empire, ever so far away. The sense of this, if it is left to itself, diminishes and may even extinguish any religious impression made on us by the historical Jesus; in spite of the hope with which we set out to return to Him, the end of our voyage finds us far from home; and no historical imagination, be it ever so lively, can bring us into a religious relation to a purely historical person. We can no more catch the glow of faith from a past so remote than we can warm our hands at the stars. A Christian reader of the Gospels, of course, does not use them in this purely historical way. Christ is not for him a person who had His being in the past and who exhausted it there; He is a living and present person, with whom he enters into direct and immediate fellowship through the gospel story; it is not a distant past he is dealing with, but a present and eternal life. This, however, is a point of view which mere history cannot attain.

(2) But there is a second point of consequence here. To the merely historical student, there is no such thing as absolute certainty. *Ex hypothesi*, everything historical is problematical. It is a question as to what testimony is available, and no testimony amounts to demonstration. Whether Jesus spoke any given word, whether He did any given act, whether He had any given experience, is open to the same kind of historical uncertainty as if, instead of Jesus, we were to put into such sentences Pericles or Julius Caesar. It may be quite true to say with Butler that probability is the guide of life; but we know very well that it was not historical probabilities about Jesus by which Christianity was inspired from the beginning, and that it is not such historical probabilities by which it is sustained now. That in our reading of the Gospels historically we continually have to weigh evidence and balance alternative possibilities is quite true; but every Christian knows that the religious value of the Gospels depends

on something else. Whatever the historical explanation of it may be—and of that, meanwhile, I say nothing—he comes into an immediate fellowship with Christ through them in which there is nothing problematic: a fellowship in which everything in his life is involved that transcends doubt or questioning. This, again, is something beyond the reach of mere history.

(3) And to come to the third point, even if our knowledge of the past were complete and sure—even if we knew all about the historical Jesus with a certainty beyond the reach of doubt—we are haunted by philosophers who are themselves haunted by the relativity of everything in history. All that takes place passes. The past has had its day. It was there to be transcended, and it has been transcended. Nothing in it abides, nothing has absolute worth. Even if you got back to Christ ever so surely, it would be no gain; you would be face to face with something which had its value and significance for its own place and time, no doubt, but something which, like all things historical, has no more than a relative and transient importance, and cannot therefore supply the basis and rule of religion which you crave.

In one way or another, considerations of this kind have made their way into the common mind, perplexing it, and damping its enthusiasm for history. Instead of staking everything on the historical Jesus, many people seem concerned to find a type of Christianity which shall be entirely independent of history. There has been a distinct revival, I will not say with greater insight, but with a greater parade of philosophical and historical demonstration, of Lessing's famous aphorism, that accidental truths of history can never become the proof of necessary truths of reason. The assumption that the Christian religion consists of necessary truths of reason is perhaps pardonable in philosophers, who are naturally embarrassed by facts, but it is very astonishing to find it accepted by theologians. It is more than astonishing to find theological professors, men whose business it is to train the members of the Christian Church for its ministry, proclaiming and arguing that what they call Christian faith is not dependent on the historical Christ, and that it would make no difference to their faith though it were to be proved that Christ never existed. This has actually happened. Men who have given themselves to what they call the purely historical study of the Gospels have been in some cases so disenchanted with the result that they have felt inwardly impelled to find a basis for their faith less open to disturbing questions. They started on the back to Christ adventure. Their idea was to make the historical original of Christianity its standard and its basis. As opposed to modern and even to apostolic conceptions of Christ they would have nothing but the historical Jesus Himself; and now that they have had their way, the historical Jesus Himself is no better than an encumbrance to them. What they really want—or so it seems to them—is not a religion which owes all its contents and power to historical facts, but a religion which has nothing to do with history. It is some kind of absolute idealism they believe in, or want to believe in—some system of thoughts which can be realised for all it is worth quite apart from the contingencies which are the warp and woof of history. What are we to say to this curious situation, to this complete swing of the pendulum, which has made men who once, in their religion, staked everything on history, now crave in their religion to be emancipated from history?

To begin with, it is worth remarking that it is not the first time that historical religion has had this battle to fight. It is older even than the Christian era. When the religion of Israel came into contact with the higher mind of Greece, this was its position. The Greeks, in spite of their intelligence, in spite even of Thucydides, had no proper conception of history. Thucydides wrote memoirs of extraordinary political penetration, but the Greeks had no idea of a continuous and progressive purpose which was being wrought out in their national life and in which all those relations of man to God and of God to man were involved, which constitute religion. Their highest religious ideas were connected not with history but with nature, and with the conception of God as the soul, and the supreme law, of the world. They were metaphysical rather than ethical. But Israel's God was the great Being who had called the fathers, who had delivered the nation from Egyptian bondage and given it an inheritance in Canaan, who had taught it His law and through all the proud and all the dark hours of its life had dealt with it in justice and in mercy. It was tempting, and the attempt was made, to come to terms with the higher Greek religion by identifying the law of God as historically revealed to Israel with the life in harmony with nature as understood, e.g., by the Stoic philosophy; in other words, it was tempting to let the historical religion melt and disappear in a religion of ideas. But though much Jewish-Hellenistic literature represents a tendency of this kind, it was foiled in the long run. There is something irreducible and refractory in facts which gives them a value all their own, and in spite of what might seem contingent and dubious the events of Israel's history, understood as revealing God, had an endurance, a vitality and an inspiration in them with which no unhistorical metaphysic could long compete. And if we have to contemplate in our own day tension between an idealistic construction of religion, which makes it independent of uncertainty by making it independent of history, and the historic faith of Christians to which facts have hitherto been essential, I have no doubt we may look confidently to its having a similar issue. Further, I think we may fairly point out, whether to theologians or philosophers who take this line, that Christianity is itself a fact, and a fact which fills a great space in human history. It does not remain for any one at this time of day to invent it, or to define it at discretion. Whoever deals with Christian religion or with Christian faith, deals with a *datum*; and it is not open to question that that *datum* involves matters of fact and history. It ought to be clearly understood that when anything is proposed to us in which no matter of fact or history is involved, whatever its value or respectability may be, it is not Christian faith; its sponsor has overlooked the *datum*; his eye is not on the object. We have every right to be suspicious when we are asked to recognise as genuinely Christian, ideas or convictions or faiths or whatever they are called whose representatives are nervously anxious to prove that they hold them without being in any sense debtors to a historical Christ. Probably in most cases they are simply mistaken: many a man is unconsciously Christ's debtor, like the man in the Gospel of whom it is said, "He that was healed wist not who it was"; but it is an ungrateful and unhappy ignorance, not a more spiritual mode of Christian faith.

Farther still, we are entitled to protest, in the name of human nature and human worth, against that extraordinary disparagement of time, and all that men experience and learn in time, which is involved in the exclusion of history from religion. Time is evanescent, it is true, but it is also continuous; we can see that something is taking place in it which accumulates; literature is evolved in it, and art and science, and political and spiritual life; evanescent as the past is, it is not lost; it leaves something behind it which can be caught up and assimilated by the present and which can continue its life there; and it is on this that life depends for all that makes it rich. If you want a picture of spiritual beggary, contemplate the mind of man stripped of all its historical accumulations and sitting naked among the eternal truths of reason. This consideration should dispose us to caution when we are asked to believe that man's supreme interests and his final destiny cannot be supposed to depend on anything historical, but must be determined solely by ideas in which contingency has no place. As mere matter of fact, we do not know anything of such ideas unless perhaps in mathematics and formal logic, and no one has so far suggested that these interesting sciences contain the sum of saving knowledge. *All* our ethical and spiritual convictions have been historically mediated to us. But for the history whose heirs we are, we should have none of them; and if the past has this real relation to the present, this real place in it, throughout its whole extent, we have surely reason to hesitate if we are told that the very heart of the present, the religious faith which where it exists at all is the life of life and the dearest of all our possessions, must be independent of all historical relations. I admit that to say this does not fix the place of the historical Christ in Christianity. It does not define the place He ought to hold, but it prohibits any one from saying that He has no essential place at all, and that His history, as such, has no religious interest. To say this, as I have already observed, is simply to overlook the *datum*. The facts recorded in the Gospels—and we may summarily comprehend these as the fact of Christ—have had and have still an importance for Christian faith which cannot be overestimated. This is the fact about them, let them be on other grounds as distant, as problematic, as relative as you please. They have been the seat of spiritual life and force from the beginning, and they are so to this hour. There is a power of inspiration and of appeal in them with which nothing can compare. The gospel history was transacted far away and long ago, but it is not lost in time. The virtue has not gone out of it with time. Something appeals to us from it, which, though manifested at a given time, is independent of any particular time—in a word, is not merely historical, but superhistorical, not merely temporal, but eternal. This is the *datum* of Christianity, and when we are trying to determine the place of Christ—I mean the historical Christ—in the Christian religion we must not let it fall out of mind.

I will venture to use an illustration which any one who likes may deride, but which will nevertheless serve as a starting point for what I want to say about the peculiar place of Christ in Christianity. When I was in the University I read what is now, I suppose, a rather antiquated book, Merivale's *History of the Romans under the Empire*. I remember still the rather pompous sentence in which the author brings upon the stage "Caius Julius Caesar, the greatest name in history." Perhaps this description is justified. Certainly the first of the Caesars was an extraordinarily great man. But in spite of the greatness of the man, in spite of his immense achievements, in spite of the vivid account of some of them which we have from his own hand, in spite of the fact that his name is the greatest name in history, it has become a proverb to say "as dead as Julius Caesar?" The influence of his life and work, like the influence of the life and work of the meanest of his contemporaries, who has no name in history at all, no doubt survives into our time, but no effort of imagination or enthusiasm can ever bring him from the past into the present. He is a great historical character and nothing else. But neither history nor philosophy nor profanity has ever been able, or ever will be able, to put into proverbial currency such a phrase as—"as dead as Jesus Christ." It is not a matter of opinion, but a matter of fact, that to read Caesar's Commentaries is one thing, and to read the Gospels another; the relation of the reader to Caesar is a relation to a person who is historical and no more; his relation to Christ is a relation to a person who is historical, certainly, and who certainly died, but who is certainly not "as dead as Julius Caesar." He is far more living than that. In some way or other He belongs as truly to the present as to the past. The most stolid soul is conscious as he reads his history of incurring responsibilities the like of which he does not incur to any merely historical character. And this is just another way of saying that the historical Christ is more than historical: it is as present and eternal that He evokes repentance and faith in the soul, and asserts His abiding and essential place in the spiritual life. This, I repeat, is the datum of Christianity; and the man who disregards it is really not speaking of Christianity, but of something quite different. He may call it by the same name, but that does not make it the same thing.

Now what is the explanation of this more than historical character which attaches in Christianity to the historical Christ? How is it that He belongs, as ordinary historical characters do not, to the present as well as to the past? Partly it is due to the fact that the moral atmosphere in which we live in Christendom has been largely created by Him. It has come into existence through the lives and sacrifices of men who called Him Lord, and we feel instinctively as we contemplate Him in the gospel that it can only be maintained and purified—as it ought to be maintained and purified—by men who still take the same relation to Him, and recognise His personal supremacy as it was recognised by His earliest followers. This is one way in which we feel that Christ is not remote but intimately near, a historical person no doubt, but one to whose significance even in history time makes no difference. And this itself is explained in the New Testament by the resurrection and exaltation of Jesus, and by the working of His Spirit. This is what gives to the historical person a superhistorical importance, a present and eternal place in religion. There are those, of course, who tell us that the resurrection and exaltation of Jesus are ideas of which history, as such, can take no cognisance; they carry us out of the very world within the limits of which the historian works. If this were the final truth, we could only say, So much the worse for history. But it is not the final truth. It is only a matter of arbitrary definition. The one haunting error of all students of the special sciences—and history in the sense assumed is a special science—is that they unconsciously elevate that part or aspect of reality in which they are interested to be the measure of the whole. The physicist often thinks of the world in a way which makes history and morality, which nevertheless exist, inexplicable and impossible; and the historian, in the case we are supposing, thinks of the world in a way which makes the Christian religion, which also nevertheless exists, inexplicable and impossible. But physicists must apply their categories with the limitations which leave room for history and freedom, and historians must apply theirs with the limitations which leave room for the presence and spiritual action of Christ in a mode transcending time: they must do this, or the actual world of Christian life, the reality they have to deal with, will be left unexplained. That the category of posthumous influence can take the place of the resurrection of Jesus and the operation of His Spirit let him believe who can.

After all this preface, which will no doubt seem superfluous to those who are not in the fight, it is possible to come closer to the place of Christ in Christianity. It is a historical Christ we are concerned with, but one who belongs to the present though He was manifested in the past; and the question assumes this form— What is it which is vital to our religion in the present, but which we only know and possess through its historical manifestation in Jesus? The answer, it seems to me, is very simple: it is Jesus Himself in His relations to God and man. We cannot know Jesus except through His history, but it is not necessary that we should know everything about Him and be acquainted with all the details of His history. As far as we can be informed about these they have interest, and they may, though we cannot say they must, have religious value. He Himself laid stress on the value of the passing hour. "As long as I am in the world I am the light of the world." It is through what He did in the days of His flesh, through the whole life which He lived then, and so far as we know through nothing else, that, He illumines the world now. Still, the significance of His acts lay in the revelation they gave of His own character, and of His relations to God and man. What we need now for our spiritual life is not information about the contingent details of His history, but knowledge of what He essentially was in these two vital relations. We can only get such knowledge through the Gospels, but subject to the moral conditions under which alone it can be apprehended, we do get it in this way. We see Jesus; and to borrow an expression of Herrmann, to see Jesus is to see "the only untroubled manifestation of that which has full power over the soul." I was going to say we must admit, but perhaps I should rather say we are bound to assert, that history alone cannot give any man this vision. It is sadly possible to read the Gospels and not to see Jesus as the apostles saw Him. Most of us who have read much in this field have read books which tempted us to say that the authors saw everything in the Gospels except Jesus. They went over the canvas inch by inch with the microscope, saw every unevenness in the fibre, every grit in the pigments, but never had a glimpse of the picture.

This is possible and we cannot explain it, any more than St. Paul could explain the melancholy fact which confronted him when He wrote—"All men have not faith." The want of faith or the blindness of some men, whatever its explanation—and it is not for us to judge them—or whatever its cure—and purely historical study will not cure it—cannot be pleaded against the experience of those who see. The Christian Church through all generations has seen Jesus in the Gospels, has seen Him there only, and has seen Him in that very character His presence in which makes Him essential to Christian faith. I will venture to refer to the main elements of truth included in this vision—truth historically given in the life of Jesus, though the historian may be blind to it, yet raised above the reach of historical doubt, because not shut up to a distant past but present in a power which still reaches the soul.

(1) In the first place we see Jesus as the Son of God—Jesus manifesting the ideal relation of man to God by Himself living in it. This is not essentially a matter of titles or designations, it is a matter of fact. It is quite true that Jesus gave expression in words to His sense of His filial relation to God; but what made His words convincing to those who heard them, what makes them overpowering still, is that there is no schism between His words and His being; they are not, like our highest words about the spiritual life, a profession of what we would be or should be; they are a revelation of what He is. It is a revelation I should never dream of reducing to a systematic form, or of binding down to particular words of Jesus, impressive and irresistible as these may be; it has in it the variety and infinity of His whole life. There is not a word nor an act of Jesus, there is not an hour of temptation or of passion, in which He is anything else than the Son. It is this greatest of all truths about Him, the truth which makes us feel that our ideal relation to God is the filial relation, which we know most surely and, I venture to add, which we most truly understand. We may not know exactly what it covers, nor how we are to adjust our minds to it, when Jesus is represented as the Son of David, or the Messiah, or even as the Son of Man coming in the clouds of heaven; but we have an intuitive comprehension of the Son *simpliciter*, and our minds open through it to faith in the Father. To say this is not to give up the case which I am arguing for the essential place of the historical Christ in Christianity. Faith in the Father is not independent

of Him in its origin, and it never becomes independent. The very same experience in which we see that sonship is the ideal relation of man to God shows us that it is a relation realised in Him, but waiting to be realised in us through Him. Jesus is conscious of the distance of other men from God, but there is no trace anywhere of any consciousness of distance on His part. He is here to bring us to the Father. That this is one element in the broad truth of the gospel, which is spiritual indeed and eternal, but depends for its power to strike into our sinful souls on its flesh and blood reality, no one, historian or philosopher, who sees what is before our eyes in the evangelists, can possibly deny.

(2) In the second place, to bring out more distinctly another essential element in the truth, we see Jesus in the gospel as the Saviour of sinners. It is the historical Jesus we see in this character. Whatever the witnesses might have been mistaken about they could not be mistaken about Jesus' attitude to themselves in this particular. They could not possibly be misrepresenting Him when they represented Him as receiving sinners. There may indeed be people to whom this is of no interest, but for men convinced of sin it is the only interesting thing in the world. Life is worth nothing to them till they can get the conviction that sin is not final, that there is something in God which can deal with it and overcome it, that it does not permanently annul sonship and for ever exclude from the Father; and they get this conviction as they watch the Son of God receiving sinners. It is through Him they believe in forgiveness; it is through Him they receive it. This is the very thing for want of which they are perishing—a holy one who is as untouched by sin as God Himself and as inexorable to it, but who makes their sad case His own, and in a passion of love they can never fathom receives them to Himself and restores them to the Father. There may be righteous persons on whom this revelation is thrown away, but it is not thrown away on men with the sense of sin. Dr. Chalmers had a noble appreciation of the Pauline gospel that God justifies the ungodly, just because he had the simplicity to say What could I do if God did *not* justify the ungodly? and a corresponding simplicity and humility are wanted to see that on one side the sum of the Gospels is Christ receiving sinners. It is through this vision that faith arises in the characteristically Christian form of faith in Christ as the Saviour, and such faith depends absolutely on the represen-

tation of Christ by the evangelists. It attaches itself to something historical and clings to it, for that is the only reality which has an anguish in it answering to its own. What is absolute idealism, what are eternal truths of reason, to a man shut out from God by a bad conscience, and lost if he is left to himself? But to such a man the Son of God in flesh and blood receiving sinners like *him* is salvation; his conscience gives him an eye for the history and its meaning, and the inward and outward witness unite in an assurance which has history at its heart yet can never be impaired.

(3) And finally, one element of the truth which we see in the Gospels, and without which the Christian religion could not be, is that Jesus in relation to men is not only Saviour but Lord. This, again, is a point on which no mistake of the witnesses is conceivable. They simply could not be under any misapprehension as to the attitude which Jesus assumed toward them or the attitude which they felt bound to adopt towards Him. It is not a question of particular claims made on one side, or particular responses on the other; it is not a matter of words or of occasions at all; it is a matter of the whole life of Christ and His whole attitude to men. His sovereignty is not claimed or asserted here or there; it is not acknowledged or disputed here or there; it is assumed and exercised from first to last in every word and act of His life. And this again is not a matter of titles, but a matter of fact. The indirect expressions of it in the evangelists are far more impressive than the direct. It is felt and acknowledged perpetually where there is no explicit assertion of it, and though the consciousness of it, like that of the Sonship and the saving power of Jesus, is morally conditioned—for no man can call Jesus Lord but by the Holy Spirit—its historical certainty is entirely indubitable. And it is in the history of Jesus that its grounds, its meaning and its obligation are to be sought, just as it is in the same history that we are to find out what is meant by speaking of Jesus as the Son of God or the Saviour of men. One is almost ashamed to say such things, but it is not without cause. People for whom the obvious is uninteresting, no matter how true it may be, are busy persuading us just now that a great part of what is meant by the Son of God is to be traced to the *Divus* or *Divi filius*, applied to Roman Emperors, dead or living—that the conception of Christ as Saviour is to be connected with the application of σωτήρ to the gods of Greek mythology or the kings who

were deified in the flattery of Egyptian and oriental courts—nay that the Lordship of Christ is not without relation to the *Dominus* applied to persons like Domitian. The late Dr. Davidson said the best thing to do with some propositions was just to deny them. But for propositions like these, this seems hardly adequate: one would like to throw them over the window. On the plea of finding out the historical relations of Christianity they are overlooking what is vital and indubitable in the historical fact of Christ, and what for that very reason must always be central and essential in the Christian faith.

The more we become familiar with this whole field of study, the more clearly the lines of cleavage in it appear. There are those who, to make Christianity independent of history, turn it into or rather replace it by an absolute idealism in which Jesus of Nazareth has no essential place. This is simply to ignore the *datum*, to shut our eyes to the whole of the fact we pretend to explain. There are those, again, who, in order to give history all its due, shut up Jesus of Nazareth into a past growing continually more remote, and while they admit His posthumous influence do not distinguish Him otherwise from all who have lived. and died upon the earth. This does not ignore the *datum* so completely as a pure idealism, but it does ignore a vast proportion of what it has to explain. And there are those who, in order to do justice to all the phenomena with which we have to deal, lay equal emphasis on the historical Jesus and on His exaltation into eternal life, and His perpetual presence with us through His Spirit in the very character which His history reveals. In the former cases, there is no Christianity at all; all that has ever been known to history under that name—the whole *datum* in the case—disappears. In the last, Christianity subsists on the same historical basis on which it has always rested, and the place of Christ in it is not doubtful. Still, as at the beginning, He fills all things. Unto Him be glory for ever.

# 9

# Adam and Christ in St. Paul

It is not my intention in this paper to write a reply to Professor Peake. Nothing I ever read made a deeper impression on my mind than the last paragraph of Jowett's essay on *Atonement and Satisfaction*. I venture to quote a sentence or two to indicate the kind of impression I mean. "If our Saviour were to come again to earth, which of all the theories of atonement and sacrifice would He sanction with His authority? Perhaps none of them, yet perhaps all may be consistent with a true service of Him. The question has no answer. But it suggests the thought that we shrink from bringing controversy into His presence."[1] It is not, I hope, in the temper of controversy at all that I shall try to state, as clearly as possible, with reference to Professor Peake's article, the place which ought to be taken in a representation of St. Paul's thoughts by the conceptions of a racial act, and of a mystical union.

Professor Peake holds that the interpretation of St. Paul depends upon a due appreciation and use of these ideas. The conception of a racial act he finds in Romans 5:12–21, and although he is not astonished that I pass by this passage in *The Death of Christ*, it is perhaps not an unfair inference that he would have been astonished at almost any one else who did so. Yet my reason for passing it by is obvious; it does not mention the death of Christ. Not indeed that I should deny any reference in it to that subject; on the contrary, I agree with Meyer that "the obedience of the one" by which "the many shall be justified" is specifically the obedience rendered by Christ in His death. But this conception of obedience is one to which I did full justice elsewhere, and apart from it there

1. Jowett, "Atonement and Satisfaction," 266–67.

121

was (as it seemed to me) no specific interpretation of Christ's death in the passage which called for consideration. Further, there was the fact, which I will express in Professor Peake's words, of "the incompatibility of his (Paul's) statements with history as we understand it." One may argue, of course, with Professor Peake, that this is of no consequence, since Paul's interest was not historical but psychological. That is exactly what I should do, but I should feel that, in consequence of so doing, the conception of a "racial act" was one with which I could no longer operate seriously even in the interpretation of St. Paul. For the psychological truth is one which belongs to my personal experience, whereas the "racial act" is surely one to which independent historical reality is essential. If we put the psychological truth, which we know at first hand—say the truth that the human race is one in the consciousness of sin—into a historical form incompatible with history—say the form that the progenitor of the human race committed a sin which involved all his descendants—we are guilty of a μετάβασις εἰς ἄλλο γένος, and the result—the conception of the "racial act," of Adam—has no validity. This is what I meant by describing a "racial act," perhaps with needless levity, but certainly without malice, as a "fantastic abstraction."[2]

A further and a serious reason for not making the passage in Romans 5:12–21 so fundamental to an exposition of Paulinism as many excellent scholars are disposed to do is that this passage is one on which men will differ to the end of time.

This last point might be illustrated by reference to Professor Peake's own interpretation. This interpretation is dominated by the conception of the racial act, and the parallelism between Adam and Christ is worked out strictly in this sense. To what,

---

2. It may not be inappropriate to remark in passing that it is unsound as well as unwise to make Paul's testimony to Christ depend upon his idea of the inclusion of the race in Adam. *Paul knew Christ.* He knew what He had done for him, and in him, and what He was able to do for all men. He knew this at first hand in a way which is entirely independent of speculations about Adam; he preached it as he knew it, and it is the interest of the gospel to make this plain. *As for Adam, Paul did not know him at all.* Neither do we. Paul's Adam is simply the abstraction of human nature, personified and placed with a determining power at the beginning of human history. Such a figure has no reality for our minds, and I own it seems to me hopeless to seek the key to the work of Christ in the assumed "racial" action of this hypothetical entity.

then, does it amount? As far as I can make out, only to this: Through one man's disobedience—that is, through the racial act of Adam—every member of the human race, immediately, without any element of choice, was constituted sinful, in the sense of becoming liable to death. On the other hand, through the obedience of the one—that is, through the racial act of Christ—every member of the human race, in the same immediate way, without any element of choice, was constituted righteous, in the sense of securing resurrection from the dead. "That they—that is, all men—belong to a race judged guilty or declared righteous, that they experience physical death or resurrection, these are facts which happen without any reference to their individual will." So Professor Peake himself sums it up.

Now this may possibly be what St. Paul ought to have said. It may even be what he would have said had he held the conception of a racial act on which Professor Peake lays such stress, and had he applied it with the same consistency to the great decisive acts of Adam and of Christ. But I venture to think that few will agree with Professor Peake in holding that this is what he does say. Whether we are to call the act of Christ by which the act of Adam is reversed a racial act or not, it was an act importing infinitely more than is here brought into view. We must not, in order that we may be justified in calling it a racial act, eviscerate or curtail it till its consequences are such and only such as affect every member of the race. We must take the act and all that it imports as it is described by the apostle, whether we can call it racial or not. How, then, does the apostle describe it? He says the free gift takes its start ἐκ πολλῶν παραπτωμάτων: that is, it finds its motive not in the guilt of the race as impersonated in Adam, but in the multiplied offences of real men. He says that those who get the benefit of Christ's act "shall reign in life." Is the meaning of that magnificent phrase exhausted when we say that every member of the race shall be raised from the dead? He says that as sin reigned in death, even so grace shall reign through righteousness unto eternal life; the former disastrous state of affairs is related to the act of Adam, the latter to the act of Christ. In every case, what is related to the act of Christ is the complete Christian salvation; and the way to avoid universalism—which I agree with Professor Peake is not a Pauline thought—is not to clip the act of Christ till we can invest the whole race in all the credit of it without securing the salvation of one of its members, but to recognize that neither that act itself nor any consequence of it has any significance for any member of the race apart from the condition of faith.

The difficulty involved in representing the act of Christ in Romans 5 as "racial" comes out perhaps most clearly if we observe that it compels us to use the Pauline expression "in Christ" in two different senses. On the one hand, *the race is in Christ*. "In His death the race dies and atones for its sin, is pronounced righteous by God, and therefore the physical death which fell on the race as the penalty of its act in Adam is cancelled by the universal resurrection of the body."[3] But this does not mean that anybody is saved. On the other hand, *the believer is in Christ*. He cries out of his faith, I have been crucified with Christ; and although we do not find him claim that in so doing he has, like the race, atoned for his sins, his being in Christ is his salvation. Now with the utmost respect but with perfect confidence I submit that the difference between these two conceptions of being in Christ is that the second is in contact with reality and the first is not. The second is an experience, the first has no basis in experience at all; it is a purely artificial and abstract conception which we have no means of verifying, and which certainly does not verify itself. And as we cannot find an experimental verification for it, just as little can we find a scriptural basis. I cannot admit that we find a "racial" application of the expression "in Christ" in 1 Corinthians 15:22. It appears to me unquestionable that the correct interpretation of this passage is that given (for example) by Professor Findlay in the *Expositor's Greek Testament*: what Paul teaches is not that all men will be raised from the dead in virtue of the fact that the race has in Christ died and made atonement for its sin, but that in every case life—which includes the whole glory revealed in 1 Corinthians 15—depends on a connexion with Christ, just as death in every case depends on a connexion with Adam. There is no eschatology either in Romans 5:12–21, or in 1 Corinthians 15, but that of the Christian hope. The other passage to which Professor Peake refers, 2 Corinthians 5:14, is equally unconvincing. To say "one died for all, therefore all died," is quite intelligible if we suppose that the one in dying

3. Peake, "A reply to Dr. Denney," 53.

took to Himself in love by God's appointment the responsibilities represented by the death of all; but if the death of the one could be properly described as a "racial" act—that is as the act of the "all" in Him—it would not be possible to attach any clear meaning to the words which are the nerve of the New Testament—One died *for* all.

It is easier, no doubt, to conceive a "racial" act in the case of Adam—easier for the imagination, that is—assuming Adam to be a real person. When Adam sinned, he was the race: and his act implicated all who in the way of nature were to owe their being to him. They were yet in the loins of their father when he forfeited the family character and inheritance. This is the sense in which many theologians have read Romans 5:12ff., and in this sense Adam's act may fairly enough be called racial. But it is not on this that Professor Peake bases his view. Indeed he explicitly rejects this view. "Adam acts for us," he says, "in virtue of a community of nature with us." And again, "He acted as every individual in his place would have acted."[4] It is thus that his act is racial. I own that from these premises I should have drawn exactly the opposite conclusion. I should have said with the Apocalypse of Baruch: *Non est ergo Adam causa, nisi animae suae tantum: nos vero unusquisque fuit animae suae Adam.*[5] Adam, in short, is nothing real, but an abstraction for human nature. And surely it is very difficult to extend the conception of a racial act on this basis to the work of Christ. Did *He* act "as every individual in His place would have acted?" Can we point to Him, as we can point to Adam, and with the whole human race in our minds, say, *Ex uno disce omnes?*[6] The question answers itself. The old humanity *was*, in a sense, in Adam; the new humanity—that which is in Christ—has first to be created in Him; and that new creation is not the condition or the presupposition of Christ's work; it is its fruit. Whenever we realize that Adam is but the abstraction of sinful human nature, personified, we see that the attempt to assimilate the relations of humanity to Adam and to Christ respectively is an attempt to prove that the old sinful race

4. Peake, "A reply to Dr. Denney," 52.

5. [Therefore Adam is not the cause, but of his soul only; and each of us was Adam of his own soul.]

6. [Learn all from one.]

bears the same relation to its own logical shadow as the new redeemed race bears to its Redeemer. We see also how unsound it is to argue that "the interest of a merely vicarious theory is to insist on the sharp distinction between Christ and the race," while the interest of a theory operating with the conception of racial acts is "to identify them as closely as possible." Discounting the biassed "merely," it is the interest of the vicarious theory, as much as of the other, to insist on the identity. There is no salvation, all Christians are agreed, except through union with Christ. The question at issue is where that union comes in. If the death of Christ is a racial act, it comes in antecedent to it and as a condition of its atoning efficacy. According to St. Paul and common Christian belief it comes. in subsequent to it, and is the result of its atoning efficacy. I once quoted before in the *Expositor*, but venture to quote again, the glorious lines of St. Bernard, which put with the moral passion which alone justifies mysticism the final truth in the matter:

> *Propter mortem quam tulisti*
> *Quando pro me defecisti,*
> *Cordis mei cor dilectum*
> *In te meum fer affectum.*[7]

Here the union with Christ comes in its true place: it is the death of Christ *for* men, which appealing to them as an irresistible motive draws them into a union closer and ever closer with Himself.

Having said so much on the first point, on which I am quite conscious of the difference between the reading of St. Paul which approves itself to Professor Peake and that which has just been given, I pass gladly to the second, on which I believe we are far more at one—I mean the idea of Christian union with Christ. It is possible to consider this without raising the question of race relations of Christ at all; for that "being in Christ" with which we are here concerned is not the state of the race but the experience of the believer.

I do not, indeed, think it helps us to understand the Christian's union to Christ to contemplate a pre-incarnate relation of Christ to men, such as Professor Peake finds in Hebrews 2:11–17, or "a universal headship of the race," such as he finds in 1 Corinthians 11:3.

---

7. [Through death, how you support me, When you withdraw on behalf of me, Beloved heart of my heart. Carry my affection in you.]

He thinks we may press the words in the last passage—"the head of every man is Christ"—in this sense. But "man" in this passage does not refer to the race at all, but to man as opposed to woman. Paul had taught at Corinth as elsewhere that in Christ there is neither male nor female, and he found Christian women in Corinth acting on that principle in a way which he did not approve. They seemed to be carrying out the divine life of the gospel on lines which defied the equally divine constitution of nature, and in vindicating this last Paul uses the peculiar analogy that woman is to man as man is to Christ and as Christ is to God. Many have agreed with his conclusion, but did anybody ever repeat his argument? To show that I had no *animus* in using an expression which Professor Peake seems to have felt unkind, I will say frankly that the apostle himself employs here a whole series of fantastic abstractions, with the result that his argument has never weighed with any man in the world, and still less with any woman. And he was conscious himself that it would not when in verse 16 he practically threw it overboard, and appealed to the authority of universal Christian custom.

We cannot however, but agree as to the words in which Paul describes union to Christ. He speaks of a Christian as "a man in Christ." He says, "I have been crucified with Christ, and it is no longer I that live, but Christ liveth in me." He says again, "To me to live is Christ"; and "when Christ, our life, shall appear." As men in general are said to live and move and have their being in God, so from the first of his Epistles to the last Christian men, for St. Paul, live and move and have their being in Christ. To refer only to his earliest Epistles, Paul has confidence *in the Lord* toward the Thessalonians; he charges and entreats them *in the Lord Jesus Christ*; they stand *in the Lord*; he gives them commandments *through the Lord Jesus*; church rulers are those who are over them *in the Lord*; the Christians departed are *the dead in Christ*. To illustrate the place which union with Christ has in his mind would be to transcribe everything he has written about the Christian life. So far it is not possible to disagree.

Probably there would be less inclination than there is to think of disagreement on this subject if all who used such terms as mystical and moral tried to make clear to themselves what they meant by them, and in particular if they considered whether they are able to give a Christian meaning to mystical when they use it simply in contrast with moral. Professor Peake himself, if I read him rightly, never makes the contrast absolute. The conception of a moral union with Christ is one which he recognizes; though it does not seem to him to cover the language of St. Paul, it has a legitimacy within limits. But when he brings into view what he calls the mystical union, he does not seem to feel the necessity of demonstrating any relation between it and the other. The whole emphasis is laid on the contrast. He speaks of "a moral union merely." He says, "I should not describe the fact that my will was in harmony with Christ's will, that I passed the same moral judgments and sought the same ends, as a union with Christ in the strict sense at all." He refers to a passage (1 Cor 6:17) in which the context "definitely excludes the thought of a moral union." A union is intended in it far closer than anything implied in that name.

It seems to me not quite fortunate that all the emphasis should be laid on this side, and I cannot help regretting that the word "mystical" should have been naturalized in Christian theology in such an ambiguous relation to "moral." It is far more appropriate to describe what has not yet reached the moral level than what in some perfectly undefined way has transcended it. It may be piously said, Calvin tells us, provided it come from a pious heart, that nature is God. There is a mystical union of creation with the Creator, and great poets like Wordsworth, or great philosophers like Spinoza, initiate us into it; they reveal the mystery, and it enters into our intellectual being. There is a mystical union of every stone with God. The stone has its being in Him. Its nature is grounded in His. The physical and chemical laws which enter into the constitution of it, and in virtue of which it holds its place in a universe, are His laws. You can have no relation to it whatever which is not a relation to Him. The term mystical seems to me appropriate enough to describe this kind of union, but for that very reason not so appropriate when we ascend from the world of nature into the world of personality. We may speak of nature still, if we please; but when two persons, two moral natures, are to enter into union with each other, then their union, no matter how intimate and profound it may be, must at the same time be, personal and moral. We may call it mystical, if mystical for any reason seems to us an expressive or felicitous term—if there is an ardour,

an intimacy, a depth in the emotions it excites to which our ordinary ethical language fails to do justice, and to which justice is
done by this impalpable name; but we must not forget that personality lives only in a moral world, and that its most intense and
passionate experiences are moral to the core. I entirely agree with
Professor Peake that the words "he that is joined to the Lord is one
spirit" are very striking, and that "they do not readily lend themselves to anything but a personal identification." Granting the propriety of the term, I entirely agree also that "it is difficult to see
how a mystical union could be better described than by this daring sentence." But is not the act in which one person in trust and
love "identifies" himself with another, the most purely "moral" of
all conceivable acts? Is it not the kind of act which, in its motives,
its essence, its fruits, most completely manifests the moral nature?
Is there anything in it, or about it or due to it, which is not moral?
If the identification of one person with another is the type of a
mystical union, surely the contrast of mystical and moral is one
which ought to disappear. I feel quite at liberty to say this in spite
of St. Paul's reference in 1 Corinthians 6:17. There is a physical basis for the loftiest human affections, but that does not justify us in
bringing down either the union of husband and wife in Christian
marriage, or the union of the believer and the Lord, from the moral
to the physical world.

The language of "personal identification," to use Professor
Peake's expression, is undoubtedly the key to all that has been
called mystical in St. Paul. But the language of "personal identification" is the language of love; it is the language of moral passion,
and except as the expression of moral passion it has no meaning
and no truth whatever. That is why I feel that the contrast of
mystical and moral is false, and that it is essentially misleading
to speak of a mystical union as opposed to a moral one, or to one
which is "merely" moral, or "no more than" moral. When a man
abandons himself in faith to the love of God in Christ, when he
identifies himself with Christ bearing his sins in His own body on
the tree, when he casts himself on Him to die with Him and live
with Him, to die with Him and have Him henceforth as his life,
he does an act in which there is no element that is not moral, and
that has none but moral issues; and this is the act in which he is
"mystically" united to Christ. The mysticism of Paul stands in no

relation of contrast to morality: it is nothing but morality aflame with passion. Hence I think Professor Peake is unfair to himself in the sentence quoted above—"I should not describe the fact that my will was in harmony with Christ's will, that I passed the same moral judgments and sought the same moral ends, as a union with Christ in the strict sense at all." If the condition so described has been produced in any sinful man by the love of Christ, and by his own response, in love and faith, to Christ, then that man is experiencing everything that Paul experienced when he spoke of being "in Christ" or of having "Christ live" in him. These are not expressions for a truth transcending morality, they are the passionate expression of moral truth.

The danger of contrasting mystical with moral is that it leads people to speak of union with Christ as a thing to be believed and talked about apart from the passionate moral experience in which it was realized in St. Paul. Everybody who has read "good books" will know what I mean. The language of the apostle about union to Christ, when taken up at a moral temperature lower than his, does not express a truth of the gospel which a "merely moral" union fails to reach; it expresses nothing at all but the mental and moral deadness of those who can handle holy things without feeling them. Professor Peake thinks I have an "almost fanatical hatred of mysticism": in the legitimate sense of the word, I hope not. But one may be excused if he feels a certain amount of impatience when words of Scripture which live and move and have their being in moral passion—which are born of that passion and serve only to express it—are read as if they belonged to another than the moral world, and expressed truths of that other world to which a union with Christ that is "no more than moral" is a poor and insignificant thing. Of mysticism in this sense I am still thankful to find nothing in the New Testament.

There is something paradoxical in the fact that this way of representing union to Christ should appear to any one to be prejudicial to moral interests—disastrous, as Professor Peake puts it, "in the sphere of the Christian life." I cannot conceive it possible that Christians should differ, if they understand each other, about the place of gratitude in their life, or about its power as a motive. To give it a central place, to make it an all-pervading motive, is not to be guilty of Deism, or of accepting the notion of an absentee

Christ. From such modes of thought I dissent as heartily as Professor Peake. But for the simple reason that the Christian life is a moral life, it must be conceived as produced not mechanically, but through motives. It is not the mechanical outcome of union with Christ; it is the process in which that personal identification of the believer with Christ which alone is the truth of such union, and which is itself a great moral act, is morally expressed and realized. And the all-embracing motive under which it proceeds, and by which it is morally generated, is the sense of obligation to Christ. Christ is present all the time, present clothed in His gospel, making for ever a *moral* appeal to man, and calling forth uninterruptedly a *moral* response—the response of a "personal identification" of the sinner with the Saviour who has suffered and died for him. There is no real truth in the idea of a mystical union—no truth, I mean, for the verification of which we can appeal to experience—that is not covered by this reading of the facts; and I cannot understand why gratitude, which is the psychological co-efficient of this in the sphere of motive, should be supposed inadequate to the effects which it actually produces. Everything in the Christian life has to be produced by motives, and if it is a weak motive to say "I am not my own, I was bought with a price," and to say so in presence of Christ who bought us with His blood, what motive is strong? Professor Peake speaks of men "whose sense of guilt is but feeble: they appreciate only very faintly what sacrifice Christ has made for them; their gratitude is but a wisp of straw to check the mad career of their desires"; and he adds, "yet it is men like these that the gospel cleanses and saves and keeps." But how does the gospel do this? Must we not say that it does it morally, by intensifying the sense of guilt in such men, by deepening their consciousness of what Christ has done for them, and by making their gratitude a strong cord that cannot be broken, and that binds them for ever to their Lord? We delude ourselves, consciously or unconsciously, when we appeal to a union with Christ which has any other contents than these. To reduce it to the simplest expression, we are saved by grace, and the correlative of grace is gratitude. That is why I still hold that the fundamental doctrine of St. Paul is justification by faith; for faith is the acceptance of grace as what it is, the surrender to it on the unconditional terms which it prescribes. It is only a formal objection to this to say that the fundamental doctrine in theology is the doctrine of God. Of course it is. But what is the Christian doctrine of God? I hope Professor Peake will not be scandalized if I quote St. Paul once more, and say it is this: God as He is revealed and preached in the gospel is He who justifies the ungodly. And it is the abandonment of the sinful soul to this God in unbounded gratitude which morally unites it to Christ and launches it on all the hopes and joys of the new life.

# 10

# He That Came by Water and Blood

The idea from which the apostle starts in this passage (1 John 5:6–8) is that of the victory of faith. Who, he asks, is he that overcometh the world but he that believeth that Jesus is the Son of God? So to believe makes us partakers in Jesus' own victory (John 16:33). In faith, however, the object is everything; if we are really to overcome, we must be very sure of Christ. To convey such an assurance is the apostle's aim in the passage. He seeks to show that Jesus is evinced or demonstrated to be the Son of God by the most conclusive tokens; and when he has summed up what may be called the external evidences by which we identify Him as what He is, he clinches them by adding, He that believeth hath the witness in himself.

It is from this point of view that we must read the opening sentence, This is He who came by water and blood, Jesus Christ (or perhaps Jesus the Christ). The past tense makes it quite clear that the reference is to the historical Jesus, and that the water and the blood allude to incidents and experiences of His life on earth in which His character as Son of God, the object of a world-subduing faith, is revealed. Looking to the Gospel and the Epistle of John as a whole, it can hardly be doubted what the incidents or experiences in question are. Jesus came through water when He was baptized by John in Jordan. It is beside the mark to argue that John's baptism, which was one of water only, was no proof that Jesus was Son of God; it was submitted to or bestowed upon multitudes to whom it bore no such testimony. This is not the point of view of the apostle. "For this end," he represents the baptist saying, "did I come baptizing with water, that He might be manifested to Israel"

(John 1:31). It is quite true that ordinarily baptism with water is opposed by John to baptism with the Spirit; but in the case of Jesus they are not contrasted, they coincide. This is the proof, or an essential part of it, that Jesus is what Christian faith holds Him to be. "I knew Him not, but He that sent me to baptize in water, He said unto me: On whomsoever thou shalt see the Spirit descending and abiding on Him, the same is He that baptizeth in the Holy Spirit. And I have seen and have borne witness that this is the Son of God" (John 1:33f.). This is John's primary conception of the Son of God; the Son is the person who has the perpetual fulness of the Spirit and the perpetual power to bestow it, and Jesus is attested by the historical event and experience of His baptism—by His coming by water—to be this person.

From the same point of view it is apparent that the coming by blood must refer to the death of Jesus. He came by blood when He died upon the cross. Like His baptism, His death must be conceived as demonstrating Him in some way to be the Son of God. We know that this was one of the great difficulties of the first believers. To a superficial view the cross was anything but an evidence that Jesus was what the apostolic gospel declared Him to be. To Jews it was an offence, and to Greeks folly. We seem even in the New Testament to see Christian minds which felt its power groping uncertainly for the means of explaining it. It is perhaps an instance of such groping when the evangelist, referring to the spear thrust into the side of Jesus, points out that the law regarding the paschal lamb—a bone of it shall not be broken—was thus fulfilled in Him, finding, so to speak, in Jesus the reality of which the ancient covenant sacrifice was only a symbol. But whatever intellectual embarrassments it may once have occasioned, the death of Christ is not a mere mystery to the writer of this Epistle. He tells us again and again of its meaning, and its power. "The Blood of Jesus His Son cleanses us from all sin" (1 John 1:7). "He is the propitiation for our sins, and not for ours only, but also for the whole world" (1 John 2:2). "Herein is love, not that we loved God, but that He loved us, and sent His Son to be the propitiation for our sins" (1 John 4:10). That the propitiation is made in the blood of Jesus can only be questioned by those who refuse to admit that the New Testament writers had any cohesion in their thoughts at all. It is in virtue of its propitiatory meaning and power that the death of Jesus is pointed to in the Epistle as proving Him to be the Son of God. No one will overcome the world if he faces it under the crushing weight of a bad conscience; it is because Jesus, who died for sins, can lift this weight, that we recognize Him to be what the gospel declares. Because, to this wonderful intent of being a propitiation for the whole world, He came by blood, we say He is the Son of God. It is the work of atonement which reveals Him as what He is, and holds Him up as the object for a faith which has the world to overcome.

In this interpretation water and blood are taken literally; the reference is to the historical events of the baptism and death of Jesus. But literal or historical is not synonymous with accidental, or spiritually insignificant and powerless. The water and the blood could not be thought of by John except as implying and declaring the possession and communication of the Spirit by Jesus, and the expiation and conquest of sin. How the baptism and the death of Jesus, with the powers involved in them, are related to one another there is nothing here to explain. They were separated in time, but Jesus Himself spoke of His death as an awful baptism (Luke 12:50; Mark 10:38f.), and there is a passage in the Gospel (John 19:34) where John brings the water and the blood into the closest connexion with one another. "One of the soldiers with a spear pierced His side, and straightway there came out blood and water. And he that hath seen hath borne witness, and his witness is true, and he knoweth that he saith true, that ye also may believe." The extraordinary solemnity with which this is attested shows the importance it had for the evangelist, and it is impossible to agree with Godet that the passage in the Epistle has nothing whatever to do with the one in the Gospel. Surely it is clear that in Gospel and Epistle alike incidents and experiences in the history of Jesus are being emphasized which prove Him to be the true object of faith. And surely it is clear further that in Gospel and Epistle alike a protest is being made against those who not merely distinguished but separated the water and the blood, and claimed the benefit of the one while disowning any obligation to the other. This is evident in the Epistle at all events. When John writes, "Not with the water only, but with the water and with the blood," he has unquestionably before his mind people who admitted that Jesus came with the first, but not with the second.[1] It is not legitimate, perhaps, to say that these were people who accepted regeneration but rejected the atonement, who consented to receive from Christ a new life, but not to be in debt to Him for the expiation of sins. We may have grounds for believing that this attitude to Christ is not uncommon, and even for holding that of all causes which contribute to the misunderstanding of the New Testament the most profound and far-reaching is the failure to see that nothing but the atonement can regenerate; but it is necessary to look to the writer's own age for more precise illustration of his meaning. He tells us himself in 1 John 4:1ff. of false prophets, in whom the spirit of the Antichrist is at work, and who deny that Jesus Christ has come in flesh. The very early gloss in 1 John 4:3—*omnis spiritus qui solvit Jesum*—points to teachers like Cerinthus, "the enemy of the truth"[2] as the truth was preached by John. Cerinthus, according to Irenaeus, held that Jesus was the son of Joseph and Mary, that after His baptism the Christ descended on Him in the form of a dove from the supreme God, that He then revealed the unknown Father and worked miracles, but that at the end the Christ departed from Jesus; so that Jesus suffered and was raised, while the Christ as a spiritual being continued impassible.[3] This seems to be precisely what the apostle is striking at—a Saviour, an object of faith, a Son of God, who comes by water only. Cerinthus (it might be put) saw divinity in the life of Jesus, but not in His death. He acknowledged the redemptive power of all that He did in virtue of His baptism, of all the teachings and healings which He accomplished in the power of the Spirit He received at the Jordan; but it seemed to him incredible and unworthy that a divine being should be dragged through the squalid tragedy of the Crucifixion. His Son of God did not come by blood: the passion of Jesus had nothing in it redemptive or divine. Formally this belongs to the first century and

---

1. The difference between διά and ἐν in διὰ ὕδατος καὶ αἵματος and ἐν τῷ ὕδατι καὶ ἐν τῷ αἵματι is not to be pressed. The διά is more appropriate to the historical incident or experience through which Jesus *passed*, the ἐν to the spiritual virtue involved in it, in possession of which Jesus *abides* as the object of faith; but the two prepositions are used indistinguishably in a very similar connexion in Hebrews 9:12, 14, 25.

2. Eusebius, *Ecclesiastical History*, 3, 28.6.

3. Irenaeus, *Against Heresies*, 1, 26.1.

is grotesque enough, but in reality, as has been suggested above, it is widely represented in our own world. There are many who are glad to acknowledge a general debt to the teaching and example of Jesus, but not a special debt to His death; many to whom regeneration, or moral stimulus, is as attractive as expiation is repellent, and who fail to see that in the Christian religion the two cannot be separated. The Person who makes propitiation in His blood is the same who baptizes with the Holy Spirit; it is because He does the one as well as the other—because He came not with the water only but with the water and with the blood—that we know Him to be what He is, the Christ, the Son of God, who has overcome the world and can enable us to overcome, the one adequate object of faith.

For a believer, it may be said, this is presumably convincing: but what of one who does not believe? What of the man who looks at the life of Jesus and at the death of Jesus as they are attested by the apostles—who contemplates Him as He came with the water and the blood—who tries to realize in some vague fashion what is meant by words like propitiation and regeneration—and who after all remains quite unmoved? It is perhaps in the sense of his own ineffectiveness and helplessness that the apostle, after emphasizing the water and the blood as realities which attest Jesus as the Redeemer, appeals directly to God. "And it is the Spirit that beareth witness, because the Spirit is the truth." It is not enough that the facts should be there in indubitable historical reality, it is not enough that an apostle should be there to interpret and enforce them on the conscience in the full assurance of his own faith; if faith is to be born in sinful souls, even under these propitious circumstances, *God* must be there to bear the supreme testimony to His Son. There is this point of mystery in all true religion, the point at which God and the soul meet. Not indeed that it is mere mystery: the Spirit does not work in the dark, but takes the things of Christ, the water and the blood, and makes them real, significant, present and powerful to the soul. Only the Spirit can do this. All the essential facts, all the presuppositions of faith, so to speak, may be present, yet faith itself is not born till the touch of God completes the spiritual circuit, and the heart is suddenly thrilled with the atoning and regenerating power of Him who came by water and blood. What was remote, inert and unintelligible flames up under the witness of the Spirit into the present, living, all-powerful love of the Redeemer. In a sense the Spirit is the only witness: it belongs to it alone to make the past present, the historical eternal. We call the New Testament an inspired book because as we hearken to its testimony to Christ the past ceases to be past, and everything is transacted before our eyes, and in relation to ourselves. Time disappears, and Christ is with us in His Spirit which is the Truth. It is not our experience that He spoke these words, but that He speaks them; not that He received sinners and ate with them, but that He receives sinners and spreads His table for them; not that He prayed for His own, but that He makes intercession for us. We do not even say, He came by blood, but He is here, clothed in His crimson robe, in the power of His atonement, mighty to save. This is what the Spirit, which, properly speaking, is the supreme and sole witness, does for us in attesting, interpreting and applying the historical facts of the life of Jesus. But the apostle has also another way of looking at the matter. There are three, he says, who bear witness, the Spirit and the water and the blood; and the three agree in one. At first the Spirit is a witness to the water and the blood, sealing their meaning and their power upon the soul; but it is possible also to think of all three as bearing one concordant testimony to the Son of God. How are we to understand this?

It does not seem possible to explain it unless we admit at this point an allusion to the Christian sacraments. Sometimes this has been very strongly denied. Dr. Charles Watson, for example, in his profound and beautiful commentary on this Epistle, writes: "St. John neither in his Gospel nor in his Epistles takes any notice whatever of the sacraments of baptism and the Lord's supper. This fact makes it unlikely that he was thinking of them when he speaks of the water and the blood as witnesses to Christ." Even Bishop Westcott says no more than that we are led to the ideas which underlie the two sacraments. When we remember the time at which John wrote, and the place which baptism and the supper, as we see from almost every New Testament writer, soon came to hold in Christian worship, it seems fair to use much stronger language. It is to the writer quite incredible that any Christian reader should ever have heard John 3 without thinking of baptism, or John 6 without thinking of the supper, or this passage without thinking of both. Baptism and the supper are perpetually present in the Church, and they are a perpetual attestation of the water and the blood. They remind us unceasingly of those great events in the life of Jesus by which He is identified as the Son of God and Saviour of men—His baptism in water, with which His baptism with the Spirit coincided, so that it became the type of all Christian baptism, in which also the coincidence of water and spirit is conceived as normal; and His death upon the cross, in which He became a propitiation for the whole world. The sacraments are a standing testimony to these great facts and to their meaning and power. They guard the realities which are vital to the Christian religion. They speak ceaselessly of Christ as able in virtue of His life and death to regenerate men and to atone for sins. In them, to put it strongly, we have the water and the blood always with us. We need not hesitate to say so because the words are capable of being abused. They are true when spoken at the moral temperature at which their meaning is realized; they are not true as a theological doctrine, defined in cold blood. Very probably superstitious ideas had gathered round the truth even before John wrote, just as they had gathered round the sacraments at Corinth (see 1 Cor 10), but it is as absurd to make John responsible for this in the one case as Paul in the other. The representatives of the religio-historical method, who interpret everything *in malam partem* and who are never so sure they are right as when they convict the apostles of religious materialism or primeval superstition, have lost their balance. In St. John's words about the sacraments in this passage there is a mingling of history, of symbolism, and of the spiritual experience of fellowship with the Son of God in the power of His life and death; but it is only an unsympathetic, one is almost tempted to say an unchristian, reader, who can find any trace in them of the magical sacramentalism of the pagan mysteries. It is far more plausible to argue that in every place in his writings in which John touches on the sacraments he is careful to leave the primacy with the Spirit. Thus in the third chapter of the Gospel he speaks once of being born of water and spirit, because that is the Christian norm as illustrated by the baptism of Jesus, but afterwards omits the water, and says born of the Spirit only. In chapter six, after saying the strongest things about eating the flesh and drinking the blood of the Son of Man—which the writer believes to be sacramental language—he precludes misconception (or tries to do so) by adding, It is the Spirit that gives life; the flesh profits nothing. And finally, in the Epistle, while the water and the blood, perpetuated in the sacraments, are themselves witnesses to Christ, the supreme witness is that of the Spirit, apart from which neither the water and the blood as historical facts, nor their perpetuation in the sacraments, have any power at all. Taking his words, however, as they stand, their effect is not to disparage the sacraments but to magnify their work as witnesses to the great experiences of Jesus by which He is evinced to be the proper object of faith.

It is in this connexion also that we become conscious of the value of the passage for all time. The apostle's interest is not in the sacraments, but in the historical realities on which the life of Christianity depends, and he refers to the sacraments only because they guarantee these realities and keep them in evidence in the Church. History will always have its difficulties, and there will always be efforts made to free religion from any dependence upon it. The Spirit, or what is called the Spirit, will always be appealed to against the more or less uncertain facts. Even a religion like the Christian, which from the beginning rested on a narrative of historical events, is subjected to this treatment. The important thing in Christianity, men say to themselves, is its ethical principle; grasp this, and everything else is indifferent. Jesus may have been the first to apprehend it clearly, but in essence it is quite independent of Him; once we realize it in its purity and truth, we do not need to vex ourselves about the truth or falsehood of the Gospel story. Die to live, as He no doubt did, or had it as His principle to do; sacrifice the lower life for the sake of the higher, and what question remains to be asked? It is not the business of any one who pleads the cause of Christianity to contemn those who seek to live by a Christian rule; but if the apostle is any authority upon the subject, this substitution of abstract principles for the passion of the Son of God is not Christianity at all. It is not the reality of abstract principles, however true or sublime, on which his faith leans; it is the reality of blood. It is no poetic or philosophic *Stirb und werde*,[4] nothing which can be learned from Goethe or Hegel, which makes us Christians; it is the pierced side, the thorn-crowned brow, the rent hands and feet of Jesus. Our faith is evoked by one who came

4. [Die and become.]

by blood, and it rests on Him alone. What can a religion of ethical principles merely do to provide a propitiation? What can it offer to lost men? What are the ethical principles from which we can deduce that profound and grateful assurance of the forgiveness of sins which inspires the doxologies of the apostolic Church?

These considerations are of special importance at present when the historical criticism of Scripture is raising so many problems for faith, and when attempts are made to allay anxiety on lines which are substantially those here denounced by the apostle. Often we hear it said to perplexed souls, "There is really nothing to be anxious about. Faith and criticism move on different planes; they can never touch, and therefore can never come into collision. Criticism may come to any conclusion whatever about the truth of facts or what are alleged to be facts in the Bible, and it will make no difference to religion." It is difficult to understand how this is believed by those who say it, and it is certainly not believed by those who hear it. It never mitigated any Christian's anxiety, but it has often added exasperation to alarm. To a simple and earnest spirit it means too obviously that religion is only to have the kind of reality which belongs to ideas and principles, not the reality of blood; and with the change all the specifically Christian virtue has departed from it. To say that faith cannot be affected by any critical result is to say that religion is independent of any historical basis, and that is to teach the false spirituality which the apostle here rejects. The Christian religion, at all events as he knew it, lives and has its being in the historical. Instead of saying to men, "nothing historical matters," we ought rather to say, "See how unimpeachable is the evidence by which the essential historical facts are guaranteed. Look, to go no further, at the sacraments of baptism and the Lord's supper. They were celebrated universally in the Church before any part of the New Testament was written. They bear witness still to Him who came by water and by blood. Every one of the countless millions who since the day of Pentecost to this day has been baptized in the name of Jesus is a witness to the baptism of Jesus Himself. Every one who since the night on which He was betrayed has eaten the bread and drunk of the cup in the Lord's supper is a witness to the reality of His passion." There are things which cannot be shaken, and it is absurd to speak as if they could be shaken and leave our religion untouched. It is because the Spirit of God has these historical realities to attest that there is such a thing as Christianity in the world. Without them preaching is vain and faith is vain; there is no love of God known to us on which we can lean as Christians have leaned hitherto on the passion of their Lord.

The emphasis which the apostle lays on the blood, when he speaks of the coming of Jesus, should have something which reflects it in the life of the believer. Christianity should be as real as the passion of the Saviour on which it rests. No deliberate aim at a sheltered life is Christian. It is possible to fall short here with the most amiable intentions. Often this is the result when the Christian life is lived in coteries, and the relations of believers are all to each other and none to the world. The sanctification of the soul then takes the place of the consecration of the life, and passion disappears. So few make holiness in any sense their chief end that it may seem rash to speak against this, yet it is painfully true that even Christian faith becomes insipid and ineffective unless it confronts the world, comes with blood, and is proved in the actualities and conflicts of life. But coteries and conventions do not perhaps mislead so many as the charm and happiness of what is probably counted a Christian home. It is not uncommon to see life narrowed in such circumstances to the circle of the domestic affections. It is pure, beautiful, amiable, truly happy; but it has no interests beyond itself. The conflicts of the world rage around it but it is not troubled by them; all that calls for effort, sacrifice, blood, is ignored. The Lord's battle is going on against powerful forces of evil—pride, sensuality, secularism, false patriotism, drunkenness, greed—but the members of such families are not in it. Their life is refined, retired, accomplished perhaps, but bloodless. Is that Christian? Can One who came by blood see in lives like these of the travail of His soul? Or does not reality like that of His passion call for something far more intensely and vividly real in those who believe in His name?

# 11

# Preaching Christ

The purpose of this article is to explain what is meant by "preaching Christ." It is assumed that to preach Christ is the preacher's function, and the intention is to show what such preaching involved in the beginning, and what it must include still if it is to be true to its original. Changing conditions may demand for it different forms, but presumably under all forms there will be a vital continuity or rather identity in the substance which is preached.

1. The New Testament as a whole presents Jesus in the character of *the Christ*. When the first preachers preached Him, it was in this character. "God," says Peter, "hath made this same Jesus both Lord and Christ" (Acts 2:36). "Saul confounded the Jews that dwelt in Damascus, proving that this is the Christ" (Acts 9:22). All the evangelists agree with this: see Matthew 1:1–18, Mark 1:1, Luke 2:11, John 20:31. Now "the Christ," or "the Messiah," was not a meaningless expression for Jews: it had a distinct meaning, and a great range of ideas and hopes attached to it. There was a Messianic dogmatic, as it has been called, among the Jews, quite apart from the question who was to be the Messiah; or, to put it otherwise, Jewish disciples had a Christology before they became believers in Jesus as the Christ. It is easy to see the dangers connected with this situation. If we take the sentence, "Jesus is the Christ," we may put the emphasis either on the subject or the predicate. We can conceive how a Jew, whose imagination was on flame with the apocalyptic hopes associated with the Messiah, might allow these hopes, when he accepted the Christian faith, to overpower the person of Jesus; Jesus, so to speak, would become nothing to him but the person through whom expectations were

to be realized which in their origin had nothing to do with Jesus. There may be occasions in the New Testament where we have to ask whether something of this kind has not taken place, but they are not conspicuous. In the New Testament, when it is said that Jesus is the Christ, the emphasis is always as much on the subject as on the predicate. The proof of the proposition is always found in something which has been done by or to *Jesus*. In point of fact, it is found in the first instance in His resurrection and exaltation to God's right hand. It is this participation in the sovereignty of God that makes Him Lord and Christ; and the content of this, in all essentials, is not derived from the Messianic dogmatic of the Jewish schools, but from the experience of the apostles themselves. This experience has two aspects, the one in the stricter sense historical, the other in the stricter sense spiritual. The one, put briefly, is, "We have seen the Lord"; the other, "He hath poured forth this—the new life at Pentecost—which ye see and hear" (Acts 2:33). The one is represented by the series of witnesses to the resurrection cited by St. Paul in 1 Corinthians 15:5–9, the other by the series of new spiritual experiences and convictions to which he can appeal in 1 Corinthians 15:12–19. It is the testimony of the apostles to the resurrection of Jesus, and experience of the new life in His Spirit, not any pre-Christian Christology, or Jewish Messianic dogmatic, that define for the first Christians the content of the title "the Christ." And it may safely be said, to begin with, that there is no such thing as preaching Christ unless it is the preaching of *One who lives and reigns*. If Jesus is at the right hand of God,—if He is behind every revival of spiritual life in the Church,—then He is the Christ, and can be preached as such; but if not, not.

2. At first, naturally, great stress was laid upon this. The apostles sincerely believed that they had seen the Lord, and they could not conceive of their calling as having anything in it to take precedence of this—that they were witnesses of the resurrection, and therefore of the Messiahship of Jesus. No doubt this gave its whole character to primitive Christianity; but if we accept the testimony of the apostles to the resurrection, we shall be slow to say that it transformed its character, and made it a new and essentially an inferior thing as compared with the religion of Jesus. Jesus was not forgotten when the apostles, appealing to the resurrection and to Pentecost, argued that He was the Christ,

God's King, through whom all the hopes which God had inspired were to be fulfilled. Harnack, indeed, has argued that in its eagerness to prove that Jesus is the Christ—that is, to discharge a task in apologetic theology—the Church spent too much of the force which ought to have been given to teaching men to observe all things whatsoever He had commanded.[1] But there is no necessary antagonism between the two things, and except for their faith in His exaltation as the Christ the apostles would never have taught anything at all. Weinel[2] represents the same tendency in a much less guarded form. "After the death of Jesus," he says, "the ethical religion of redemption, which had entered the world with Jesus, underwent its most decisive transformation of a formal kind; it ceased to be the religion of sonship to God, and became faith in the Christ-nature of the man Jesus. . . . The disciples demanded faith in Him as the Messiah exalted to God, and in the conception of His death as an atonement appointed by God for sins. With the experience of the resurrection and with this dogma of the death of the Messiah, the Christ-religion, Christianity in the narrower sense, begins." One almost wonders if Weinel thinks it a pity that Jesus rose from the dead, or that His disciples believed that He did, and were overpoweringly influenced by a faith so tremendous; but this apart, the assumption in all criticism of this sort is that when the apostles preached Jesus as the Christ they concentrated all their attention on the predicate of the proposition, which owed no part of its import to Jesus, and treated the subject as if it had no meaning. Even on *a priori* grounds we should say this was improbable, and there is a very significant piece of evidence that it is not true. This is found in the qualifications of the man appointed to take the place of Judas. His function was to be a witness to the resurrection—that is, to the Messiahship of Jesus; he was, in other words, to be a preacher of the Christ. But he was chosen from "the men that have companied with us all the time that the Lord Jesus went in and went out among us, beginning from the baptism of John unto the day that he was received up from us" (Acts 1:21f.). To preach Christ, even in the days when belief in the resurrection was so overpowering, one

1. Harnack, *Dogmengeschichte*, 1:57f.
2. Weinel, *Paulus*, 108f.

required to have a full knowledge of Jesus. It is idle to say that Jesus is the Christ if we do not know who or what Jesus is. It has no meaning to say that an unknown person is at God's right hand, exalted and sovereign; the more ardently men believed that God had given them a Prince and a Saviour in this exaltation, the more eager would they be to know all that could possibly be learned about Him. If there were men alive who had lived in His company, they would wait assiduously on their teaching (Acts 2:42). They would be more than curious to know what spirit He was of, and whether they could detect in His appearance and career on earth "the works of the Christ" (Matt 11:2). They would expect to find some kind of moral congruity between His life on the one hand, and His transcendent dignity and calling on the other; there would be a demand, from the very beginning, for facts about Him. From this point of view, then, we may say that preaching Christ is not taking leave of Jesus in any sense or to any extent; it is preaching Jesus exalted and sovereign.

The passage just quoted (Acts 1:21f.) is practically coterminous with the oldest form of gospel which we possess. "Beginning from the baptism of John unto the day that he was taken up": these are the limits within which lies the Gospel according to Mark. Hence we might say that to preach this gospel is to preach Christ, on condition, of course, that it is preached in its connexion with Jesus exalted. Merely to narrate the history of Jesus, even if we had the materials for it, would not be to preach Christ. We need, of course, to know the historical Jesus, as the qualifications for apostleship show; but to preach Christ means to preach that Person as present in the sovereignty of His resurrection. It is not preaching Christ if we tell the story of the life and death merely as events in a past continually growing more remote. It is not preaching Christ though we tell this story in the most vivid and moving fashion, and gather round it, by the exercise of historical imagination or dramatic skill, the liveliest emotions; it is not preaching Christ to present the life and death of Jesus as a high and solemn tragedy, with power in it to purify the soul by pity and terror. There is no preaching of Christ, possessed of religious significance, that does not rest on the basis on which the apostolic preaching rested: His exaltation in power, and therefore His perpetual presence. The historical Jesus is indispensable; but if we are to have a Christian religion, the historical must become present and eternal. This it does through the resurrection as apprehended by faith.

3. For the purposes of this article it is assumed that the Synoptic Gospels give such a knowledge of the historical Jesus as is sufficient for the preacher's ends. No doubt He is depicted for us there by writers who believed in Him as the Christ, and for whom the light of His exaltation was reflected on the lowliness of His earthly career; but this light is not necessarily a distorting one. We have no reason to say that there is anything in these Gospels which is untrue to the historical personality of Jesus, anything which represents Him in mind, in will, in temper, in character, in His consciousness as a whole of His relations to God and man, as other than He really was. Extravagant things have been said by many writers of *Lives of Jesus*, from Strauss downwards, on the imperfection of our knowledge, and on the way in which the real Jesus has been disguised from the very beginning by the idealization of His figure in the faith and love of those who preached Him— and especially in the Gospels. If we concentrate our attention on the character of Jesus, on the spirit of His words and deeds and death, on His consciousness of His relations to God and men—in a word, on what He was and achieved in the spiritual world—it is the present writer's conviction that we shall feel the very reverse of this to be the truth. We may be dubious about this or that word, this or that incident in the Gospels, but we have no dubiety at all about the Person. The great life that stands out before us in the Gospels is more real than anything in the world; and Jesus is so far from being hidden from us that it is no exaggeration to say that we know Him better than anybody who has ever lived on earth.

It does not follow from this that we accept the evangelists' proofs that Jesus was the Christ, or that in preaching Christ we employ the same arguments as they to show that Jesus has the unique significance for religion which was represented for them by the Messianic title. Broadly speaking, these arguments were two—one from prophecy and one from miracles. Both may be accepted in principle without being accepted in form. The argument from prophecy is an assertion of the continuity of revelation, of the one purpose of God running through it all, and culminating in Jesus. Jesus is the fulfilment of all the hopes contained in the ancient revelation, and we look for no other: "How many soever are the promises of God, in him is the yea" (2 Cor 1:20); we recognize this, and the absolute significance which it secures for Jesus in religion. But we no longer prove it to ourselves by emphasizing, in the manner of the First Gospel, particular correspondences between incidents in the life of Jesus and passages in the Old Testament. There is no religious and no intellectual value for us in such fulfilments of prophecy as Matthew 2:15; 2:18; 2:23. We should apply the Pauline principle (2 Cor 1:20) quite differently, recognizing that correspondence is one thing, fulfilment another. Jesus did not really come to fulfil prophecy in the sense of carrying out a programme the details of which were fixed beforehand; He came to fulfil Himself, or to fulfil the will of the Father, as the Father made it plain to Him from step to step; and though, on one occasion (Mark 11:1–10), He Himself arranged an incident in which a literal correspondence with a prophecy was secured, it is not such a phenomenon which makes Him the Christ to us. Its value now lies in showing that He regarded Himself as the Christ, the promised King. And so with the argument from miracles, which, though not formally put, is perhaps as characteristic of the Second Gospel as the argument from prophecy is of the First. The works of Jesus, in the largest sense,—all that He did and the power which it implied,—go to give Him the importance He has in our minds. But we do not limit His works to the class commonly called miraculous; the impression left on the minds of men by His whole being and action gathers up into itself much more than this. The arguments from prophecy and from miracles are formal ways of expressing truths which really contain much more than these forms can carry; and our impression of the truths is too direct, immediate, and complex to have justice done it by such arguments.

4. While, however, the inadequacy of such arguments to their purpose must be admitted, the purpose of the arguments is not to be overlooked. What those who first called Jesus the Christ, or preached Him as such, intended to do, was to put Him in a place which no other could share. Whatever else the name meant, it meant the King; and there was only one King. In the Christian religion Jesus was never one of a series, a person who could be classified, and be shown to His proper place in the line of great personalities who have contributed to the spiritual uplifting of the race. The study of Comparative Religion has fostered a tendency

to regard Him in this light; but it cannot be said too strongly that to admit the legitimacy of such a tendency is to abandon from the very root all that has ever been known to history as Christianity. The New Testament is quite unequivocal about this. From the beginning Christians call Jesus "Lord" (1 Cor 12:3), and recognize that God has given Him the name which is above every name (Phil 2:9). All other men in the New Testament meet as equals on the same level, and all bow before Him as King. In His exaltation He confronts men as one divine causality with the Father, working for their salvation. Historical Christianity, said Emerson,[3] has dwelt and dwells with noxious exaggeration about the *person* of Jesus. As a criticism of some kinds of interest in dogmatic Christology, this may be true; but if it is meant to reflect on the devotion of Christians to Jesus as a Person, it is completely beside the mark. To Christians this Person has been from the beginning, and will be for ever, what no other can be. To talk of Him as the same in kind with other prophets or founders of religions,—with Moses and Isaiah, with Confucius or Buddha, or, what is even harder to understand, with Mohammed,—is to surrender anything that a New Testament Christian could have recognized as Christianity. To preach Christ at all we must preach Him as κύριος and μονογενής. The first name secures His unshared place in relation to men, as the latter does in relation to God; and unless He fills such a place, Christianity has no *raison d'être*. That it has is the assumption of this article, as it is the fact presented in the New Testament. It is, in fact, the *differentia* of Christianity as a religion that the distinction which can sometimes be drawn between a person and the cause for which he stands is in it no longer valid. To preach what Jesus preached is not preaching Christianity unless the thing preached is preached in its essential relation to Him. The truth which He announces is not independent of Himself; it is in the world only as it is incarnate in *Him*. Thus, to take as an example what many regard as the supreme category in the teaching of Jesus—the Kingdom of God: what is meant by preaching Christ here? It is very likely impossible for us to understand precisely what the expression "Kingdom of God" conveyed in the mental atmosphere of Judaism or of the first century generally. It may be impossible for us even to

---

3. Emerson, *Works*, 2:195.

understand with certainty and precision what Jesus Himself on any given occasion meant it to convey. All shades of meaning run through it,—political, eschatological, spiritual; national, universal; here, coming: how can anyone tell whether in preaching the Kingdom of God he is preaching Christ? The answer is clear if we remember that the Kingdom of God in His sense could come only in and through Him, and that its character is ultimately determined by that fact. He Himself, in the sense at least of being God's representative, is King in it (Matt 13:41; 20:21; 25:34; Luke 23:42), and it is from what we know of Him, including ultimately His resurrection and exaltation, that all our conceptions of the Kingdom must be derived. To preach the cause and ignore the Person, or to preach the cause as of universal import and to assign to the Person an importance in relation to it which He only shares with an indefinite number of others, is to be untrue to the facts as the Gospels present them. Even preaching the Kingdom of God is not preaching Christ unless the Kingdom is preached as one which owes its character to the fact that Jesus is its King, and the certainty of its consummation to the fact that Jesus shares the throne of God. Christianity is not abstract optimism; it is optimism based on the exaltation of Jesus, and on the knowledge of God as revealed in Him.

5. If we bring these ideas to a point, we shall say that to preach Christ means to preach Jesus in the absolute significance for God and man which He had to His own consciousness and to the faith of the first witnesses; and to preach Him as exalted, and as having this absolute significance now and for ever. The question then arises, In what forms did Jesus Himself present this absolute significance to His own mind? How did He conceive it, and body it forth to others, so as to make an adequate impression on them? And are the forms of thought and of imagination which He employed for this purpose in a given historical environment as indispensable to us, and as binding in our totally different environment, as they were for those with whom Jesus stood face to face? To preach Christ it is necessary to be able to answer these questions not at haphazard, but on principle; and the answer may sometimes seem difficult.

To proceed by illustration: (*a*) One of the ways in which Jesus represented His absolute significance for the true religion was this: He regarded Himself as the Messiah. The Messianic role was one which could be filled only by one Person, and He Himself was the Person in question; He and no other was the Christ. But is "the Christ" a conception of which we, in another age and with other antecedents, can make use for the same purpose? Only, it must be answered, if we employ the term with much latitude. What it suggests to us, as already pointed out, is the continuity of revelation, and the fulfilment through Jesus of all the hopes which, through history and prophecy, God had kindled in human hearts; it is the possibility of using it to express this that justifies us in retaining the name. But it is certain that for those who first came to believe in Jesus as the Christ the name was much more definite than it is for us; it had a shape and colour that it has no longer; it had expectations connected with it which for us have lost the vitality they once possessed. In particular, the eschatological associations of the term have not, in their New Testament form, the importance for us which they had for the first believers. In the teaching of Jesus these associations cluster round the title "the Son of Man," which, at least after the confession of Peter at Caesarea Philippi, is used as synonymous with "the Christ"; the Son of Man is identified with Jesus, and comes again, after His suffering and death, to establish the Kingdom, in the glory of His Father with the holy angels (Mark 8:31; 8:38; Matt 10:33; 16:27). This coming again, or, as the original disciples conceived it, this coming (παρουσία) in the character of the Christ, was expected, by those who first preached and received the gospel, to take place in their own generation; and it is difficult to argue that this expectation could have any other basis than the teaching of Jesus Himself. Nothing was more characteristic of primitive Christianity; it was the very essence of what the early Church meant by *hope*; it was for it part of the very meaning of "the Christ." Account has been taken, in "Authority of Christ,"[4] of any considerations which go to qualify the certainty with which we ascribe to Jesus Himself this eschatological conception of the consummation of God's Kingdom, and especially this conviction as to its imminence; but if we do connect it with Him, and regard it as part of what is meant when He represents Himself as the Christ, clearly history requires us to recognize the inadequacy of that conception to be the vehicle

4. [Chapter 7 of this volume.]

of the truth. The Kingdom of God has been coming ever since Jesus left the world; but Jesus Himself, after nearly two thousand years, has not yet come in like manner as the disciples saw Him going into heaven (Acts 1:11). We still believe that the Kingdom of God is coming; we believe this because we believe in Jesus; we believe that it is coming only through Him and as He comes; that is what the Christian of to-day means when he says we believe in Him as the Christ. But even the belief in His exaltation to God's right hand does not make possible for us that particular kind of expectation of His coming which burnt with so intense a flame in the breast of the apostolic Church; quite apart from any preference or effort, our outlook on the future is different from theirs; and, while we do not abate in the least our recognition of the sole sovereignty of Jesus, and our assurance that God's Kingdom can come and God's promises be fulfilled through Him alone, we are compelled, apparently, to recognize that in infusing into the disciples His own assurance of the final triumph of God's cause in His own person, our Lord had to make use of representations which have turned out unequal to the truth. He had to put His sense of the absolute significance of His Person for God and man into a form which was relative to the mind of the time. The eschatological Christ, coming on the clouds of heaven, and coming in the lifetime of some who heard His voice, was one expression for Jesus of this absolute significance; and it is as such an expression—that is, as an assurance of the speedy triumph of God's cause in and through Him, and not in its spectacular detail—that we believe in it. It is not rejecting the absolute significance of Jesus to say that this spectacular detail is relative to the age and its mental outlook; but it would be a rejection of it, and a repudiation of Jesus as the Christ, if we denied that the Kingdom of God—however experience enables us to picture its coming and consummation—comes and is consummated through Him alone. This truth must be preached if we really preach Christ.

(*b*) Jesus, however, has other ways of conveying His absolute significance. One of the simplest is that in which He represents Himself as judge of men, arbiter of their eternal destinies. It may be argued, no doubt, that the form in which this is expressed in Matthew 7:21ff.; Matthew 25:31ff. is, in part at least, due to the evangelist; "prophesying in the name of Jesus" was a phenomenon which came into the world only after His death, and such an allusion to it as Matthew 7:22, where it is treated as an obvious thing, would hardly have been intelligible in His lifetime. But there is no reason whatever to doubt that both this passage and the other convey the mind of Jesus about His own significance for men. Whatever be the rule of the judgment—doing the will of *His Father* (Matt 7:21), or humanity exhibited in practice in relation to those whom He calls *His brethren* (Matt 25:40)—it is a rule which has been finally embodied in Him. It is in Him that we see what doing the will of the Father means; it is in Him also that we see the law of humanity fulfilled. It is what we are when measured by His standard, judged by His judgment, that discloses the very truth about us. It has been urged that this prerogative of judgment is merely an element in the Jewish conception of the Messiah, and as such has been formally transferred to Jesus in the Gospels; but nothing is less formal in the New Testament than the conception of Jesus as judge. It does not rest on any borrowings from a pre-Christian Messianic dogmatic, but on the most real experiences of men in the presence of Jesus: "Depart from me, for I am a sinful man, O Lord" (Luke 5:8); "Come, see a man who told me all things that ever I did" (John 4:29). The experiences by which words like these were inspired give reality and solemnity to all the representations of Jesus as judge. Here again we may say that the spectacular representations of the judgment are a form which we may recognize to have only a relative value, while yet we do not dispute in the least the absolute truth that the standard of reality and of worth in the spiritual world is Jesus, and that no life can be finally estimated except by its relation to Him. The Gospel according to John is distinguished from the others by emphasizing the function of Christ as judge, and the continuous exercise of it in what might almost be called an automatic fashion. The Father has committed all judgment to the Son (John 5:23); and the process of judging goes on in the Gospel under our eyes. The very presence of Jesus sifts men; they gather round Him or are repelled from Him according to what they are. Something of absolute and final significance, it may be said, is transacted before our faces, as men show that they will or will not have anything to do with Jesus. It is eternal judgment revealed in the field of time, and Jesus is the judge. No one else could fill His place in this character, and we do not preach

Christ as He was and is except by making this plain. Probably, however, in this case more than in any other it is rash to discount too cheaply what we think, rightly enough in principle, are but forms of conveying this truth, and forms unequal to the reality. The picture of the last judgment in Matthew 25:31–46 may not be true as a picture, the moral reality of the judgment may not be dependent at all on the scenic details here presented, but whether or not it is true as a picture, it is true in the moral impression it leaves on the mind, and this is the truth that is important. There is such a thing, if there is any truth in Christ at all, as final judgment; there is a right hand of the judge and a left, an inside of the door and an outside, a character that abides for ever and a character that collapses in irreparable ruin; and to realize of what kind character is, or where it must stand at last, we have only to confront it with Him. The man who cannot withstand the attraction of Jesus does not come into judgment, he has passed from death into life (John 5:24); the man who will not yield to the attraction of Jesus is judged already (John 3:18), and the judgment will be revealed at last. To recognize and proclaim the absolute significance of Jesus here is an essential part of preaching Christ.

(c) The supreme illustration of this incomparable significance of Jesus remains. It is given in what we may call *His consciousness of His relation to God*. To Jesus, God was the Father, and He Himself was the Son. It does not matter that God is a universal Father, and that all men are or are called to be His sons; Jesus recognizes this, and insists upon it, but He claims Sonship in a peculiar sense for Himself. He never speaks of Himself as *a* child of God, but as *the* Son, *simpliciter*. In speaking of God and Himself He uses ὁ πατήρ and ὁ υἱός in a way which implies that there could no more be a plural on the one side than on the other: see esp. Matthew 11:27f., Mark 13:32. It is natural to suppose that in the account of Jesus' baptism (Matt 3:17 and parallels) the heavenly voice which pronounces Him Son of God, in words borrowed from Psalms 2, means the term there to be taken in the Messianic "official" sense; it is the Messianic consciousness of Jesus, as the accompanying narrative of the Temptation proves, which is expressed in ὁ υἱός μου. What the relation may have been in His mind between this (which defines His calling by relation to Old Testament hopes) and the divine Sonship exhibited in Matthew 11:27, we may not be able to tell. It has been argued by some that the official Messianic Sonship, the calling to be God's King in Israel, widened and deepened in the mind of Jesus Himself into the consciousness of a unique relation to God, which found its most adequate expression in the language of Matthew 11:27; by others, that only such a consciousness as is disclosed in Matthew 11:27 enables us to understand how Jesus could ever have regarded Himself as the Messiah. The Messianic categories have been considered above; what we have here to do is to look at the less specifically Jewish way in which Jesus here reveals His absolute significance for religion. "All things have been delivered to me by my Father: and no one knoweth the Son, save the Father; neither knoweth any one the Father, save the Son, and he to whomsoever the Son willeth to reveal him."[5] Here Jesus claims in the most explicit terms to have had the whole task of revealing God to men—the whole task of saving men, so far as that depends upon their coming to know God—committed to Him.[6] It is a task to which He is equal, and for which no other has any competence at all. Everything connected with it has been entrusted to Him, and to Him alone; there is not a man upon the earth who can know the Father except by becoming a debtor to Jesus. There is no such thing as preaching Christ unless we preach this: He is the mediator for all men of the knowledge of God as Father; that is, of that knowledge of God on which eternal life depends. This is the loftiest, the most universal, and the most gracious form in which the absolute significance of Jesus can be expressed: the loftiest, because it declares Him unequivocally to be the μονογενής, having His being in a relation to God constituted by perfect mutual understanding, and belonging to Him alone; the most universal, because the relation of Father and Son, while it can only be symbolic of the reality, uses a symbolism based on nature, not on history, and is therefore intelligible to all men, and not only (like Messiah) to one race; and the most gracious, for it suggests directly not only mutual understanding but mutual love, the love which unites the Father and the Son in the work of enlightening and redeeming men (cf. Matt 11:28f.). It

5. See "Authority of Christ" [chapter 7 of this volume].

6. It is fanciful, on account of παρεδόθη, to suppose that Jesus is here contrasting His παράδοσις, which has its starting-point in the Father, with the "traditions" of the elders.

is not necessary, however, to dwell on this: the point is that in this central passage Jesus emphasizes His absolute significance in the two main directions in which it can be understood: He is to God what no other is, and He can therefore do for man what no other can do. He is the only-begotten Son, and the only Mediator between God and man. In preaching Christ in this sense, we have much more to go upon than this single utterance. The truth which it conveys, indeed, is not so much a truth revealed by Christ, as the truth which is embodied in Him; in order to appreciate it, it is necessary to have the experience of coming through Him to the Father, and of recognizing the Father in the Son. The interest of the Fourth Gospel consists to a large extent in this—that it is an expansion and illustration of these words. Jesus is presented there as the Word made flesh—the principle of revelation embodied in a human life; it is His work, so to speak, to enlighten every man, and apart from His work men remain in darkness. "No man hath seen God at any time: the only-begotten Son, who is in the bosom of the Father, he hath declared—or interpreted (ἐξηγήσατο)—him" (John 1:18); "He that hath seen me hath seen the Father" (John 14:9); "I am the way and the truth and the life: no one cometh to the Father but through me" (John 14:6). This is the key to the peculiar passages in the Gospel in which Jesus says ἐγώ εἰμι without any expressed predicate (John 4:26; 8:24; 8:28; 13:19): we are meant to think of Him as the great decisive Personality, who stands in a place which is His alone, and by relation to whom all men finally stand or fall. It may be that the expression given to this in the Fourth Gospel owes something to the writer as well as to Jesus; but what the writer expresses is at least the impression made on him by Jesus, and, as Matthew 11:27 and Mark 13:32 show, the impression is one which answers exactly to Jesus' consciousness of Himself. The words quoted above from John only do justice to Jesus' sense of what He was in relation to God and man, and it is not possible to preach Christ in any adequate sense if we ignore or deny the truth they convey. To do so would be to reject both what Jesus said and what He was in the experience of those who first believed on Him.

6. With the rest of the New Testament in mind, the question is naturally raised at this point, whether Jesus gave any further definition to the idea of mediation than that which we find in this

passage. All men owe to Him the knowledge of God as Father, but how does He impart it? All men must become His debtors if they are to have the benefit of this supreme revelation: is there anything which more than another enables us to estimate the dimensions of this debt? If there is, then in preaching Christ that thing would require to have a corresponding prominence. It is obvious that Jesus mediates the knowledge of God to men, not by His words only, but, as is shown elsewhere,[7] by His being and life as well. It is the Son in whom the Father is revealed, and everything in the Son contributes to the revelation: His teaching, His works, His intercourse with others, His sufferings and death. The revelation is made in and through all these, and none of them can be omitted in preaching Christ. To borrow words of Wellhausen which are not without a misleading element: "His religion is found not only in what He taught publicly, but in His nature and bearing under all circumstances, at home and on the street, in what He said and did not say, in what He did consciously or without being conscious of it, in the way in which He ate and drank and rejoiced and suffered. His Person, with which they had the privilege of intercourse in daily life, made an even deeper impression on His disciples than His teaching."[8] All this is true, but not the whole truth. The New Testament in all its parts lays a quite peculiar emphasis on the death of Christ, and in doing so it is not false to His own conception of the way in which He mediated the knowledge of the Father to men. His death, it may be said, does not require to be interpreted otherwise than His life; it is His life carried to a consistent consummation under the circumstances of the time; it is part of His life, not something distinct from it. This also is true, but, according to the representation in the Gospels, it is less than the whole truth. His death is a part of His life which has an essential relation to His work as the revealer of the Father, and the King in the Kingdom of God; it was recognized by Jesus Himself as divinely necessary, it was the subject of frequent instruction to His disciples, and it is commemorated by His will in the most solemn rite of Christian worship (see Mark 8:31; 9:31; 10:33; 10:45; 14:24 and parallels). It is a fair inference from this, combined with the place taken by the

---

7. [Chapter 7 of this volume.]

8. Wellhausen, *Einleitung in die drei ersten Evangelien*, 114.

passion in the evangelic narratives, and the place given to the interpretation of Christ's death in the Epistles, that to preach Christ it is necessary to represent His death as a main part, or rather as *the* main part, of the cost at which His work of mediation is done. In what particular way it is to be construed is an ulterior question. Our general conception of the moral order of the world, our sense of individuality and of the solidarity of the race, our apprehension of sin as generic, or constitutional, or voluntary, the mental equipment with which we approach the whole subject, may determine us to interpret it in ways which are intellectually distinguishable; no given explanation of the death of Jesus can claim finality any more than any given interpretation of His Person. But just as we may say that Christ is not preached unless the Person of Christ is presented in its absolute significance for religion, as the one Person through whom the knowledge of the Father is mediated to men, so we may say further that Christ is not preached in the sense which answers to His own consciousness of what He was doing, unless it is made clear and central that His mediation necessitated and therefore cost His death. In the simplest words, it is necessary to say, in preaching Christ, not only that He is μονογενής and Mediator, but that He died for men. It was not for Him to insist on this as a doctrine; it was for the Church to apprehend it as a fact, and to put it into doxologies (Rev 1:5; 5:9); but in doing so, it could go back to unmistakable words of Jesus Himself, and to the sacrament which speaks for Him more impressively than any words.

7. Jesus' consciousness of Himself, which, however hard it may be for us to apprehend it, has certainly the character just described—in other words, is a consciousness of His absolute and incomparable significance for all the relations of God and man—must lie at the heart of all preaching of which He is the object. He had this significance while He moved among men on the earth, and it was declared and made unmistakable to His disciples when He rose from the dead. It is on Jesus' consciousness of Himself, therefore, including His consciousness of His vocation, and on His exaltation to God's right hand, that the preaching of Christ rests. As has already been remarked (see §3), the writer of this article assumes that in the Synoptic Gospels we have a representation given of the consciousness of Jesus, on the truth of which we can quite securely proceed. No doubt this has been questioned,

most recently and radically by Wellhausen. The Gospels (to put it concisely) were written by Christians, and Jesus was not a Christian. They contain the gospel, that is, the Christian religion; but He knew nothing about the gospel, although it is put into His lips. He was a Jew. He preached no new faith. He taught men to do the will of God, which like all Jews He found in the Law and the other sacred books. The only difference was that He knew a better way of doing the will of God than that which the scribes of His day enforced on the people, and that He called men to leave their traditions and learn of Him. Wellhausen not only removes from the mind of Christ in this way everything that in Christian preaching has ever been known as gospel, everything that could by any possibility be regarded as contributing to Christology and Soteriology, but the great mass of what up till now has been regarded by criticism as the best attested part of the evangelic record, the words of Jesus common to Matthew and Luke. Most of the parables, too, are sacrificed. Even the few in Mark are not all genuine, and Wellhausen feels free to pass severe strictures alike on those of Matthew and of Luke. All that need be said of this is, that if Jesus had been no more than Wellhausen represents Him to be, then it is inconceivable that either the Gospels or the gospel could ever have been generated from any impulse He could impart to human minds. As Jülicher puts it, the primitive Church is thus made to appear richer, greater, and freer than its Head: in Jerusalem it surpasses Him by producing the marvellous evangelic history, in St. Paul it surpasses Him by producing a new imposing theory of redemption. The historian looks in vain for anything analogous to this elsewhere. We do not understand how it could be done. We do not understand how the Church so suddenly lost the power of doing it. We do not understand how a man like St. Paul, we may say how men like those who wrote all the New Testament books except the Gospels, should have been so incapable of writing a page which reminds us of them. Although it is true to say that truth guarantees only itself, not its author, the truths exhibited by the evangelists have a way of coalescing into a sum of truth which is identical with Jesus. As Deissmann has expressed it,[9] they are not separate pearls threaded on a string,

9. Deissmann, "Evangelium und Urchristentum," 85.

but flashes of the same diamond. Separately they guarantee themselves, but collectively they are a spiritual evidence to the historical reality of the great Person to whom the gospel owes its being, and to whom all preaching is a testimony. There is a kind of criticism which tacitly assumes that it is a mistake to believe in Christ as those who first preached Him believed; He was a Person who appeared in history, and therefore cannot have the absolute significance which must attach to the object of religious faith, and which does attach to Jesus throughout the New Testament. Such criticism makes it its business to reduce this figure to a true scale—which means to make His personality exactly like our own, and His consciousness exactly what our own may be. Wellhausen illustrates the direct application of this criticism to the Gospels; we see how it is brought to bear on the Epistles in such a remark as Wernle's, that a faith in Christ like that of St. Paul (which as good as deified its object) implies a certain want of faith in the living God. The consciousness of God must have decayed or lost its vital intensity in the apostle before he could write the Epistle to the Colossians. Such a writing, we are almost invited to think, is on the way to justify the Jewish sneer: the creed of Christians is that there is no God, but that Jesus is His Son. In the face of criticism of this type, we hold with confidence the trustworthiness of the evangelic representation, and venture to say that no New Testament writer, not even St. Paul or St. John, has anything to say of the absolute significance of Jesus, in all the relations of God and man, which goes beyond Jesus' consciousness of Himself as the Gospels preserve it. And, further, we venture to say that no New Testament writing, however casual or informal, falls short of the testimony which Jesus, according to the evangelists, bears to Himself. Everywhere Jesus has the place which He claims for Himself, and Christians are conscious of an absolute dependence on Him for their standing towards God. To give Him this place is the only way to preach Christ.

8. The earliest specimens of apostolic preaching are the sermons of St. Peter in Acts. Their value is universally acknowledged. According to Schmiedel, "almost the only element that is historically important (in the early chapters of Acts) is the Christology of the speeches of Peter. This, however, is important in the highest degree. . . . It is hardly possible not to believe that this Christology of

the speeches of Peter must have come from a primitive source."[10] It starts with the historical person as such: "Jesus of Nazareth, a man approved of God to you by miracles and portents and signs which God wrought through him, as you yourselves know" (Acts 2:22). This approbation of Jesus by His wonderful works might seem confuted by His death, but to this the apostle has a twofold answer. On the one hand, the death itself was divinely necessary; He was delivered up by the determinate counsel and foreknowledge of God, evidence of which was found in the Scriptures (Acts 2:23; cf. 1 Cor 15:4). On the other hand, it was annulled by the resurrection of Jesus and His exaltation to God's right hand. It was this that made Him both Lord and Christ, and in this character He determined for the apostles and for all men their whole relation to God. To Him they owed already the gift of the Holy Ghost; and, as St. Peter explicitly states elsewhere (Acts 11:15; 11:17; 15:8), to receive the Holy Ghost is to be religiously complete. To His coming they looked for times of refreshing, indeed for the "times of the restoration of all things, whereof God spake by the mouth of his holy prophets that have been from of old" (Acts 3:21). All prophecy, to put it otherwise, is conceived as Messianic; all the hopes which God has inspired are hopes to be fulfilled through Christ. He is Prince of life (Acts 3:15), Lord of all (Acts 10:36), ordained of God as Judge of living and dead (Acts 10:42). Those who repent, believe, and are baptized in His name receive remission of sins and the gift of the Holy Ghost (Acts 2:38; 10:43). All these expressions imply that from the very beginning Jesus had for His disciples that absolute significance which we have seen belonged to His own consciousness of Himself; but in addition to this, it is put with singular force in a passage which expresses nothing else: "There is not salvation in any other: for there is no other name under heaven given among men, whereby we must be saved" (Acts 4:12). It may be possible to strip from the gospel of St. Peter, without detriment to its essence, some of that vesture of eschatological Messianism which it necessarily wore at the time; but it is not possible that religion should be to us what it was to him,—it is not possible, in the original sense of the words, to preach Christ— unless we give to Christ that same significance in all the relations

---

10. Schmiedel, "Acts of the Apostles," 48.

of God and man which He has in St. Peter's preaching. It is not too much to say that side by side with his frank recognition of Jesus as a man (Acts 2:22), whose career in history he could himself look back upon, St. Peter regarded Jesus in His exaltation as forming with God His Father one divine causality at work for the salvation of men. It was only in virtue of so regarding Him that he could preach Him as he did, and essentially similar convictions are still necessary if preaching is to be called preaching *Christ*. It is not necessary to argue that the Christology of the First Epistle of Peter is on a level with this. In many respects it is more explicit. There has been more reflexion on the absolute significance of Jesus in religion, on His relation to the Old Testament, on the power of His resurrection, on the virtue of His passion as connected with redemption from sin, and on the example set in His life and death. But two passages may be briefly referred to as going to the root of the matter. The first is Acts 1:21, where Christians are described as "you who through him [Jesus] are believers in God." It is to Him that Christian faith owes its peculiar qualities and virtues: men may be theists apart from Him, but to have specifically Christian faith in God we must be His debtors. The other is the longer passage, so much discussed, Acts 3:18—4:6. Whatever else this passage reveals, it reveals the writer's conviction that for the dead as well as the living there is no hope of salvation but Christ. Not only in this world, but in all worlds, whatever is called redemption owes its being to Him. All spiritual beings, angels, principalities, and powers, are subject to Him. The Christian is a person who is in Him (Acts 5:14), and accordingly by Him everything in the Christian life is determined. To give Christ this place in our spiritual world, though a different mode of conceiving the world of the spirit may modify the intellectual form in which we do so, is indispensable to preaching Christ. Apart from His holding such a place it is possible only to preach *about* Him, not to make *Him* the sum of our preaching.

9. To pass from St. Peter to St. Paul is to pass from one who had the most vivid personal recollections of the Man Christ Jesus to one who had no such recollections at all; and it is all the more striking to find that both of them preach Christ in the same sense; or, perhaps, we should say, mean the same thing by preaching Christ. St. Paul's acquaintance with Christ began when the Lord

appeared to him on the way to Damascus, and for him Jesus is predominantly the Lord of Glory (1 Cor 2:8). When he preaches Him it is as Lord (2 Cor 4:5); that is, as exalted at God's right hand. To call Him "Lord," to acknowledge His exaltation, is to make the fundamental Christian confession (1 Cor 12:3, Rom 10:9). It is often asserted that whatever differences may have existed between St. Paul and the Jerusalem Church, there can have been no difference of a Christological character; but it is not vital to Christianity that this should be so. It is just as plausible to argue from 2 Corinthians 1:19 that the Corinthians had heard preachers who did not preach Christ precisely as Paul and Silvanus and Timothy did; and the argument might be supported by reference to 2 Corinthians 5:16; 11:4. Further, the fact that St. Paul has something which he calls "my gospel," a conception of Christianity and a mode of presenting it which had peculiarities due to the peculiarity of his religious experience, might be adduced on the same side. And the presumption thus raised could not be overturned simply by an appeal to 1 Corinthians 15:4; 15:11, which would prove only that his gospel rested, exactly as did that of the Twelve, on the great facts of the death and resurrection of Jesus interpreted in the light of Scripture. What it is important to see is that, be the variations in mode of thought or conception what they may, the apostle ascribes to Jesus that absolute significance for religion which we have already seen attach to Him both in His own mind and in the preaching of St. Peter. This is the basis and the content of preaching Christ.

It might seem enough to refer to the salutations of the Epistles, in which St. Paul wishes the Churches grace and peace from God our Father and the Lord Jesus Christ (Rom 1:7), or addresses them as having their being in God the Father and the Lord Jesus Christ (1 Thess 1:1). Here we have the Father and Christ confronting men, so to speak, on the same plane, co-operating as one divine power for their salvation. When St. Paul preaches Christ it is as a Person who has this power and importance, and stands in this relation to God and men. Or we might refer to what perhaps comes closest in form to Jesus' own mode of expression, the passage in 1 Corinthians 15:28, in which "the Son" is used absolutely, as in Mark 13:32. There is a subordination of the Son to the Father here, and yet no more here than in Mark 13:32 or in Matthew 11:27 could we conceive of either word in the plural. Or again, we might refer to such passages as those in which St. Paul contrasts all other persons with Christ. "What is Apollos? what is Paul? Was Paul crucified for you? or were you baptized in the name of Paul?" (1 Cor 3:5; 1:13). This is entirely in the line of the contrast between the many servants and the one beloved Son in Mark 12:1–12, or of the sayings of Jesus in Matthew 23:8–10. Of course both these evangelic passages have been disputed, but the present writer sees no reason to doubt that in substance both are rightly assigned to Jesus. What St. Paul means in the words cited is that any other person has only a relative importance in Christianity, while Christ's importance is absolute. The Church would have missed Paul and Apollos, but it would have been there; whereas but for Christ it could not have been there at all. It existed only *in* Him. This is assumed in all preaching of which He is the object. His significance for the Church is not in the same line with that of Paul and Apollos; it is on the same line with that of the Father. No matter what the mode in which St. Paul conceives of Christ, he always conceives of Him as having this incomparable significance, and it is worth while to note the ways in which it appears.

(*a*) Sometimes they are, so to speak, unstudied: the truth is put, and possibly with emphasis, but there is no particular reflexion upon it. Thus, in 1 Corinthians 3:11 "other foundation can no man lay than that is laid, which is Christ Jesus." This comes very close to Acts 4:11f. (see above). Again, when we read in 2 Corinthians 1:20 "how many soever are the promises of God, in him is the yea," we are confronted with the same truth. There is not a single promise God has made, not a single hope with which He has inspired human hearts, which is to have any fulfilment except in Him. The mental attitude is the same in Galatians 1:8f. The form of St. Paul's arguments is sometimes more disconcerting to us in Galatians than in any other of his Epistles, yet nowhere does he keep closer to the heart of his gospel. What these two seemingly intolerant verses mean is that Christ is the whole of the Christian religion, and that to introduce other things side by side with Him, as if they could supplement Him, or share in His absolute significance for salvation, is treason to Christ Himself. Christ crucified—the whole revelation of God's redeeming love to sinners is there; the sinful soul abandoning itself in unreserved faith to this revelation—the whole of the Christian religion

is there. Whoever brings into religion anything else than Christ
and faith, as though anything else could conceivably stand on the
same plane, is, wittingly or unwittingly, the deadly enemy of the
gospel. Such expressions as these exhibit the absolute significance
which Christ had for the apostle in the most unquestionable way,
but they imply no speculative Christology. We may hold them, and
to preach Christ we must hold them, but we may do so without
raising any of the theological questions which have been raised in
connexion with them. There is hardly a page of St. Paul's writings
which could not be quoted in illustration. Confining ourselves to
the Epistles to the Thessalonians, as his earliest letters, and omit-
ting the salutations referred to above, we find everywhere the absolute dependence of the Christian on Christ,—a kind of relation
which would be not only inconceivable but immoral if any other
than Christ were the subject of it. Just as men in general are said
to live and move and have their being in God, Christians live and
move and have, their being "in Christ." What space is to bodies,
Christ is to believing souls: they live in Him, and all the functions
of their life are determined by Him. St. Paul has confidence *in the
Lord* toward the Thessalonians (2 Thess 3:4); he charges and entreats them *in the Lord Jesus Christ* (2 Thess 3:12); they stand *in the
Lord* (1 Thess 3:8); he gives them commandments *through the Lord
Jesus* (1 Thess 4:2); church rulers are those who are over them *in the
Lord* (1 Thess 5:12); the Christian rule of life is the will of God *in
Christ Jesus* concerning them (1 Thess 5:18); the Christian departed
are the dead *in Christ* (1 Thess 4:16); all benediction is summed up
in the grace of our Lord Jesus Christ (1 Thess 5:28; 2 Thess 1:12;
3:18); Jesus and the Father are co-ordinated as the object of prayer
(1 Thess 3:11), and prayer is directly addressed to the Lord, i.e.,
to Christ (1 Thess 3:12). Our Lord Jesus Christ, through whom we
are to obtain salvation at the great day, is He who died for us, that
whether we wake or sleep we should live together with Him (1
Thess 5:10). It is as though all that God does for us were done in
and through Him; so that He confronts us as Saviour in divine
glory and omnipotence. We may trust Him as God is trusted, live
in Him as we live in God, appeal to Him to save us as only God
can save; and it is only as we do so that we have in Him a Person whom we can preach. Such a Person we can have, as the passages cited show, without raising any of the questions with which

St. Paul himself subsequently wrestled. But the right way to express all this—which does not first appear in Colossians, but is of the essence of Christianity from the beginning—is not to say with Wernle that the consciousness of God has been weakened, but that the idea of God has been Christianized: the Father is known in the Son, and is known as working through Him to the end of our salvation. And this, it need hardly be repeated, is identical in religious import with what we have found in the mind of Christ Himself.

(*b*) Sometimes, however, the apostle presents us with more speculative conceptions of Christ. He is not simply a Person who has appeared in history, and has been exalted in divine power and glory. He is what may be called a universal Person, a typical or representative Person, who has for the new humanity the same kind of significance as Adam had for the old. Adam was the head of the one, Christ is the head of the other. As in Adam all die, so in Christ shall all be made alive. The acts of Christ have a representative or universal character: the death that He died for all has somehow the significance which the death of all would itself have; in His resurrection we see the first-fruits of a new race which shall wear the image of the heavenly. Broadly speaking, this way of conceiving Christ, in which the individual historical Person is elevated or expanded into a universal or representative Person, pervades the Epistles to the Romans, Corinthians, and Galatians (see esp. Rom 5:12ff.; 1 Cor 15:21–49). As these Epistles are central in St. Paul's writings, there is a certain justification for laying this conception of Christ—the second Adam—at the basis of a Pauline Christology (as was done by Somerville in his *St. Paul's Conception of Christ*). It is the conception which lends itself most readily to "mystical" interpretations of Christ's work and of Christian experience. To bear the Christian name we must "identify ourselves" with all the experiences of the Second Adam. But though it is eminently characteristic of St. Paul, it is neither his first nor his last way of representing the absolute significance of Christ. It belongs to the controversial period in which everything Christian was defined by contrast. What St. Paul wanted to annihilate was legalism, the influence of the statutory in religion; and he argues that the really important categories in the religious history of humanity, those of universal and abiding significance, are not law, but sin and grace. The great figures in the history are not Moses, but Adam and Christ. He works out the parallel or rather the contrast between them with enthusiasm; but when we realize what he is doing, we feel that this is only one way of giving Christ His peculiar place. It is, however, a way which will maintain itself as long as the antithesis of sin and grace determines the religious life; and as this is a limit beyond which we cannot see, it seems involved in any adequate preaching of Christ that He should be preached in this universal character as the head of a new humanity.

(c) In his later Epistles, St. Paul preaches Christ in what seems a more wonderful light. Christ is presented to us not merely as a historical, or as a universal, but also as an eternal or divine Person. That which is manifested to the world in Him does not originate with its manifestation. The explanation of it is not to be sought merely in the history of Israel (as though Jesus were no more than a national Messiah), nor even in the history of humanity (as though He were no more than the restorer of the ruin which began with Adam): it is to be sought in the eternal being of God. When St. Paul came in contact with Jesus, he came in contact with what he felt instinctively was the ultimate reality in the universe. Here, he could not but be conscious, is the Alpha and the Omega, the beginning and the end, all that is meant—all that has ever been meant—by "God." Here is "all the fulness of the Godhead bodily" (Col 1:19; 2:9); here is the revelation of what God essentially and eternally is, and here therefore is that by which all our thinking must be ruled. Christ belongs to, or is involved in, because He is the manifestation of, the eternal being and nature of God. How far does this carry us when we try to think it out? Possibly not further, in some respects, than we have come already. Christ, it may be said, is represented as an eternal Person when He is spoken of as *final Judge of all* (Acts 10:42; 2 Cor 5:10); that is eternity as apprehended in *conscience*. Again, He is represented as an eternal Person when we speak of Him as *final Heir* or *Lord of all things* (Heb 1:2; Matt 28:18); that is eternity as apprehended in *imagination*. But in Colossians it is not through the conscience or the imagination, but through a more *speculative faculty*, that St. Paul interprets his conception of the eternal being of Christ. If Christ really has the absolute significance which all Christian experience implies,—for in all such experience we meet with *God* in Him,—then *all things* must be defined by relation to Christ; the universe must be reconstituted with Him as its principle, its centre of unity, its goal. Nature must be conceived as an order of things brought into being with a view to His Kingdom, and this implies that He was present in the constitution of nature. To say that He was ideally but not actually present,— present only in the mind of God as the intended consummation of the process,—would have been to St. Paul to introduce a distinction which we have no means of applying where God is concerned. The true doctrine of Christ—this is what St. Paul teaches in Colossians—involves a doctrine of the universe. The doctrine of the universe is put only negatively, or so as to exclude error, when we say that God created all things out of nothing; such a formula teaches only the absolute dependence of nature on God. But it is put positively, or so as to convey the truth in which the world is interested, when we say that all things were created in Christ. St. Paul's conviction of this truth is based (he believes) on experience: in his consciousness as a Christian man he is assured that in Christ he has touched the last reality in the universe, the *ens realissimum*, the truth through which all other truths are to be defined and understood. In other words, a true apprehension of the absolute significance of Christ involves a specifically Christian conception of the universe. The Christian religion is not true to Christ (as St. Paul understood His significance) unless it has the courage to conceive a Christian metaphysic, or, in simpler words, *to Christianize all its thoughts of God and the world*. Put in this form, we can see that in the last resort it is still necessary to share the apostle's convictions at this point if we mean to preach Christ. For if there is any region of reality which does not depend for its meaning and value on its relation to Him,—if the truth with which we come in contact in Him is not the ultimate truth of God, the master light of all our seeing,—then His importance is only relative, and He has no abiding place in religion which requires that He should be preached at all. But in reality He is a Person so great that all nature and history and religion have to be interpreted through Him. All we call being, and all we call redemption, need Him to explain them. The love revealed in Him is the key to all mysteries. The categories we use to make His redemption intelligible are the only categories by which we can completely understand anything. Once Christ's absolute significance has become clear to us,—and, as already said, it is involved in every Christian experience,—we discover that our task, if we would understand the system of things in which we live, is not to find natural law in the spiritual world, but rather to find spiritual law—indeed, specifically Christian law—in the natural world. So far as we do so we are providing scientific attestation for the conception of Christ as a divine and eternal Person.

10. The Epistle to the Hebrews and the Fourth Gospel, it need hardly be added, share in this conception of Christ. In neither is it allowed to infringe on the truth of His human nature while He lived on earth: indeed, of all the New Testament writings, these two in various ways make most use of Christ's humanity for religions and moral ends. But as the subject of this article is not Christology, it is not necessary to go into details. The prologue to the Fourth Gospel has precisely the same Christian experience behind it as the first chapter of Colossians, and the same experience, when taken seriously, will always inspire the mind to think along the same lines. The conception of the Logos, as has often been remarked, is not carried by the writer beyond the prologue: it may in reality affect the evangelist's way of representing certain things, but it is not formally embodied in the Gospel. It was a conception widely current in the writer's time, whatever its sources, and he used it to introduce Jesus in circles which naturally thought in such terms. It does not follow that to introduce or to explain Christ among men who think in other categories, the preacher is still bound to make use of this one. "There is only one thing," says Dr. Sanday, "that he [the evangelist] seeks. He wants a formula to express the cosmical significance of the person of Christ."[11] That in which we must agree with him if we in turn would preach Christ, is his conviction of this significance, not the formula in which it suited him at the close of the first century to express it. That like Paul he *had* such a conviction, based on experience, there is no doubt. The Son of God was not to St. John a lay figure to be draped in the borrowed robes either of Messianic dogmatic or of Alexandrian philosophy. He was a Being so great, and had left on the soul of His witness an impression so deep, that the latter felt it could be satisfied by nothing but a reconstitution of his universe in

11. Sanday, *The Criticism of the Fourth Gospel*, 198.

which this wonderful Person was put at the heart of everything—creation, providence, revelation, and redemption being all referred to Him. In St. John as in St. Paul the absolute significance of Christ in the relations of God and man, which is the immediate certainty of Christian experience, stamps Him as a divine and eternal Person, by relation to whom the world and all that is in it must be described anew. We may say if we will that he uses the Logos as a formula to describe the cosmical significance of Christ, but that is perhaps less than the truth. He uses it rather to suggest that truth, as truth is in Jesus, is the deepest truth of all, and the most comprehensive, and that under its inspiration and guidance we must Christianize all our conceptions of God, nature, and history. He who is not in sympathy with this conviction will not find it easy to preach Christ in any sense in which the New Testament will support him.

11. If, however, we are in sympathy with this conviction, it may fairly be argued that we can preach Christ without raising any further questions. We must find the absolute significance of Jesus in the area within which Jesus presented Himself to men, "beginning from the baptism of John until the day when he was taken up" (Acts 1:22). This was the basis on which the gospel was launched into history, faith evoked, and the Church founded. This was the gospel of the original apostolic testimony, and it is within its limits that the power of Christ must be felt. Once we do recognize this power, and its incomparable and unique significance, we are prepared to let our minds go further, and to appreciate at its true value what the apostles and evangelists tell us of such things as the preexistence of Christ and the condescension of His entrance into the world. But these can never be the first things in preaching Christ. To put them first is really to put stumbling-blocks in the way of faith. Faith is evoked by seeing Jesus and hearing Him, and we see and hear Him only within the range indicated above. It is only faith, too, that preaches; preaching is faith's testimony to Christ. Hence, although faith must amount to a conviction of Christ's absolute significance, it must find the basis of this conviction in the historical Saviour, and it is only by appeal to the historical Saviour that it can reproduce itself in others. Accordingly it may exist and may render effective testimony to Christ without raising questions that carry us beyond this area. How we are to think of the

superhistorical relation to God of the Person whose absolute significance we recognize in history, how we are to think of what is
usually called His pre-existence, and of the marvel of His entrance
into the world of nature and of history: these are questions which
faith's conviction as to Christ's significance will dispose us to face
in a certain spirit rather than another, but they are not questions
on which the existence of the gospel, or the possibility of faith, or
of preaching Christ, is dependent. With such faculties as we have,
and especially such an inability to make clear to ourselves what
we mean by the relation of the temporal to the eternal,—a relation which is involved in all such questions,—it may even be that
we recognize our inability to grasp truth about them in forms for
which we can challenge the assent of others. We can be certain
from Christ's life that His very presence in the world is the assurance of an extraordinary condescension and grace in God, even if
we are baffled in trying to think out all that is involved either in
His coming forth from the Father or in His entrance into humanity.
But if on the basis of an experience evoked by the apostolic testimony we can call Him Lord and Saviour, recognizing in Him the
only-begotten Son through whom alone we are brought to the Father, then we can preach Him, be our ignorance otherwise as deep
as it may be.

12. It might have seemed natural, in the discussion of such a
question, to refer more directly to the various *criteria* of Christianity which the New Testament itself suggests, e.g., Romans 10:9, 1
John 4:2f. But the last of these two passages only emphasizes the
historical character of Christianity, the truth of our Lord's manhood, and the first the exaltation of Jesus: and to both of these justice has been done. The combination of the two is indeed required
in preaching Christ, and it is all that is required. The reality of Jesus' life on earth as He Himself was conscious of it, the life of One
uniquely related to God, and present in our world to make us all
His debtors for revelation and redemption; and the exaltation of
such a One to the right hand of God: it is on this that preaching
Christ depends. Into this we can put all the convictions by which
the New Testament writers were inspired, and all that we know
of the words and deeds of Jesus: and while we share at the heart
the faith of apostles and evangelists, we do not feel bound by all
the forms in which they cast their thoughts. The faith which stim-

ulated intelligence so wonderfully in them will have the same effect on all Christians, and they will not disown any who call Jesus Lord, and give Him the name which is above every name.

# 12

# Elemental Religion

"O Lord, thou hast searched me and known me."—
Psalm 139:1.

I once heard a well-known man, speaking of difficulties in the Bible, express himself between jest and earnest in this fashion: "The Gospels are a story, and a story may conceivably be untrue; the epistles are arguments, and arguments may conceivably be unsound; but the Psalms are the immediate reflection of personal experiences, and we can take them as they stand without asking any questions." Certainly that is true of the 139th Psalm, which even in the Psalter has an eminence of its own, and brings us into contact with elemental religion, with the soul's direct and overwhelming experience of God. None of us could have written it, but there is none of us in whom there is not an echo to its sublime and solemn utterance; and that echo is the Spirit of God, bearing witness by and with His word in our hearts.

The Psalm has four strophes, each of six verses; and in each of the four an essential aspect or element in the soul's experience of God absorbs the mind of the writer. It will repay us if in following his thought his experience in any degree becomes ours.

1. First, he is overpowered by the experience of God's perfect knowledge of him.

We are apt to speak in this connexion of God's omniscience, but there is nothing about omniscience in the Psalm. Omniscience is an abstract noun, and abstract nouns are unequal to the intense feeling of the passage. The important thing in religion is not the belief that God is omniscient, but the experience that God knows me, and it is on this the Psalmist dwells. It is almost implied in

173

the connexion of his words that in the heart of the writer there was a kind of passive resistance to this experience, a resistance which God's Spirit overcame, piercing and discovering all his inner life. We are slow to know ourselves, and sometimes do not wish to; purposes form in the background of our minds, of which we are hardly conscious; latent motives actuate us; perhaps our own words or deeds, in which they suddenly issue, startle us; we are amazed that we should have said or done such a thing. But it is no surprise to Him. "Thou understandest my thought afar off." Such knowledge of man by God is quite different from omniscience. Omniscience is a divine attribute, but what is here experienced is a divine action—it is God through His searching knowledge of us entering with power into our lives. It is God besetting us behind and before, and laying His hand upon us. The Psalmist does not dwell particularly on the divine motive, so to speak, in this searching of man. It might be felt as the shadowing of the soul by an enemy, or as the over-shadowing presence of a friend. The one thing on which he does dwell is its reality and its completeness. It is too wonderful for him; it baffles him when he tries to understand it; but incomprehensible as it is, it is real. He only knows himself as he is conscious of being searched and known by God.

I suppose most of us have wrestled with arguments intended to prove the existence or the personality of God. Well, I am not going to raise any philosophical question about the powers or the incapacities of human reasoning in this matter. No religion ever took its origin in such reasoning, however it may have succeeded or been baffled in trying to justify itself at reason's bar. The being and the personality of God, so far as there is any religious interest in them, are not to be *proved* by arguments; they are to be *experienced* in the kind of experience here described. The man who can say, *O Lord, Thou hast searched me and known me*, does not need any arguments to prove that God is, and that He is a person, and that He has an intimate and importunate interest in his life. If that is a real experience—as who will deny that it is?—and if it is not a morbid phenomenon, but one which is sane and normal, then the *thou* in it is just as real as the *me*. The Psalmist is as certain of God as he is of his own existence; indeed it is not too much to say that it is only as he is conscious of being searched and known by God—only as he is overwhelmed by contact with a Spirit which knows him better than he knows himself —that he rises to any adequate sense of what his own being and personality mean. He is revealed to himself by God's search; he knows himself through God. Speaking practically—and in religion everything is practical—God alone can overcome atheism, and this is how He overcomes it. He does not put arguments within our reach which point to theistic conclusions; He gives us the experience which makes this Psalm intelligible, and forces us also to cry, O Lord, Thou hast searched me and known me. "After that ye have known God," says St. Paul to the Galatians, "or rather"—correcting himself—"have been known by God." Yes, it is the overpowering sense that we are known through and through by another which seals upon our hearts that knowledge of God on which religion rests.

2. The second strophe of the Psalm deals with another aspect or element in the writer's experience of God. There is indeed something unreal in calling it another, for all experiences of God are interdependent. Still, it inspires the Psalmist anew; his soul, which has sunk exhausted under the thought of God's absolute knowledge of him, rallies itself to speak of God's wonderful and inevitable presence with him. And here again we should take care not to lose ourselves and the profit of this high experience by speaking of God's omnipresence. No doubt if we were constructing a doctrine of God, we should have need and room for such a term; but in religion the important thing is not the idea that God is everywhere, but the experience that wherever I am God is with me. "Whither shall I go from Thy Spirit, or whither shall I flee from Thy presence?" Why, it may be asked, should we want to go anywhere? Why should we try to escape from God? The answer does not need to be given, because every one can give it for himself. The first man tried to hide from God, and so have all his children, but always in vain. Wilful boys try, experimenting with their new-found liberty, and God makes His presence felt through all their riot. Worldly men try, absorbed in affairs they had rather keep to themselves, renouncing church and sabbath, Bible and reflexion; but when they least expect it, a light or a shadow falls on their path, and they know that God is there; sensual men try it in dissipation, and desperate men even in death; but there is no height nor depth nor distance nor darkness that can shut Him out of our life. As St. Augustine says, the only way to flee from God is

to flee to Him. The voice which says in our hearts, Where art thou? is not meant to drive us from Him, but to make us conscious of His presence, and to urge us to turn consciously to Him. There is only one thing which can really separate us from God, and that is a secret. A secret always divides. It divides more in proportion as the relation which it annuls is close. It may divide fatally husband and wife; it divides fatally the soul and God, raising an invisible but insuperable wall between them, and keeping us far from Him even while He is intimately near to us. Do not cut yourself off from God by any unconfessed sin, by any unavowed hope, by anything that makes you restrain prayer or try to avoid His presence. It is not far to seek and to find Him. He is near to all that call upon Him in truth. To find His presence not a dread but an inspiration, He asks nothing of us but that we should walk in the light as He is in the light, and have no secrets from Him.

3. The third strophe of the Psalm, the third element in the Psalmist's experience of God, seems at the first glance to be of a different character, yet it is closely connected with what precedes. Observe how it is linked on by *for*. "For Thou hast formed my reins: Thou hast knit me together in my mother's womb." Here, it may be said, we are not dealing with immediate experience; there is an element of inference in the writer's conviction which is introduced by the *for*. God is at first, so to speak, an observer, and then a companion; but what is implied in an observer so searching, in a companion so close and inseparable? To the mind of the Psalmist what is implied is that his very being has its ground in God, and that the whole marvel and mystery of what he is go back to Him. If it were not so, God could not have the knowledge of him or the nearness to him by which he is so deeply impressed. At first he thinks of himself as an inhabitant of the moral world, and there God is an awful observer, an inevitable presence; now he thinks of himself as a native of what we call the physical universe, only to realize that there also the presence and action of God are as pervasive as in the higher sphere. It is not exaggerating or misrepresenting him if we say that the truth to which expression is given in the third section of the Psalm is the truth that the physical and the moral worlds, as we call them, are one in God—that He whose moral sovereignty has been so deeply felt and so wonderfully described in the world of conscious life is

the author of nature too—and that nature and human nature, in each individual human being, through all variations of condition and circumstance, are determined by Him and are continually in His hand. "My frame was not hidden from Thee when I was made in secret . . . in Thy book were they all written, even the days which were ordained, when as yet there was none of them." In all that we are, in the very frame and texture of our being; in all that befalls us, in the length of our life and its vicissitudes, we are absolutely dependent on God. That in a manner explains how we can have the wonderful experiences of God before described; only the author of our being could have such a close and unremitting interest in us.

There are few things more to be desired at the present moment than the power to realize this truth. Partly we have got into the habit of defining the physical and the moral worlds simply by contrast with each other, as if we had not to live at the same time in both, and as if that did not imply their ultimate unity; and partly we are accustomed to appeal to the lower against the higher. How, a man asks, can I, a creature with such a nature, face a spiritual calling? How can I ever be anything but what I am? There is no proportion between the constitution which nature has given me and the vocation with which God summons me. Or the same thing is said about circumstances. How can anyone born in the conditions in which I was, and compelled to live in the environment in which I live, be anything but the miserable creature you see? These are dangerous things to say. No one ever says them for himself with quite a good conscience, and their moral unsoundness is shown by the fact that the compassion for others which they inspire turns only too easily into contempt. Surely the Psalmist has the deep truth in his grasp when he reminds us that God is not only intimately with us in our moral life, but that He is in and behind our nature and our circumstances—that He fashioned us in the womb and that all our days were written in His book—that He commits us to no conflict in which He does not stand behind us—that no nature is so disabled, no circumstances so disabling, as to shut a man out from the care and the providence of his Maker. One of the striking things in the Psalm is the tone in which the writer speaks of this at the close of this strophe. The omniscience and omnipresence of God, as they come home to the individual conscience in the moral world, have something oppressive in them; they awe and overwhelm us; but as resting on God's creation of us, and His providential ordering of our lives, they are transfigured with tenderness; the Psalmist is not haunted by God, but abandons himself with joy to His care. "How precious also are Thy thoughts unto me, O God; how great is the sum of them! If I should count them, they are more in number than the sand; when I awake, I am still with Thee." No doubt these words repeat in a new connexion what has been already said in the first section—"such knowledge is too wonderful for me; it is high, I cannot attain unto it"—but they contain something more. They are an echo of the touching words in the 103rd Psalm: "Like as a father pitieth his children, the Lord pitieth them that fear Him"; they are an anticipation of St. Peter's words in the New Testament—"Commit your souls to Him in well doing as to a faithful Creator." Whoever betrays us, our Creator will not. With all its disabilities and limitations, and in spite of all its corruptions, human nature is dear to its author. "I will give thanks unto Thee, for I am awfully and wonderfully made; wonderful are Thy works, and that my soul knoweth right well." It is only when we shut God out of nature—as no one can do who has had in his nature the experience out of which man cries, O Lord, Thou hast searched me and known me—that we can look on it in ourselves or others with contempt or despair. For the human creature to know the faithful Creator is to know that he has not been made in vain, and to be assured that through whatever conflicts he can rise and live in a world where inspired utterances like those of this Psalm will fall upon his ear through nature and awaken echoes in his inmost soul.

4. And now we come to the last strophe of the Psalm. I have spoken of all the others as expressing some aspect or element of religion in its simplest and deepest form—as uttering the soul's fundamental experiences of God—but can we say the same of this? or does it not carry us into another world when we read: "Oh that thou wouldest slay the wicked, God! Depart from me, therefore, ye bloodthirsty men. Do not I hate them, O Lord, that hate Thee, and do not I loathe them that rise up against Thee? I hate them with perfect hatred, I count them mine enemies." How, it may be asked, can a soul which has been flooded with the consciousness of God, of His intimate nearness, of His all penetrating love, how can such

a soul be overcome by such a temper? Surely these are not pious prayers; but savage and inhuman, a melancholy illustration of the inconsistencies which lower human nature even at its height.

I cannot think that in a mind so great as that of the writer of this Psalm—and one might even say in a work of art so perfect—there should be an unprovoked and sudden lapse into mere inconsistency. There must be a connexion in thought between these passionate words and what precedes, and I believe it is not hard to find. The Psalmist has been dwelling on what I have called the unity of the natural and the moral worlds, the truth that God is behind both, that it is the same power which speaks in conscience, revealing man to himself, and which originates and sustains that physical being in which man lives his moral life. These are real truths and experiences, and religion depends for its very being on the recognition of them. But it is possible to recognize them in a way which is fatal to religion. It is possible to lose in the sense of the unity of nature and the moral life as alike dependent on God the sense of the vital differences with which they confront us. It is possible to become insensible to the fact that God is not only the source of all being, but of the distinction between good and evil, and that to assert the distinction is as essential to religion as to assert the unity of God and the dependence of all things on Him. Christ, says a French writer, has two great enemies, the God Priapus and the God Pan, and the latter is the more impracticable of the two. The most dangerous enemy of religion is the mood in which all the differences in the world seem to become unreal in face of the unity of God. The difference between nature and spirit, between the personal and the impersonal, between freedom and necessity, between what we are born and what we make of ourselves, between corporate responsibility and the responsibility of the individual—the difference in the last resort of right and wrong—all these are relative, evanescent, never to be fixed; they dissolve, when we try to grasp them, in a kind of moral or non-moral haze. This is the supreme illustration of the truth that the corruption of the best is worst; for there is no better or more inspiring truth than that of the dependence of all being, natural and moral, upon God; and no error more deadly or degrading than that to God all things are alike. It is against the temptation to let the truth which he has just recognized in such moving words sink into this deadly falsehood that the soul of the Psalmist reacts with instinctive and passionate vehemence. He knows that the world and every human being in it are absolutely dependent upon God; but he knows also that what is going on in the world is a battle, and that it is the Lord's battle, and that it is vital to be on the Lord's side. No doubt the passion with which he casts himself into the battle is less than Christian passion. He is ready to kill in the battle, and perhaps not ready to die. But in the Lord's battle the sign under which we conquer is the cross. It is not by shedding the blood of others, but by the sacrifice of our own life, that we can contribute to the Lord's victory. But where the Psalmist is right, and where we must not fall beneath his insight, is in the clear perception that the reality of religion involves conflict—that what is going on among men in the world is a battle in which the cause of God is at stake—a battle, and not a sham fight. God is not in the same sense on both sides. It is not a game of draughts in which the same hand moves the blacks and the whites. It is a matter of life and death, and the Psalmist is *in* it for life or death, with his whole heart. So must every one be who would prove what the presence of God in life means. The cross of Christ, where He died for the difference between right and wrong, and declared it to be as real as His agony and passion, teaches the same truth as the vehement Psalmist, and makes the same appeal. "Who is on the Lord's side?" it calls to us as we look out upon life. And it is only as we enlist under that ensign, and commit ourselves to fight the good fight to the last, that we can share in the experiences which inspired this wonderful Psalm.

There is something peculiarly touching in the closing lines. "Search me, O God, and know my heart; try me, and know my thoughts; and see if there be any wicked way in me, and lead me in the way everlasting." It is as if the Psalmist shrank suddenly from his own impetuosity, felt his rashness in judging others, and realized that it is easier to slay the wicked than to be inwardly separated from sin. In this humbler mood he does not shrink from God's eye, but longs for it. He feels that for God to take knowledge of him is his hope. Salvation does not come from his zeal, but from the Lord, who knows him altogether. It is exactly in the key in which the Samaritan woman speaks of Jesus: "Come, see a man which told me all things that ever I did; is not this the Christ?" It is only one who knows us better than we know ourselves who can give us the life which is life indeed.

# 13

# Man's Claims in Religion, and God's Response

"Jews ask for signs, and Greeks seek after wisdom: but
we preach Christ crucified . . . Christ the power of
God and the wisdom of God."—1 Cor 1:22–24

Many men, many minds, says the proverb, and there is no de-
partment of human affairs in which it is more true than the spiritual. It is not, as it has been sceptically put, that everyone con-
structs his own *roman de l'infini* to suit his taste, but that men who
are quite serious have their own ideas of what religion ought to
be. They know what they want it to do for them, and they think
they know the proper kind of evidence by which it ought to be
supported. If it does not meet the conditions they prescribe, they
feel at liberty to withhold their assent from it. This is not done with
any sense of arrogance, but naturally and as a matter of course. If
religion does not meet our needs, if it does not come supported by
what we regard as the indispensable evidence, how can we have
anything to do with it? It does not occur to those who think thus,
that they are prescribing to God the manner in which He shall
make Himself known, or giving Him notice of the only terms on
which they will recognize Him. Yet this is what it amounts to. And
while in all such operations of the mind man's need of God is attested, there may quite possibly be something in them which God
cannot meet in the way required.

In his work as a preacher of the gospel, Paul encountered many
types of mind, and in this text he describes the two chief. "Jews
claim signs, and Greeks are in quest of wisdom". The very form
of the sentence shows that Jews and Greeks are to be taken, not in
their nationality, but as representative of intellectual types; and it

is because such types survive among ourselves that we can make a profitable application of the words.

1. *Jews claim signs.*—For them the evidence of religion was to be given in works of power. They would not believe in God unless He appealed to their senses by doing something extraordinary—something which He was not doing meanwhile. We know how constantly this demand was made upon our Lord. It was a temptation which beset Him from the very beginning of His ministry. If He had cast Himself down from the pinnacle of the temple He would have provided the kind of evidence for His mission that some people required. Show us a sign from Heaven, they said to Him again and again. Even in His agony they taunted Him with His inability to produce that proof that He was from God which they were entitled to claim. "If He be the King of Israel let Him now come down from the cross, and we will believe Him." The modern equivalent of all this is commoner than many people think. When Carlyle said of God, the God in whom Christians believe, "He *does* nothing," he gave expression to precisely this mental temper. It is the temper of all to whom it is a religious difficulty that there is a constitution and course of nature and of human life in which things go on according to general laws, and in which there is much that is baffling, mysterious, and unjust. If we are to believe in God, they say, let Him do something. Let Him *signalize* His presence in the world by wonderful works of power. "We see not our signs." Let Him make bare His holy arm; let Him break the oppressor in pieces, heal the terrible diseases that fill us with fear and humiliation, interpose visibly and decisively to arrest wrong; let Him satisfy this natural and legitimate demand for an exhibition of His power, and we will believe in Him. But apparently He does not do so. As far as such signal demonstrations are concerned, all things go on as they have done since the beginning of the creation. Some people call this a trial to faith; others describe it as an objection to religion; but there it is. God does not accept the dictation of the Jew in us as to the way in which He is to make Himself known.

2. *Greeks seek after wisdom.*—As distinct from natures which crave a demonstration of power, there are those which long for nothing so much as a key to the world and to the life of man. This is what they want in religion, and they will not look at anything

as religion which does not put such a key into their hands. The Greeks are a type of this class. They are the most intellectual people known to history. We owe to them all that we call philosophy and science. They believed in the mind, in its powers, its duties, its right to be sincerely dealt with and to have its legitimate demands met. Even in religion they sought intellectual satisfaction. They wanted its preachers to have excellency of speech and of wisdom. They required of religion itself to give them an intellectual grasp of the world in which they lived, an intelligible interpretation of it; what was it good for if it did not do so, justifying the ways of God to man, solving the problems which vexed both brain and conscience, reconciling man intellectually to his environment? It hardly needs to be stated that this type of mind is common enough. It is represented more or less adequately by every one who has what are called intellectual difficulties about religion. A poet of our own day speaks about the burden and the mystery of all this unintelligible world, and what many really crave in religion is such a light upon its nature and destiny as will alleviate the burden and dissipate the mystery. A religion that does not bring such a light, that does not yield a rational explanation of nature and of human life, is not for them. Perhaps the most signal illustration of this is that great estrangement from the Christian faith commonly known as Agnosticism. The Agnostic is a man who has been baffled in the Greek quest for wisdom, and has given up religion as the sphere of insoluble problems. He is a Greek, with a natural instinct for wisdom, which disappointment has paralyzed. He no longer *seeks* wisdom; he has abandoned such vain adventures; he stays at home and realizes, with such resignation as he can command, how poorly the house is furnished. God does not meet his claim, any more than that of the Jew, in the way which he prescribes. There may be a key to all mysteries, but it is not put in his hand to start with.

This apparently negative attitude of the gospel to the claims of Jew and Greek has, I believe, misled many. The impression left on their minds is that the true religion has nothing to do with signs or with wisdom: it reveals a God to whom miracles and philosophy are alike indifferent. He does not signalize His presence by works of power; He does not cast an interpretative light on the mystery of the world. But this is a mistake, due to breaking off

in the middle of the apostle's sentence. The demands of the Jew
and of the Greek are in a sense just, and a true religion must be
able to meet them. There must be power in God, and therefore in
the true religion; there must be wisdom in God, and therefore the
true religion must have a key to the world, a way of looking at
life in which the mind can rest. These are not presumptuous but
legitimate demands, and the apostle does not repel them: the very
claim he makes for his gospel is that it meets them. It meets them
indeed in a way so startling as to be at first sight almost incredible,
but it does meet them. "We preach Christ crucified . . . Christ *the
power* of God and *the wisdom* of God"—the very thing which Jews
and Greeks required. Jews claim signs? Well, if you want to see all
that God can do, the supreme demonstration of His power, look at
Christ on His cross, and at what God accomplishes through Him.
Greeks are in quest of wisdom? Once more, if you want to find the
key to the world's perplexities, to see the very splendour of the
light with which God lightens up its gloomiest and most oppressive mysteries, look at Christ on His cross. The one heart-breaking
and hopeless mystery of life is sin; the one thing in presence of
which it vanishes is redeeming love, the love revealed in the crucified Son of God. Man's claim upon God for a demonstration of
power and wisdom is not repelled; it is fully met and satisfied—
but at the cross.

No doubt it is very difficult to take this in, and it was probably
more difficult for those who could distinctly envisage crucifixion
and its horrors than it is for us. Crucifixion was public execution,
the shameful death of the lowest criminals. The Jewish name of
contempt for Jesus was "the hanged". But the repulsiveness has
been felt under all circumstances, and the temptation has often
come to the church to ignore or to spiritualize what the apostle
here puts into the forefront as God's answer to man's need—the
real person, and the real and shameful death of Christ, recorded
in the Gospels. One of the purposes served by the Lord's supper,
which we celebrate to-day, is to provide a check to such tendencies.
At first sight it seems strange to find this material element, so to
speak, in a spiritual religion. It is so inconsistent, apparently, with
the worship of God in spirit and in truth, that some Christians
like the Quakers disregard it, and many in all the churches are
embarrassed by it, and even when they observe it do not know

what to think of it, and could wish they did not need to think of it at all. But in any case it does this for us: it brings us back whether we will or not to the heart of the revelation on which our religion rests: Christ crucified. As often as we eat this bread and drink this cup we show the Lord's death. We are withdrawn from all our prepossessions about God, from all the requirements we address to Him, from all our preconceptions as to the way in which He must or ought to act, and are set down before the reality which shows us how it has actually pleased Him to display His power and His wisdom to men. Here, however startling it may be, is the seat of God's omnipotence; here and nowhere else is the key to all that is mysterious in life.

We must notice that the power is uniformly put first: it is of it that we first have experience, and it is only through it that we have access to the wisdom. You want an almighty God, the apostle says. Where then can you find God exerting omnipotent power, doing what it baffles every other power in the universe to do, except here? If a child were asked to point to the signs of God's power, he might naturally think of the storm which tosses the sea and the ships; or of the earthquake which levels cities in a moment and engulfs the pride of man; or of the lightning flash which shatters trees and towers. Those who are no longer children know better than this even about the forces of nature. They know that the fiercest storm which ever swept the ocean has no power in it at all compared with the silent irresistible swell of the tide. They know that the earthquakes which appalled the world at Lisbon and Messina were insignificant forces compared with the invisible pull of the sun which holds the planets in their orbits. They know that no thunderbolt has potency in it to compare with the sunshine in which we bask on a summer morning. And they know also, if they know anything of themselves and their necessities, that God has more wonderful and difficult things to do than can be done by storm or tide, by earthquake or gravitation, by lightning or sunshine. He has to make bad men good. He has to win again those who have been alienated from him by an evil life. He has to reach their hearts through a bad conscience, and without weakening conscience, nay while vindicating all its claims, He has to prevail with them to come to Himself. He has to overcome the distrust and fear of men, and to evoke their confidence. He has to subdue them to penitence, to faith, to devotion. He has to do this not for one, but for all; He has to reconcile the world to Himself. It needs an inconceivable power to do that—a power far more wonderful than any that could be exerted through nature, whether in mercy or in wrath. To fill men's hearts with food and gladness would not do it; to blight them with pestilence and famine would not do it. But God does it through Christ crucified. There, at the cross, he wields a power far more wonderful than any of which the Jews dreamed—a supernatural power transcending everything that could have been displayed in such signs as they claimed—an unmistakable, immeasurable, divine power: a final guarantee of the presence of God.

Paul knew this from his experience as a preacher, and it was because he knew it he magnified his calling. "I am not ashamed of the gospel, for it is a divine power to save all who believe." He had seen its efficacy, when he wrote to the Corinthians, through a ministry of more than twenty years. We have entered now on the twentieth Christian century, and as we look back on that long stretch of time we can say that the supreme power in the world for good from the beginning of it till this day has been the power of Christ crucified. All reconciling, regenerating, healing influences which have blessed the world have had their seat and centre in the cross. And is it not possible for us to add our individual testimony to the great testimony borne by history? When *we* are bad—when we are selfish, angry, indolent, indulgent, ungodly—can we keep it up in the presence of Christ crucified? Or if we are determined to keep it up, must we not shut our eyes to this great sight, or go to some place where it sinks below the horizon? To give it the opportunity of telling upon us—to expose ourselves to the power which issues from it—is to give it the victory. This is what we profess to-day as we gather round the Lord's Table. We long to be better men and women, to get dominion over our sins, to be thoroughly right with God. We long for truer penitence, for more whole-hearted, loving, devoted obedience to God. Where in all the world is the divine power to be found which can work these miracles in us? It is to be found—this is the very meaning of the supper—in Christ crucified. Our one hope for all this is that He may become dominant in us, establishing His ascendency in our hearts. The power of God to save, the highest and divinest power God can exercise, is the power manifested in His passion and operating through it. The Lord reigns from the tree. This is the paradoxical but sufficient answer of God to all who ask signs. He is working wonders all the time which transcend any of which nature could be the scene; and to them, the miracles wrought by the passion of Jesus, the final appeal lies.

Let us look now at the gospel as God's response to those who seek wisdom: Christ crucified . . . the wisdom of God. Wisdom is always a hard word, and perhaps it is not possible for us to be sure of what precisely it meant to the apostle. But we know in what direction to look for the meaning. We know generally that wisdom is that which enables us to recognize the end if not the plan of life—that it is that which brings light to its mysteries, and even in our dark strivings makes us conscious of the right way. The great mystery of life, in presence of which the others hardly count, is sin. This is the one thing which after all speculation remains opaque and impenetrable. No reason can cast the faintest gleam of real light upon it. Those who explain it as a mere negation, an unreality—those who regard it simply as an imperfection, and to be outgrown—those who tell us it is but good in the making, and that a bad conscience is the growing pains of the soul—are all alike, when the conscience listens to them, madmen. It is they who are unreal, and whose ingenuities appal by their frivolity and irrelevance the soul which is actually at grips with evil. But though no philosophy as such has ever been able to rationalize sin, though in a world created and sustained by a good God it is and remains an enigma to the mind, at the cross some light falls upon it: we see that whatever its origin, God takes the burden of it on Himself. He does not stand afar off, and decline to have anything to do with the sinful world which owes to Him its being. He *bears* its sin. He enters into the situation sin has created. He takes the pain, the shame, the death it involves, upon Himself: and in so doing He overcomes it and enables us to overcome. The only thing which goes any way to make sin intelligible—in other words, the only thing which in this connexion puts wisdom even imaginably within our reach—is redemption. It is not a new thought, or a new combination of thoughts; it is not anything which the mind could compass by its own efforts; it is a new fact; a new revelation of reality given in a mighty act of God. Here is wisdom for a world baffled and stupefied by sin: here, in the redemption which is in Christ crucified, sin gets at last a meaning as a foil to grace, and God's love shines out with a power and splendour which but for sin we could not have conceived.

Difficult as the idea of wisdom is, there are two ideas which are always involved in it—unity and purpose; and Christ crucified appears as the wisdom of God in this respect also, that through the power which issues from Him unity and purpose are brought into our lives. Many people are conscious that their life has neither; it is fragmentary and aimless; they do one thing and then another, but they have no dominant motive, no chief end. Life is a thing of shreds and patches, dissipated in a hundred inconsistent directions: there is no wisdom in it, no worthy end, method, or plan. They will never be happy, they will never feel that they have found the key to life, nay they never will find it, till something enters into their being which enables them to say: This one thing I do. And this they will never say till their life comes under the power of Christ crucified. The life consummated in that death is great enough, comprehensive enough, commanding enough, to gather our little lives into its vast eternal sweep, and to bear them on to God. It has absolute unity, absolute certainty of itself and of its goal, absolute consistency and worth. When Christ crucified subdues and impels us—when we can say with the apostle, I live no longer but Christ liveth in me—we are delivered from inconsistency, futility, and folly, and made wise with the wisdom of God.

Under the guidance of the apostle we may take one step further, and try to look not at the blackness of sin, nor at the perplexed individual life, but at the whole world of nature in the light cast by the cross. We are quite familiar with the interpretation of nature which is given by science, and in which everything is explained by reference to antecedent conditions. In the nature of things such explanation is endless. Science can never answer all its own questions, and even if it had done so a further question remains, the only question the answer to which raises us from the world of science into that of wisdom: What is all this world of nature for? We are overwhelmed by its vastness—its boundless spaces, its immeasurable duration, its inexhaustible life: is there any key to it? Has it any unity or purpose? Is there any intelligible law which pervades it all and directs it to one end? Paul is bold enough, and I admit it is the utmost reach of boldness of which the human mind is capable, to answer all these questions in the affirmative, and to say that he knows the supreme law of the world, and that he has found it at the cross. What is revealed there is redeeming love, and it is revealed as the last reality in the universe, the eternal truth of what God is. It is before the foundation of the world; nay the very foundations of the world are laid in it. Christ is the key to creation; nature is constituted to be the Redeemer's Kingdom. This is not science, but wisdom—this conviction that in Him were all things created, and that all things therefore work together for good to them that love Him; this assurance that things visible and invisible, things past and to come, all times and spaces and all that fill them, are the destined inheritance of the crucified Christ.

If anyone is disposed to repel all this in words like the Psalmist's—such knowledge is too strange for me; it is high; I cannot attain unto it—I admit it is not easy. But the simple fact about Christ crucified is that when He enters into our life it is to fill all things. He will be everything or nothing. It is His destiny to have all things put under His feet, and it is our only wisdom to look at all things in this light. Think what it means to say: We preach Christ crucified. Here, in this place, at this hour, he is held up on His cross, the Son of God, bearing the sin of the world. You wish to know the final truth about God? Here it is, eternal love, bearing sin. Can you think of a power so wonderful as that which bears the sin of the whole world? a power so able to regenerate you, and to put the key of life, and of all the mysteries with which it confronts you, into your hand? Can you want anything better to trust, anything worthier to inspire, anything abler to throw upon all the dark places of life the light of hope and joy? There is not anything. It is here or nowhere we must learn what the power and wisdom of God mean; and whatever we may have been seeking or expecting or claiming, it is here, in the presence of Christ crucified, that the voice of God comes to us at last: "Look unto Me and be ye saved, all the ends of the earth: I am God, and there is none else."

# Bibliography

Bruce, Alexander Balmain. *The Kingdom of God.* New York: Scribner & Welford, 1889.

Cremer, Hermann. *Die paulinische Rechtfertigungslehre im Zusammenhange ihrer geschichtlichen Voraussetzungen.* Vol. 1. C. Bertelsmann, 1899.

Deissmann, Gustav Adolf. "Evangelium und Urchristentum." In *Beiträge zur Weiterentwicklung der Christlichen Religion,* 77–138. Munich: J. F. Lehmann's Verlag, 1905.

Denney, James. "Adam and Christ in St. Paul." *The Expositor,* sixth series, no. 52 (1904) 147–60.

———. *The Atonement and the Modern Mind.* New York: A.C. Armstrong, 1903.

———. "Authority of Christ." In *A Dictionary of Christ and the Gospels,* edited by James Hastings, 1:146–53. Edinburgh: T & T Clark, 1906–8.

———. *The Christian Doctrine of Reconciliation.* London: Hodder & Stoughton, 1917.

———. "Christianity and the Historical Christ." *The Expositor* 5, no. 2 (1913) 12–28.

———. *The Death of Christ: Its Place and Interpretation in the New Testament.* 4th ed. Hodder & Stoughton, 1902.

———. "Elemental Religion." In *The Way Everlasting: Sermons by James Denney,* 1–12. London: Hodder & Stoughton, 1911.

———. "He That Came by Water and Blood." *The Expositor* 5, no. 27 (1908) 416–28.

———. "Holy Spirit." In *A Dictionary of Christ and the Gospels,* edited by James Hastings, 1:731–44. Edinburgh: T & T Clark, 1906–8.

Denney, James. "Man's Claims in Religion, and God's Response." In *The Way Everlasting: Sermons by James Denney*, 13–25. London: Hodder & Stoughton, 1911.

———. "Preaching Christ." In *A Dictionary of Christ and the Gospels*, edited by James Hastings, 1:393–403. Edinburgh: T & T Clark, 1906–8.

———. *Studies in Theology*. London: Hodder & Stoughton, 1895.

———. "The Theology of the Epistle to the Romans: II. The Doctrine of Sin." *The Expositor* 3, no. 12 (1901) 172–81.

———. "The Theology of the Epistle to the Romans: III. The Doctrine of Sin." *The Expositor* 3, no. 19 (1901) 283–95.

———. "The Theology of the Epistle to the Romans: IV. The Gospel a Divine Righteousness." *The Expositor* 3, no. 28 (1901) 433–50.

———. "The Theology of the Epistle to the Romans: V. Faith and the Righteousness of God." *The Expositor* 4, no. 6 (1901) 81–95.

———. "The Theology of the Epistle to the Romans: VI. The Righteousness of God and the New Life." *The Expositor* 4, no. 20 (1901) 299–311.

———. "The Theology of the Epistle to the Romans: VII. The New Life and the Spirit." *The Expositor* 4, no. 28 (1901) 422–36.

Emerson, Ralph Waldo. *The Works of Ralph Waldo Emerson*. London: George Bell and Sons, 1882.

Eusebius. *Eusebius: The Ecclesiastical History*. Translated by Kirsopp Lake. Vol. I. William Heinemann, 1926.

Feine, Paul. *Das Gesetzesfreie Evangelium des Paulus: nach seinem Werdegang*. Leipzig: JC Hinrichs, 1899.

Findlay, George Gillanders. "St. Paul's First Epistle to the Corinthians." In *The Expositor's Greek Testament*, edited by W. Robertson Nicoll, 2:727–953. London: Hodder & Stoughton Limited, 1897.

Gordon, James M. *James Denney (1856–1917): An Intellectual and Contextual Biography*. Milton Keynes, UK: Paternoster, 2006.

Harnack, Adolf. *Das Wesen des Christentums*. Leipzig: J. C. Hinrichs'sche Buchhandlung, 1902.

———. *Lehrbuch der Dogmengeschichte*. Freiburg I. B., 1888.

Irenaeus. *Five Books of S. Irenaeus Bishop of Lyons Against Heresies*. Translated by John Keble. London: James Parker and Co., 1872.

Jowett, Benjamin. "Essay on Atonement and Satisfaction." In *Theological Essays of the Late Benjamin Jowett*, edited by Lewis Campbell, 209–67. London: Henry Frowde, 1906.

Loisy, Alfred. *Autour D'Un Petit Livre*. Paris: Alphonse Picard et Fils, 1903.

———. *L'Évangile et LÉglise*. Paris: Alphonse Picard et Fils, 1902.

Merivale, Charles. *A History of the Romans Under the Empire*. London: Longman, Brown, Green, and Longmans, 1850.

Moser, Paul K. *Paul's Gospel of Divine Self-Sacrifice*. Cambridge: Cambridge University Press, 2022.

Peake, Arthur Samuel. "A reply to Dr. Denney." *The Expositor*, sixth series, 9, no. 5 (1904) 47–66.

Sanday, William. *The Criticism of the Fourth Gospel*. New York: Charles Scribner's Sons, 1905.

Sanday, William, and Arthur Cayley Headlam. *A Critical and Exegetical Commentary on the Epistle to the Romans*. Edinburgh: T. & T. Clark, 1900.

Schmiedel, Paul Wilhelm. "Acts of the Apostles." In *Encyclopædia Biblica*, edited by Thomas Kelly Cheyne, 1:37–57. Toronto: George N. Morang & Company, 1899.

———. "John, Son of Zebedee." In *Encyclopædia Biblica*, edited by Thomas Kelly Cheyne, 2:2503–62. New York: Macmillan, 1901.

Somerville, David. *St. Paul's Conception of Christ*. Edinburgh: T. & T. Clark, 1897.

Taylor, John Randolph. *God Loves Like That!: The Theology of James Denney*. London: SCM Press, 1962.

Weinel, Heinrich. *Paulus als kirchlicher Organisator*. Leipzig: Freiburg I. B., 1899.

Wellhausen, Julius. *Einleitung in die drei ersten Evangelien*. Berlin: Druck Und Verlag Von Georg Reimer, 1905.

Wendt, Hans Hinrich. *The Teaching of Jesus*. Translated by John Wilson. New York: Charles Scribner's Sons, 1892.

# Name Index

Augustine, 22, 35, 175

Bentham, Jeremy, 26
Bernard of Clairvaux, 57, 126
Bruce, Alexander Balmain, 99
Bunyan, John, 22, 29
Butler, Joseph, 109

Caesar, Julius, 109, 114
Calvin, John, 128
Carlyle, Thomas, 183
Cerinthus, 136
Chalmers, Thomas, 118
Coleridge, Samuel Taylor, 89
Cremer, Hermann, 41, 46

Davidson, Andrew Bruce, 120
Deissmann, Gustav Adolf, 159
Domitian, 120

Emerson, Ralph, 149
Eusebius of Caesarea, 136

Feine, Paul, 24
Findlay, George Gillanders, 124

Godet, Frédéric Louis, 135
von Goethe, Johann Wolfgang, 140

von Harnack, Adolf, 98, 145
Headlam, Arthur Cayley, 40, 46
Hegel, Georg Wilhelm Friedrich, 140
Herrmann, Johann Georg Wilhelm, 116
Holtzmann, Heinrich Julius, 68
Hort, Fenton, 48

Irenaeus, 136

Jowett, Benjamin, 121
Jülicher, Adolf, 159

Lessing, Gotthold Ephraim, 110
Lipsius, Richard Adelbert, 81
Loisy, Alfred, 97, 98
Luther, Martin, 29

Merivale, Charles, 114
Meyer, Heinrich August Wilhelm, 121

Peake, Arthur Samuel, 121–24, 126–32
Pericles, 109
Pfleiderer, Otto, 54, 81

Ritschl, Albrecht, 41–43, 46, 68

Sainte-Beuve, Charles Augustin, 63
Sanday, William, 40, 46, 169
Schmiedel, Paul Wilhelm, 98, 160
Smith, Robertson, 49
Somerville, David, 166
Spinoza, Baruch, 128
Strauss, David Friedrich, 147

Thucydides, 111

Watson, Charles, 138
Weinel, Heinrich, 145
Weiss, Johannes, 68, 98
Wellhausen, Julius, 49, 157, 159, 160
Wendt, Hans Hinrich, 99
Wernle, Paul, 160, 166
Westcott, Brooke Foss, 138
Wordsworth, William, 128

# Subject Index

CPSIA information can be obtained
at www.ICGtesting.com
Printed in the USA
LVHW021536280622
722301LV00009B/508